Teach Yourself VISUALLY™

MacBook Air™

Visual™

by Brad Miser

WILEY

Wiley Publishing, Inc.

Teach Yourself VISUALLY™
MacBook Air™

Published by
Wiley Publishing, Inc.
10475 Crosspoint Blvd.
Indianapolis, IN 46256

Published simultaneously in Canada

Library of Congress Control Number: 2008935817

ISBN: 978-0-470-37613-3

Manufactured in the United States of America

10 9 8 7 6 5 4 3 2 1

Trademark Acknowledgments

Contact Us

For general information on our other products and services please contact our Customer Care Department within the U.S. at 800-762-2974, outside the U.S. at 317-572-3993, or fax 317-572-4002.

For technical support please visit www.wiley.com/techsupport.

Wiley Publishing, Inc.

Sales

Contact Wiley
at (800) 762-2974 or
fax (317) 572-4002.

Praise for Visual Books

"Like a lot of other people, I understand things best when I see them visually. Your books really make learning easy and life more fun."

John T. Frey (Cadillac, MI)

"I have quite a few of your Visual books and have been very pleased with all of them. I love the way the lessons are presented!"

Mary Jane Newman (Yorba Linda, CA)

"I just purchased my third Visual book (my first two are dog-eared now!), and, once again, your product has surpassed my expectations.

Tracey Moore (Memphis, TN)

"I am an avid fan of your Visual books. If I need to learn anything, I just buy one of your books and learn the topic in no time. Wonders! I have even trained my friends to give me Visual books as gifts."

Illona Bergstrom (Aventura, FL)

"Thank you for making it so clear. I appreciate it. I will buy many more Visual books."

J.P. Sangdong (North York, Ontario, Canada)

"I have several books from the Visual series and have always found them to be valuable resources."

Stephen P. Miller (Ballston Spa, NY)

"Thank you for the wonderful books you produce. It wasn't until I was an adult that I discovered how I learn – visually. Nothing compares to Visual books. I love the simple layout. I can just grab a book and use it at my computer, lesson by lesson. And I understand the material! You really know the way I think and learn. Thanks so much!"

Stacey Han (Avondale, AZ)

"I absolutely admire your company's work. Your books are terrific. The format is perfect, especially for visual learners like me. Keep them coming!"

Frederick A. Taylor, Jr. (New Port Richey, FL)

"I have several of your Visual books and they are the best I have ever used."

Stanley Clark (Crawfordville, FL)

"I bought my first Teach Yourself VISUALLY book last month. Wow. Now I want to learn everything in this easy format!"

Tom Vial (New York, NY)

"Thank you, thank you, thank you...for making it so easy for me to break into this high-tech world. I now own four of your books. I recommend them to anyone who is a beginner like myself."

Gay O'Donnell (Calgary, Alberta, Canada)

"I write to extend my thanks and appreciation for your books. They are clear, easy to follow, and straight to the point. Keep up the good work! I bought several of your books and they are just right! No regrets! I will always buy your books because they are the best."

Seward Kollie (Dakar, Senegal)

"Compliments to the chef!! Your books are extraordinary! Or, simply put, extra-ordinary, meaning way above the rest! THANK YOU THANK YOU THANK YOU! I buy them for friends, family, and colleagues."

Christine J. Manfrin (Castle Rock, CO)

"What fantastic teaching books you have produced! Congratulations to you and your staff. You deserve the Nobel Prize in Education in the Software category. Thanks for helping me understand computers."

Bruno Tonon (Melbourne, Australia)

"Over time, I have bought a number of your 'Read Less - Learn More' books. For me, they are THE way to learn anything easily. I learn easiest using your method of teaching."

José A. Mazón (Cuba, NY)

"I am an avid purchaser and reader of the Visual series, and they are the greatest computer books I've seen. The Visual books are perfect for people like myself who enjoy the computer, but want to know how to use it more efficiently. Your books have definitely given me a greater understanding of my computer, and have taught me to use it more effectively. Thank you very much for the hard work, effort, and dedication that you put into this series."

Alex Diaz (Las Vegas, NV)

Credits

Project Editor
Sarah Hellert

Sr. Acquisitions Editor
Stephanie McComb

Copy Editor
Marylouise Wiack

Technical Editor
Geoff Coryell

Editorial Manager
Robyn Siesky

Business Manager
Amy Knies

Sr. Marketing Manager
Sandy Smith

Editorial Assistant
Laura Sinise

Special Help
Tobin Wilkerson

Manufacturing
Allan Conley
Linda Cook
Paul Gilchrist
Jennifer Guynn

Book Design
Kathie Rickard

Production Coordinator
Erin Smith

Layout
Carrie A. Cesavice
Andrea Hornberger
Jennifer Mayberry

Screen Artist
Ana Carrillo
Jill A. Proll

Illustrators
Ronda David-Burroughs
Cheryl Grubbs
Shane Johnson

Proofreader
Linda Quigley

Quality Control
Caitie Kelly

Indexer
Sherry Massey

Vice President and Executive Group Publisher
Richard Swadley

Vice President and Publisher
Barry Pruett

Composition Director
Debbie Stailey

About the Author

Brad Miser has written more than 30 books, his favorite topics being anything related to Mac computers. In addition to *Teach Yourself VISUALLY MacBook Air*, Brad has written *MacBook Pro Portable Genius*, *Teach Yourself VISUALLY MacBook*, and *MacBook Portable Genius*. He has also been an co-author, development editor, or technical editor on more than 50 other titles.

In addition to his passion for silicon-based technology, Brad enjoys steel-based technology and rides his motorcycle whenever and wherever possible. A native of California, Brad now lives in Indiana with his wife Amy; their three daughters, Jill, Emily, and Grace; and a rabbit named Bun-Bun.

Brad would love to hear about your experiences with this book (the good, the bad, and the ugly). You can write to him at bradmacosx@mac.com.

Author's Acknowledgments

While my name is on the cover, it takes many people to build a book like this one. Thanks to Stephanie McComb who made this project possible and allowed me to be involved. Sarah Hellert deserves extra credit for leading me through the details; I'm sure working with me was a challenge at times. Geoff Coryell did a great job of keeping me on my toes to make sure this book contains fewer technical gaffs than it would have without his help. Marylouise Wiack transformed my stumbling text into something people can read and understand. Thanks also to my agent, Marta Justak, for managing the business of the project and being a support for me during the writing process.

On my personal team, I'd like to thank my wife Amy for her tolerance of the author lifestyle, which can be both odd and challenging. My delightful daughters Jill, Emily, and Grace are always a source of joy and inspiration for all that I do, for which I'm ever grateful.

Table of Contents

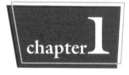 **chapter 1** Exploring MacBook Air

chapter 2 Looking Through Mac OS X Finder Windows

chapter 3 Using the Dock, Exposé, Spaces, and the Dashboard

chapter 4 Working on the Mac Desktop

chapter 5 Working with Mac Applications

Table of Contents

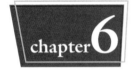

chapter 6   Personalizing MacBook Air

GETTING CONNECTED

chapter 7   Connecting to a Network and the Internet

chapter **8** Traveling with MacBook Air

chapter **9** Connecting MacBook Air to Other Devices

Table of Contents

chapter 10 Using MobileMe Online Services

chapter 11 Surfing the Web

Table of Contents

chapter 14 Managing Contacts

chapter 15 Managing Calendars

chapter 16 Printing on Paper or Electronically

chapter 17 Maintaining and Troubleshooting MacBook Air

Table of Contents

chapter **18** Listening to Music and Watching Video with iTunes

chapter 19

Creating Photo Books and Other Projects with iPhoto

How to use this book

Do you look at the pictures in a book or newspaper before anything else on a page? Would you rather see an image instead of read about how to do something? Search no further. This book is for you. Opening *Teach Yourself VISUALLY MacBook Air* allows you to read less and learn more about MacBook Air computers.

Who Needs This Book

This book is for a reader who has never used a MacBook Air, and it is also for more computer literate individuals who want to expand their knowledge of the different features that MacBook Air has to offer. You do not need much experience with MacBook Air to be able to learn from this book because it begins at the beginning, covering topics such as using MacBook Air's multi-touch trackpad. If you already know how to do these tasks, do not worry because they are only the start. As you read through this book, you will know how to get the most out of MacBook Air, even if you have used it for some time, when you learn about networking, managing the desktop, and other techniques.

Book Organization

Teach Yourself VISUALLY MacBook Air has 19 chapters.

Chapter 1 gets you started with powering up MacBook Air, using the trackpad, and other essential tasks.

Chapter 2 helps you learn to look at the world through Mac OS X Finder windows, including changing views, using the Sidebar, and making the toolbar work for you.

In Chapter 3, you take command of the desktop using Expose, Spaces, and the Dashboard.

Chapter 4 teaches you how to move around on MacBook Air's desktop, create and use files and folders, and work with disks and discs.

You explore how to use applications on MacBook Air in Chapter 5. Topics include installing applications, opening documents, and saving documents.

In Chapter 6, you learn how to make MacBook Air your own by personalizing it. These include setting desktop pictures, configuring the keyboard, and creating and managing user accounts.

No MacBook Air is an island. In Chapter 7, you learn how to connect MacBook Air to different kinds of networks, the most important of which is the Internet.

One of the great things about MacBook Air is that you can take it with you. Chapter 8 provides information about moving around with yours.

While MacBook Air contains all the hardware devices you must have, there are lots more you need, such as external hard drives and mice. In Chapter 9, you learn how to connect MacBook Air to these devices.

A MobileMe account empowers you to do a lot of great things, including accessing an online disk, creating and publishing your photo galleries, and keeping information in sync. Chapter 10 shows you how.

In Chapter 11, you learn how to use Safari to take advantage of the Web. You also learn about Firefox, which is another (and some say better) Web browsing application.

Chapter 12 helps you e-mail like a pro (is there really a professional e-mailer?). You learn how to set up e-mail accounts and how to use Mac OS X's excellent Mail application to read, send, and organize e-mail.

If you like to communicate with other people in real time, chatting is a great way to do it. With iChat, you can chat with text, audio, and video. Chapter 13 shows you how.

When you communicate with people, you need to manage and use contact information. Chapter 14 explains how using Mac OS X's Address Book.

Chapter 15 enters the picture with iCal. If you are memory challenged like I am (and even if you are not), having a way to manage the times and dates that are important is helpful. You can use iCal to create and manage your own calendars, share those calendars with others, and access calendars people share with you.

Computers certainly did not eliminate the need for paper; in Chapter 16, you learn how to print your documents in a number of ways. If you want to save a few trees and distribute documents electronically, you learn that too.

In Chapter 17 you focus on tasks that are important to keep MacBook Air running in top form. You also learn what to do if MacBook Air's condition becomes something less than that.

Chapter 18 fills you in on the basics of iTunes music and video. You learn how to stock the shelves of your iTunes Library and how to listen and watch the great content you store there.

Digital photos are great, and iPhoto is just the application you need to store, organize, and use your own photos. In Chapter 19, you can see how easy these tasks are.

Chapter Organization

This book consists of sections, all listed in the book's table of contents. A section is a set of steps that show you how to complete a specific task.

Each section, usually contained on two facing pages, has an introduction to the task at hand, a set of full-color screen shots and steps that walk you through the task, and a set of tips. This format allows you to quickly look at a topic of interest and learn it instantly.

Chapters group together three or more sections with a common theme. A chapter may also contain pages that give you the background information needed to understand the sections in a chapter.

What You Need to Use This Book

To use this book, you need a MacBook Air running Mac OS X (of course, you can read the book even if you do not have a MacBook Air, but it will not be nearly as much fun). The book's screen shots and steps are for the Leopard version of Mac OS X, which is the operating system the MacBook Air runs.

Using the Trackpad

This book uses the following conventions to describe the actions you perform when using the trackpad:

Point

Slide your finger on the trackpad. The pointer on the screen follows your finger motion on the trackpad. Pointing to something is how you indicate that you want to do something with whatever you point to.

Click

Press the trackpad button once. You generally click the trackpad button on something to select it. This is equivalent to a single mouse click and to a left-button click on a two-button mouse.

Double-click

Press the trackpad button twice. Double-clicking something on the computer screen generally opens whatever item you have double-clicked.

Control+click (also known as Right-click)

Hold the Control key down and press the trackpad button; this is the equivalent of pressing the right button on a two-button mouse. When you right-click anything on the computer screen, a shortcut menu containing commands specific to the selected item is shown (this is called a contextual menu).

Click and Drag, and Release the Trackpad Button

Drag your finger on the trackpad to point to an item on the screen. Press and hold down the trackpad button to select that item. While holding the button down, move your finger so the pointer (to which the item will be attached) moves to where you want to place the item and then release the button. You use this method to move an item from one area of the computer to another.

The Conventions in This Book

A number of typographic and layout styles have been used throughout Teach Yourself VISUALLY MacBook Air to distinguish different types of information.

Bold

Bold type represents the names of commands and options that you interact with. Bold type also indicates text and numbers that you must type into a dialog or window.

Italics

Italic words introduce a new term and are followed by a definition.

Numbered Steps

You must perform the instructions in numbered steps in order to successfully complete a section and achieve the final results.

Bulleted Steps

These steps point out various optional features. You do not have to perform these steps; they simply give additional information about a feature.

Indented Text

Indented text tells you what the program does in response to you following a numbered step. For example, if you click a certain menu command, a dialog may appear, or a window may open. Indented text may also tell you what the final result is when you follow a set of numbered steps.

Notes

Notes give additional information. They may describe special conditions that may occur during an operation. They may warn you of a situation that you want to avoid, for example the loss of data. A note may also cross reference a related area of the book. A cross reference may guide you to another chapter, or another section with the current chapter.

Icons and buttons

Icons and buttons are graphical representations within the text. They show you exactly what you need to click to perform a step.

 You can easily identify the tips in any section by looking for the TIPS icon. Tips offer additional information, including tips, hints, and tricks. You can use the TIPS information to go beyond what you have learned in the steps.

Discovering MacBook Air

MacBook Air might be the most amazing laptop ever; it combines outstanding capabilities with sophisticated design, creating a computer that is unique. MacBook Air is powerful and intuitive, and its compact size and low weight make it an ideal traveling companion. In this part, you learn fundamentals to guide you on your journey of discovery toward MacBook Air mastery.

Tour MacBook Air

You can learn about the major features of MacBook Air from the outside, including its controls, ports, and other areas that you use to control your MacBook Air and to connect it to other devices.

MacBook Air is elegantly designed and easy to use. But do not let that fool you; it is a very powerful and capable computer that can do just about anything you want it to.

MACBOOK AIR

● **Display**

The MacBook Air display provides a sharp, bright, and colorful view into all that you do

● **Ambient light sensor**

MacBook Air has a backlit keyboard that illuminates when this sensor detects low light conditions

● **iSight camera**

Use the built-in iSight camera to video conference, take photos, and more

● **Microphone**

Use the microphone to speak during audio- and video- conferences and record your voice or other sounds

● **Keyboard**

Along with the standard letter and number keys, you can use function keys to control your MacBook Air

● **Ports**

Connect MacBook Air to other devices, such as hard drives and iPods

● **Sleep indicator light**

Pulses when MacBook Air is asleep, and glows solid when MacBook Air is on but its display is dimmed

● **Trackpad**

You can control MacBook Air by sliding your fingers on the trackpad

● **Trackpad button**

Click this button to perform actions

● **Power port**

Connect the power adapter here to run the computer from a power outlet and charge the MacBook Air battery

MACBOOK AIR KEYBOARD

● **Brightness keys**

Press F1 to decrease your screen's brightness, or F2 to increase it

● **Exposé key**

Press F3 to activate Exposé

● **Dashboard key**

Press F4 to open the Dashboard

● **Backlighting brightness keys**

Press F5 to decrease the brightness of the keyboard backlighting, or F6 to increase it

● **Playback control keys**

Controls media playback in iTunes or other applications; press F7 to move back, F8 to play or pause, or F9 to move forward.

● **Volume keys**

F10 mutes MacBook Air, F11 turns the volume down, and F12 turns it up

● **Eject key**

Press ⏏ to eject an iPod, hard disk, CD, or DVD

● **Power button**

Press to turn MacBook Air on; press and hold to force MacBook Air to turn off.

● **Scroll keys**

Press to move around the screen

● **Modifier keys**

Press to invoke keyboard shortcuts

● **Alternate function key**

Hold down Fn while pressing a function key to perform the alternate task (such as activating a function control within an application) instead of the preprogrammed action (such as changing volume)

MacBook Air is wrapped in a sleek, elegant, and extremely lightweight package that makes it the envy of every technology fan. The MacBook Air design is simple and uncluttered.

Getting familiar with the external ports on your MacBook Air will not take long because there are not many of them. And, the useful accessories you received with your MacBook Air, such as the video adapter, can be used with these ports.

MACBOOK AIR PORTS

- **Closed port hatch**

  In the closed positions, the ports are not accessible

- **Open port hatch**

  Flip the port hatch down to expose the ports

- **Headphones/audio out**

  Connect headphones or analog speakers

- **USB**

  Connect USB devices, such as iPods and disk drives

- **Micro-DVI**

  Use the included adapter to connect MacBook Air to external displays or projectors

- **Power**

  Connect MacBook Air to power

INCLUDED ACCESSORIES

● **Power adapter**

Powers MacBook Air and charges its battery

● **Power cord**

Extends the reach of the power adapter

● **Micro-DVI to VGA adapter**

Connects MacBook Air to VGA monitors and projectors

● **Micro-DVI to DVI adapter**

Connects MacBook Air to DVI monitors and projectors

MACBOOK AIR COMPANIONS

● **MacBook Air SuperDrive**

Connect to the MacBook Air USB port to be able to run and burn CDs and DVDs

● **External hard drive**

Every MacBook Air user should have an external hard drive to back up important files and for extra working room

● **Time Capsule**

Combines an AirPort Extreme Base Station with a hard drive to enable you to create a wireless network and to back up MacBook Air wirelessly

● **Bluetooth mouse**

Wirelessly connect to a mouse when you want to use it instead of the MacBook Air trackpad

● **Remote**

Control MacBook Air from a distance, such as when you are listening to music or watching movies

Explore the Mac OS X Desktop

MacBook Air operates through the Mac operating system, which is currently in version 10.5, more commonly called Mac OS X Leopard.

The Mac OS X desktop is the overall window through which you view all that happens on MacBook Air, such as looking at the contents of folders, working on documents, and surfing the Web.

MAC OS X DESKTOP

● **Menu bar**

A menu bar always appears at the top of the screen so that you can access the commands it contains

● **Drives**

MacBook Air stores its data, including the software it needs to work, on hard drives or solid-state drives. It includes one internal drive, but you can also connect external drives.

● **Remote Disc**

You can access CDs or DVDs using Remote Disc, which enables you to use the disc as if it were inserted into a drive connected to MacBook Air

● **Folders**

Containers that you use to organize files and other folders stored on MacBook Air

● **Files**

Documents (such as text, graphics, movies, and songs), applications, or other sources of data

● **Finder windows**

You view the contents of folders in Finder windows

● **Application and document windows**

When you use applications, you use the windows that those applications present, for documents, Web pages, games, and so on.

FINDER MENU BAR AND MENUS

● **Apple menu**

This menu is always visible so that you can access special commands, such as Shut Down and Log Out

● **Finder menu**

This is where you control the Finder application itself, such as to empty the Trash or set preferences

● **File menu**

Use commands on this menu to work with files and Finder windows

● **Edit menu**

This menu is not as useful in the Finder as it is in other applications, but here you can undo what you have done or copy and paste information

● **View menu**

Enables you to determine how you view the desktop; it is especially useful for choosing Finder window views.

● **Go menu**

Takes you to various places, such as specific folders

● **Window menu**

Enables you to work with open Finder windows

● **Help menu**

Use when you need help with Mac OS X or the other applications

● **Configurable menus**

You can configure the menu bar to include specific menus, such as Displays, Volume, AirPort, Battery, and many more

● **Clock**

Here you see the current time and day

● **Spotlight menu**

Enables you to search for information on MacBook Air

The Finder application controls the Mac OS X desktop, and so you see its menu bar whenever you work with this application. When you view the contents of a folder, you do so through a Finder window.

The Dock and Sidebar on the desktop enable you to access items quickly and easily.

FINDER WINDOWS

● **Close button**

Click to close a window

● **Minimize button**

Click to shrink a window and move it onto the Dock

● **Maximize button**

Click to expand a Finder window to the maximum size possible; click it again to return to the previous size.

● **Window title**

The name of the location whose contents you see in the window

● **Toolbar**

Contains tools you use to work with files and folders

● **Search bar**

Use this tool to find files, folders, and other information

● **Hide/Show toolbar and Sidebar**

Click to show or hide the toolbar and Sidebar

● **Sidebar**

Enables you to quickly access devices, folders, and files, as well as searches you have saved

● **Files and folders**

Within a window, the contents of a location are shown; this example shows the icon view.

● **Status information**

Shows information about the current location, such as the amount of free space when you are viewing the MacBook Air drive

● **Resize handle**

Drag this handle to change the size of a window

DOCK AND SIDEBAR

● **Devices**

Contains your iDisk (MobileMe members), the internal drive, Remote Disc, and hard drives that your MacBook Air can access

● **Shared**

Computers and other resources being shared on a network

● **Places**

Files and folders that you can open by clicking them

● **Searches**

Saved searches that you can run by clicking them

● **Dock**

Shows files and folders you can access along with applications that are currently running

● **Applications**

Icons on the left side of the Dock are for applications; open applications have a glowing dot under their icon.

● **Files and folders**

Icons on the right side of the Dock are for files and folders. The default Dock includes the Downloads folder for files you download from the Internet.

● **Trash/Eject**

Items you delete go here (to get rid of them, empty the Trash); when you select an ejectable device, such as an iPod, this becomes the Eject icon.

Understand Disks, Volumes, Optical Discs, Folders, and Files

As you use MacBook Air, you work with data. Underlying all this data is the need to store and organize it. The major items that MacBook Air uses for storing and organizing data are described in this section.

These items include disks, volumes, optical discs, folders, and files. Each of these items is managed by the Finder, and you access them directly from the desktop or from within applications.

Disks

Disks are the physical means that MacBook Air uses to store data internally. Some MacBook Airs have a hard disk on which data is stored on a magnetic disk accessed through a read/write head. Other MacBook Airs have a solid-state drive that uses only electronic elements to store data. MacBook Air has one internal drive that contains the software it needs to work with the operating system (OS), applications you install, and documents you create. You can connect external hard disks to MacBook Air through its USB port to expand the storage room that is available. Drives come in various storage capacities, such as 160GB, and operate at different speeds (faster is better). Disks are represented on MacBook Air with icons, each under a different name. Different kinds of disks have different icons.

Volume

A volume is an area of a disk created using software rather than a physical space. A drive can be partitioned into multiple volumes, where each volume acts like a separate disk. A volume performs the same task as a disk, which is to store data. In fact, when you work with a volume, you might not be able to tell the difference. You can also access volumes being shared with you over a network. Application installers often appear as volumes that you use as if they were on a disk. Volumes are used to organize data in different ways and to represent various resources with which you work.

Optical Discs

CDs and DVDs serve many purposes. For example, you can put your own data on CD or DVD by burning audio CDs with iTunes, creating DVDs with iDVD, and backing up your data on DVD. One of the reasons why MacBook Air is so thin is that it does not have an internal disc drive. To work with discs, you can use Remote Disc to access a disc inserted into a different computer, or you can use the MacBook Air External SuperDrive.

Folders

Like manila folders in the physical world, folders on MacBook Air are a means to organize things, such as files and other folders. Mac OS X includes many folders by default. You can create, name, delete, and organize folders in any way you see fit (mostly any way — there are some folders you cannot or should not change). You open a folder in a Finder window to view its contents.

Files

A file is a container for data. Files can contain many different kinds of data. For example, some files are documents, such as text documents you create with a word processor. Files can also be images, songs, movies, and other kinds of content. Files also make up the operating system that runs MacBook Air; you typically do not interact with system files directly. Files have names that include filename extensions, such as .jpg and .doc (which can be hidden), and are represented by icons in Finder windows and e-mail attachments.

Configure and Use the Multi-Touch Trackpad

Another of the innovations introduced in MacBook Air is its multi-touch trackpad. With this trackpad, you can make gestures on the trackpad to cause something to happen on the screen. For example, suppose that you want to rotate a photo in iPhoto. Instead of clicking a button, you can simply rotate your fingers on the trackpad, making the action even more intuitive.

You can configure the trackpad to use as much of this functionality as you like. Even better, MacBook Air shows you exactly what each gesture is as you configure it.

Configure and Use the Multi-Touch Trackpad

① Open the **Apple** menu (🍎) and choose **System Preferences**.

② Click the **Keyboard & Mouse** icon.

The Keyboard & Mouse pane appears.

③ Click the **Trackpad** tab.

You see the trackpad's configuration options.

④ Drag the **Tracking Speed** slider to the right to make the pointer move more with the same amount of finger movement, or to the left to cause it to move less.

⑤ Drag the **Double-Click Speed** slider to the right to reduce the time between presses of the trackpad button to register a double-click, or to the left to increase time.

⑥ Drag the **Scrolling Speed** slider to the right to increase the amount of scrolling for the same amount of finger motion on the trackpad, or to the left to decrease the amount of scrolling for the same movement on the trackpad.

7 Select the **Tap to Click** gesture.

● A video plays, showing you what the gesture is and what it does; at the top of the video window you see the desktop, while in the lower part, you see the gestures you make. With the Tap to Click gesture, you can press once on the trackpad to register a single click of the trackpad button.

8 If you want to be able to use this gesture, check the **Tap to Click** check box.

9 Repeat Steps **7** and **8** for each of the gestures; select a gesture, watch the video to learn what it does, and then check its check box if you want to use it.

10 If you enable the Screen Zoom gesture, click the **Options** button.

The Options sheet appears.

11 On the **Zoom using** pop-up menu, choose the key combination you want to press to activate zooming.

12 Click the **Continuously with pointer** radio button if you want the zoomed image to always move with the pointer.

13 Click **Only when the pointer reaches an edge** if you want the zoomed image to remain stationary until your pointer reaches the edge of the screen.

14 Click **So the pointer is at or near the center of the image** if you want the zoomed image to remain centered around the pointer.

15 If movement seems sluggish when zoomed, uncheck the **Smooth images** check box.

16 Click **Done**.

The sheet closes.

17 If you plan to also use an external mouse and do not want the trackpad to work when you do, check the **Ignore trackpad when mouse is present** check box.

TIPS

I am confused by the number of gestures; what should I do?
The multi-touch trackpad supports a number of different gestures, some of which might not be intuitive to you at the start. Take your time watching the videos of each gesture because they are very helpful in showing you how each one works. If there are too many gestures to start with, disable some of them until you are comfortable and then add gestures, one at a time, until you have explored all of them.

Why would I use a mouse when the MacBook Air trackpad is so powerful?
This is a matter of personal preference. Some people are just not comfortable with trackpads even though the MacBook Air trackpad enables you to do much more than a mouse does. The good news is that you can easily use a mouse whenever you want, especially if you have a Bluetooth wireless mouse. (See Chapter 9 for the details.)

Use Remote Disc

One of the limitations of MacBook Air is that it does not have a built-in optical drive. This could be a problem when you want to install software from an optical disc; however, the Mac OS X Remote Disc feature enables you to use a CD or DVD that is inserted into another computer so that you can install software it contains.

You need to configure disc sharing on the computer with an optical drive. Then you can access a disc inserted into that drive to be able to perform some actions, such as running an installation program.

Use Remote Disc

CONFIGURE DISC SHARING

Note: To be able to use Remote Disc, MacBook Air must be on the same network as the Mac with a disc drive. To configure a network, see Chapter 7.

1 On a Mac with a disc drive, open the **Apple** menu (◼) and choose **System Preferences**.

2 Click the **Sharing** icon.

The Sharing pane appears.

3 Check the **DVD or CD Sharing** check box.

DVD or CD Sharing starts.

4 If you want to be prompted to allow sharing each time someone uses Remote Disc, check the **Ask me before allowing others to use my DVD drive** check box.

ACCESS A SHARED DISC

① Insert the disc you want to use into the Mac with a disc drive.

② On MacBook Air, select **Remote Disc** on the Sidebar.

You see the computers that are configured to share discs on the network.

③ Double-click the icon of the computer whose disc you want to share.

④ If the **Ask to use** button appears, click it; if not, skip this step.

● If permission to share the disc is given (if required), the disc that is being shared appears in the window and you can access its files by double-clicking its icon.

Understand Finder, Application, and Document Windows

Like windows in the physical world, windows on MacBook Air enable to you to view objects on-screen, such as folders, files, and documents.

In Mac OS X, most windows have common elements no matter what application you are using. In some cases, particularly with games and utilities, you might not see document windows when you run an application; instead, you see windows that are specific to the functions of those applications. it is important to be comfortable with any kind of window you encounter.

FINDER WINDOWS

● **Title**

Shows the name of the drive, folder, or other location you are currently viewing.

● **Toolbar**

Contains tools to control windows, move among them, change views, and perform actions.

● **Search tool**

Enables you to search for files or folders.

● **Files and folders**

The contents of the folder you are viewing appear within the main part of Finder windows.

● **Sidebar**

Contains icons for locations; you can click an icon to view its contents in the window or open it in its application if it is a document.

● **Status**

Displays status information for what you are viewing, such as available disk space on the current drive

● **Scroll bars**

Enable you to move up, down, left, or right within a window to see all of its contents.

● **Resize handle**

Drag this handle to change the size and shape of a window.

● **Hide/Show Sidebar and Toolbar**

Click to show or hide the Sidebar and toolbar.

APPLICATION WINDOWS

● **Document title**

The name of the document being shown in the window, or the application's name.

● **Window controls**

Enable you to close, minimize, or maximize the window.

● **Toolbar**

Provides buttons for specific actions in the application.

● **Content**

The main window of the application presents the content with which you can work in the application, such as a document or Web site.

DOCUMENT WINDOWS

● **Document title**

The name of the file being shown in the window.

● **Scroll bars**

Enable you to move up, down, left, or right within a window to see all of its contents.

● **Application-specific tools**

Most applications provide tools in their windows that are specific to the application.

View Finder Windows in Icon View

Icon view is the view that is most synonymous with Mac computers. Icons are pleasing to look at and visually indicate the kind of object they represent, such as a file or folder.

While being pretty, Icon view is not the most useful one, but it does have a few things to offer. This view is pretty because the icons themselves are pleasing to look at, and some icons are miniature works of art. You also have more control over how a window in Icon view looks because you can set the window's background color or use an image as the background.

View Finder Windows in Icon View

① Open a Finder window by clicking a folder in the Sidebar.

Note: *You can also click the **Finder** icon (the Mac "happy face") on the Dock or open a folder on the desktop to open a Finder window.*

② Click the **Icon View** button (⊞).

The objects in the window are represented with icons.

③ Click **View** and then click **Show View Options**.

The View Options dialog appears.

④ To have the folder always open in Icon view, check the **Always open in icon view** check box.

⑤ Drag the **Icon size** slider to increase or decrease the size of icons.

⑥ Drag the **Grid spacing** slider to decrease or increase the space between icons.

⑦ Click the **Text size** pop-up menu and choose the size of the text for icon labels.

⑧ To have icon labels appear at the bottom of icons, click **Bottom**, or click **Right** if you want labels to appear on the right side of icons.

⑨ To show additional information about items, check the **Show item info** check box.

⑩ To show a preview of items within the icon, check the **Show icon preview** check box.

⑪ Use the **Arrange by** pop-up menu to choose how items are arranged in the window.

Note: *Choosing **Snap to Grid** enables auto aligning of the icons in the window.*

⑫ Click **White** to make the window's background white.

13 Click **Color** to use a different color for the background.

14 Click the color button.

● The Color Picker appears.

15 Use the Color Picker to choose the color you want for the background.

16 When you have the color you want, click **OK**.

The Color Picker closes and you move back to the window, which now has the color you selected as its background.

17 To use an image as the background, click **Picture**.

The Select button appears.

18 Click **Select**.

The Select a Picture dialog appears.

19 Use the dialog to move to and select the file you want for the window's background.

20 When you have selected the file you want to use, click **Select**.

The dialog closes, and the image is applied to the window's background.

21 To have every window you open in Icon view use these settings by default, click **Use as Defaults**.

22 Close the View Options dialog by clicking its **Close** button ().

TIPS

Where does a file's icon come from?

Mac OS X automatically creates icons for documents based on their content. For example, an image file's icon is a thumbnail view of the image, while a Word document's icon is a text file with the word "DOC" on it. Application files display the application's icon. This makes it easy to identify a file's type by simply looking at its icon.

How can I change how icons are arranged in a window?

You can Control +click the window's background. The contextual menu appears. Select **Arrange By** and then choose how you want the icons to be arranged. For example, select **Kind** to have icons grouped by their kind, such as all image files together. You can straighten up the icons in a window by selecting **Clean Up** on the contextual menu.

View Finder Windows in List View

Icon view is pretty, but it does not provide a lot of information about the files and folders you see. Even if you make the icons small, they take up a lot of room, making it hard to see all the contents of a Finder window.

List view may not look as nice as Icon view, but it does provide a lot more information. Also, you can easily sort the content in windows so that the items appear in the order you want.

View Finder Windows in List View

1 Open a Finder window by clicking a folder in the Sidebar.

Note: *You can also click the **Finder** icon (the Mac "happy face") on the Dock or open a folder on the desktop to open a Finder window.*

2 Click the **List View** button (▤).

The objects in the window are shown in a list.

3 Click **View** and then click **Show View Options**.

The View Options dialog appears.

4 If you want the window to always open in List view, check the **Always open in list view** check box.

5 Choose the icon size for the view by clicking the larger or smaller icon button.

6 Use the **Text size** pop-up menu to choose the text size for the List view.

7 Check the boxes for each column you want to see.

8 If you want relative dates to be displayed, such as Yesterday or Today, check the **Use relative dates** check box.

9 If you want the sizes of folders to be displayed, check the **Calculate all sizes** check box.

10 If you want to see previews of the icons for each item, check the **Show icon preview** check box.

11 If you want other windows to use these settings by default, click **Use as Defaults**.

12 When you are done making changes, click ⊙.

⑬ To change the order in which columns appear in the window, drag a column heading that you want to move to the left or to the right.

⑭ When the column is in its new position, release the trackpad button.

The column settles into its new location.

⑮ To change the order in which the items are sorted, click the column heading by which you want to sort the items.

The items in the window are sorted by the column you selected.

⑯ To reverse the sort order, click the triangle at the far-right edge of the sort column heading.

The items in the window are sorted in the opposite order.

⑰ To open the contents of a folder, click its expansion triangle (▶ changes to ▼).

The folder expands so that you can see the folders and files it contains.

⑱ Click ▼ to collapse the folder again.

 TIPS

How do I expand all the folders within a window at the same time?
Press and hold the Option key while you click a folder's expansion triangle. The folder expands, along with all the folders contained within that folder. Press and hold the Option key and click the folder's expansion triangle to collapse it and all the folders it contains again.

How do I tell where a folder is when I view its window?
Click **View** and then click **Show Path Bar**. A bar appears at the bottom of the window that shows you the path from the startup disk to the location of the current folder.

23

View Finder Windows in Column View

Column view is best for navigating quickly around MacBook Air. This view allows you to see the contents of folders along with the locations of those folders. You can click any folder's icon to immediately see the contents of that folder in the same window.

As you learn to use MacBook Air, you should become comfortable with the Column view so that you can use it to quickly move to any location.

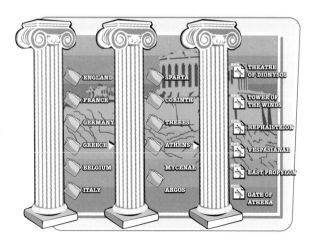

View Finder Windows in Column View

1 Open a Finder window by clicking a folder in the Sidebar.

Note: _You can also click the **Finder** icon (the Mac "happy face") on the Dock or open a folder on the desktop to open a Finder window._

2 Click the **Column View** button (▥).

The objects in the window are shown in columns.

3 Click **View** and then click **Show View Options**.

The View Options dialog appears.

4 If you want the window to always open in Column view, check the **Always open in column view** check box.

5 Use the **Text size** pop-up menu to choose a text size for the labels shown in Column view.

6 If you want to see an icon for each item, check the **Show icons** check box.

7 If you want to see a preview of items within their icons, check the **Show icon preview** check box.

8 If you want to see a preview of a file you select, check the **Show preview column** check box.

9 Use the **Arrange by** pop-up menu to determine how items in the window are listed.

10 When you are done making changes, click ⊙.

⓫ Select a location in the Sidebar to view it.

⓬ Click a folder to see its contents.

As you move through the folder hierarchy, columns shift to the left so that you always see the last column opened.

⓭ Click a file.

You see information about the file in the far-right column, including a preview of the file if that option is enabled. If the file is dynamic, such as audio or video, you can play its content in the preview.

⓮ To change the width of a column, drag its **Resize** handle (||) to the left or right.

The column resizes immediately.

⓯ To scroll in the current column, drag the scroll bar up or down.

TIPS

How do I resize all the columns at once?

Press and hold the Option key while you drag one column's **Resize** handle. All the columns are resized at the same time. If you double-click the **Resize** handle, the column expands to be the width of the longest file or folder name shown.

How do I tell the difference between a folder and a file?

In Column view, folders always have a right-facing triangle at the right edge of their column to show that when you select this triangle, the folder's contents appear in a new column. Files do not have this arrow.

THEATRE OF DIONYSOS

ATHENS ▶ TOWER OF THE WINDS

GATE OF ATHENA

View Finder Windows in Cover Flow View

Cover Flow view is a graphical way to quickly scan through contents of a Finder window. In addition to making scrolling through lots of files and folders faster, this view displays thumbnail images of each item you are browsing.

The easiest way to think about the Cover Flow view is to visualize a stack of CDs that you flip through to see each CD. A Finder window in Cover Flow view behaves similarly. You can flip through the various folders and files to browse them in the top part of the window. In the bottom part of the window, you see the items in the folder you are browsing in List view.

View Finder Windows in Cover Flow View

① Open a Finder window by clicking a folder in the Sidebar.

Note: You can also click the Finder icon (the Mac "happy face") on the Dock or open a folder on the desktop to open a Finder window.

② Click the **Cover Flow View** button (▥).

The Cover Flow viewer appears at the top of the window, and the items in the window appear at the bottom of the window in List view.

③ Click **View** and then click **Show View Options**.

The View Options dialog appears.

④ If you want the folder to always open in Cover Flow view, check the **Always open in Cover Flow** check box.

⑤ Configure the rest of the settings just as you would for List view (see "View Finder Windows in List View" earlier in this chapter).

⑥ To browse the contents of the folder quickly, drag the scroll bar to the left or right.

As you drag, a preview of each item flips by in the Cover Flow viewer at the top of the window. The item currently selected is the one directly facing you and is highlighted on the list at the bottom of the window.

⑦ To jump to a specific file or folder, click its icon.

It becomes selected and moves to the center of the Cover Flow viewer.

⑧ To make the Cover Flow part of the window larger or smaller, drag its Resize handle up or down.

Configure the Sidebar

The Finder's Sidebar makes it easy to get to specific locations on MacBook Air. It comes with a number of default locations, but you can add items to or remove them from the Sidebar so that it contains the items you use most frequently.

The Sidebar is organized into sections. *Devices* includes hard drives and other devices (such as iPods) mounted on your MacBook Air. *Shared* includes disk drives or computers you are accessing over a network. *Places* contains folders and files. *Search For* presents saved searches.

Configure the Sidebar

① To remove an item from the Sidebar, drag it from the Sidebar onto the desktop and release the trackpad button.

● The item disappears in a puff of smoke.

Note: When you remove something from the Sidebar, it is not removed from the computer. The item remains in its current location on MacBook Air; it is just no longer accessible from the Sidebar. You can always add it back again later.

② To add something to the Sidebar, drag its icon from a Finder window or the desktop onto the Sidebar.

③ When the item is over the location of the Sidebar where you want to place it, release the trackpad button.

The item's icon is added to the Sidebar and you can use it just like the default items.

④ To change the order of items in the Sidebar, drag them up or down the list.

⑤ To collapse or expand sections of the Sidebar, click their expansion triangles ([▶] changes to [▼]).

Use the Action Pop-up Menu and Quick Look

The Action pop-up menu is a powerful element of Finder windows, though you might not think so to look at it. This menu contains a list of contextual commands that you can use.

The Finder's Quick Look command enables you to view the contents of a file or group of files without actually opening them. This can save time, especially when you are looking for specific files on the desktop.

Use the Action Pop-up Menu and Quick Look

USE THE ACTION POP-UP MENU

1. Open a Finder window by clicking a folder on the Sidebar.

*Note: You can also click the **Finder** icon (the Mac "happy face") on the Dock or open a folder on the desktop to open a Finder window.*

2. Click the **Action** pop-up menu (⚙▾).

The list of available commands appears.

3. Choose the command you want to use.

The action you select is performed.

USE QUICK LOOK

1. Open a Finder window by clicking a folder on the Sidebar.

*Note: You can also click the **Finder** icon on the Dock or open a folder on the desktop.*

2. Select the files you want to view.

Note: To select multiple files at the same time, press and hold the ⌘ key while you click each file.

3. Click the **Quick Look** button (👁).

Note: You also open the Quick Look window by pressing **Spacebar**.

The Quick Look window appears.

4. Use the controls in the Quick Look window to view the files.

*Note: The controls you see depend on the kind of files you are viewing. For example, if you selected multiple images, you can click the **Play** button to see those images in a slide show.*

5. To see Quick Look in full screen, click the **Full Screen** button.

6. When you are done with Quick Look, click its **Close** button (⊗).

Configure the Finder Window Toolbar

The toolbar that appears at the top of the Finder window contains buttons that you can use to access commands quickly and easily. For example, the various View buttons appear there along with the Quick Look and Action menu buttons.

The Finder toolbar includes a number of buttons by default. However, you can configure the toolbar so that it contains the buttons you use most frequently.

Configure the Finder Window Toolbar

① Open a Finder window by clicking a folder on the Sidebar, clicking the **Finder** icon on the Dock, or opening a folder on the desktop.

② Click **View** and then click **Customize Toolbar**.

The Toolbar Customization sheet appears.

③ To remove a button from the toolbar, drag its icon from the toolbar onto the desktop.

● When you release the trackpad button, the toolbar button disappears in a puff of smoke.

④ To add a button to the toolbar, drag its icon from the sheet and drop it on the toolbar at the location in which you want to place it.

● When you release the trackpad button, the button is added to the toolbar.

⑤ To change the locations of buttons on the toolbar, drag their icons from the current location to the new one.

⑥ When you are finished customizing the toolbar, click **Done**.

The Customization sheet closes and you see your customized toolbar.

Explore the Dock, Exposé, Spaces, and the Dashboard

Mac OS X's Dock, Exposé, Spaces, and Dashboard help you use your MacBook Air's desktop more effectively.

The Dock is a bar containing many icons you can click to open the related item.

Exposé is a feature that helps you manage your open windows quickly and efficiently.

Spaces allow you to create groups of applications and windows, and switch between them easily.

The Dashboard presents mini-applications, called *widgets*, that you can quickly access and use.

THE DOCK

- **Application icons**

  Application icons can be stored on the Dock for easy access; icons for all open applications are also shown.

- **Running applications**

  Applications that are open are marked with a blue dot in their reflection.

- **Dividing line**

  On the left side of this line are application icons; on the right are folder and file icons, minimized windows, and the Trash.

- **Files and folders**

  File and folder icons can also be placed on the Dock for easy access.

- **Minimized windows**

  When you minimize a window, it shrinks and moves onto the Dock.

- **Trash**

  This is the holding place for files that you delete from MacBook Air.

EXPOSÉ

- **Thumbnail windows**

  When you activate Exposé, all open windows are shrunk and organized so that you see them on the desktop.

- **Window in focus**

  When you point to a window, you see its title and it is highlighted in blue; click a window to make it active.

SPACES

- **Spaces manager**

  When you activate Spaces, the desktop is hidden and the spaces available to you are shown.

- **Spaces**

  Each space includes a collection of open document and application windows; when you move into a space, you can use the windows it contains.

- **Applications**

  Each space can have many applications included in it.

DASHBOARD

- **Dashboard**

  When activated, the Dashboard fills the desktop and presents the active widgets.

- **Active widgets**

  To have widgets appear when you activate the Dashboard, you install them on it. You can use any of the active widgets by activating the Dashboard.

- **Available widgets**

  You can add widgets that are installed on MacBook Air to the Dashboard by dragging them onto it. You can also download and install more widgets.

Use and Configure the Dock

The Dock is a very useful part of Mac OS X because it provides quick and easy, single-click access to various items, including applications, documents, and folders.

The Dock includes a number of default icons, and you can add as many icons to your Dock as you want. You can also customize the way the Dock looks and works to suit your preferences.

USE THE DOCK

1. Point to an icon on the Dock.

   Its name appears above the icon.

2. Click the trackpad button.

   • What happens depends on the icon you click. If the icon is a closed application, for example, the application opens, and you see its initial window.

3. To open a Dock icon's menu, point to the icon, press and hold the **Control** key, and click.

Note: You can also open a Dock icon's menu by pointing to it and holding the trackpad button down for a second or two.

4. Choose the command you want to use from the menu.

Note: As more icons appear on the Dock, they get smaller and the Dock expands so that all the icons fit onto it.

CONFIGURE THE DOCK

1. Point to the dividing line so that the pointer (🔺) becomes a horizontal line with arrows on the top and bottom (⬍).

2. **Control**+click the line.

   The Dock menu appears.

3. Choose **Dock Preferences**.

The Dock pane of the System Preferences application appears.

④ Drag the **Size** slider to the left or right to make the default size of the Dock smaller or larger.

Note: The default size refers to when only installed icons are shown and no windows have been minimized. As icons are added to the Dock, its size changes accordingly.

⑤ If you want icons to be magnified when you point to them, check the **Magnification** check box and drag the slider for more or less magnification.

⑥ To position the Dock on the left, bottom, or right side of the desktop, click **Left**, **Bottom**, or **Right**.

⑦ On the Minimize using pop-up menu, choose **Genie Effect** to see windows get whisked onto the Dock when you minimize them; **Scale Effect** scales the window down as it moves onto the Dock.

⑧ To have icons bounce while their applications are opening, check the **Animate opening applications** check box.

⑨ To automatically hide the Dock when you are not pointing to it, check the **Automatically hide and show the Dock** check box.

Note: When the Dock is hidden, position the pointer over its location; it pops up so you can use it.

⑩ Press ⌘+Q to close the System Preferences application.

The Dock behaves according to your settings.

How can I add icons to or remove them from the Dock?

To add an icon to the Dock, drag it from a Finder window onto the Dock; an application's icon must be placed on the left side of the dividing line, whereas a document or folder's icon goes on the right side. When the icon is at the desired location, release the trackpad button. To remove an icon, drag it up onto the desktop and release the trackpad button.

What happens when I add folder icons to the Dock?

When you click a folder's icon, a preview window appears showing the folder's contents. You can click an icon to work with one of the items, such as a document icon to open it. You can also click the **Show in Finder** button (⊙) to open the folder in a Finder window. For example, the Dock contains the Downloads folder that is the default location for files you download from the Web, but you can add any folder to the Dock to make it instantly accessible.

Manage Open Windows with Exposé

Exposé greatly helps with the screen clutter that is inevitable as you use MacBook Air and open window after window for documents and applications.

Exposé has three modes: You can hide all open windows to show the MacBook Air desktop. You can reduce all open windows to thumbnails so that you can quickly jump into a window you want to use. You can create thumbnails of all the open windows within a specific application for quick access.

Manage Open Windows with Exposé

HIDE ALL OPEN WINDOWS WITH EXPOSÉ

1 Open as many windows as you want, including those from the Finder and from applications.

2 Press Fn + F1 on the MacBook Air keyboard.

● All the windows are moved off of the MacBook Air screen, leaving an uncluttered desktop for you to work on.

Note: *To return the desktop to its cluttered state, press* Fn + F1 *again, or click one of the sides of the windows that you see at the edges of the desktop.*

SHOW THUMBNAILS OF ALL OPEN WINDOWS WITH EXPOSÉ

1 Open as many windows as you want, including those from the Finder and from applications.

2 Press F3 on the MacBook Air keyboard.

● All windows shrink down so that they fit on the desktop.

3 Point to a window (**k** changes to 🖑).

● The window is highlighted in blue and the window's name pops up.

4 Click a window to move into it.

The window becomes active and moves to the front so that you can use it.

SHOW ALL OPEN WINDOWS FOR AN APPLICATION WITH EXPOSÉ

1. Open multiple documents within the same application.

2. Press **Fn** + **F1** on the MacBook Air keyboard.

   All windows for the application shrink down so that they all fit on the desktop.

3. Point to a window (k changes to 🖑).

   ● The window is highlighted in blue, and the window's name pops up.

4. Click a window to move into it.

   The window becomes active and moves to the front so that you can use it.

CONFIGURE EXPOSÉ

1. From the Apple menu, choose **System Preferences**.

   The System Preferences window appears.

2. Click the **Exposé & Spaces** icon.

   The Exposé & Spaces pane appears.

3. To cause an Exposé action to occur when you point to a corner of the desktop, use the pop-up menus located next to each corner of the desktop thumbnail.

   For example, select **All Windows** on the upper-left menu to perform the same action as **Fn** + **F9** when you point to the upper-left corner of the screen.

4. To change the keyboard shortcut for using Exposé with all open windows, open the **All windows** pop-up menu.

5. Choose the function keys you want to use for this Exposé command.

Note: *To select a key combination, hold down the keys you want to use while the menu is open.*

6. Use the **Application windows** and **Show Desktop** pop-up menus to configure the keyboard shortcuts for those actions.

Note: *Because the function keys are assigned to default actions, you have to hold the* **Fn** *key down while you press the key combination you select.*

7. To assign one of the actions to a trackpad button-click, use the menus on the right side of the window.

Note: *As an example, you could assign the All windows action to the "secondary mouse button" which by default equals pressing two fingers on the MacBook Air trackpad.*

8. Press **⌘** + **Q** to close the System Preferences application.

Create and Use Desktop Spaces

Spaces are collections of applications and documents that you can use to jump between sets of windows easily and quickly. When you use spaces, you do not have to bother locating individual windows, which is not always easy when you have many windows open. You can have as many spaces as you need up to 16.

For example, if you have several Internet applications that you use at the same time, you can create an Internet space and add your applications to it. To use the Internet, you just open the space, and its applications are ready to use immediately.

Create and Use Desktop Spaces

CREATE AND CONFIGURE DESKTOP SPACES

1 From the Apple menu, choose **System Preferences**.

The System Preferences window appears.

2 Click the **Exposé & Spaces** icon.

The Exposé & Spaces pane appears.

3 Click the **Spaces** tab.

The Spaces pane appears. At the top of the pane are thumbnails of the spaces you will be configuring. By default, there are four spaces.

4 Check the **Enable Spaces** check box.

5 Click the **Add** button (![+]).

The Applications sheet appears. By default, the Applications folder, where most applications are stored, is shown.

6 Click the application you want to add to the space.

Note: *You can select multiple applications at the same time by pressing and holding the* ⌘ *key while you click each application.*

7 Click **Add**.

The sheet closes. On the Spaces pane, you see the applications added to the space.

8 Repeat Steps **5** to **7** until you have added all the applications you want to include in spaces.

Note: *To remove applications from the list, select the applications you want to remove and click the* ***Remove*** *button next to the Add button. The application is removed from the Spaces list, but is not affected in any other way.*

9 To add two more spaces in a row, click the **Add** button () next to Rows.

A new row of spaces appears.

10 To add two more spaces in a column, click ⊕ next to Columns.

A new column of spaces appears.

11 Repeat Steps **9** and **10** until you have created all the spaces you want to manage.

Note: *To delete spaces, click the **Remove** button (⊖) next to Rows or Columns.*

12 Open the **Space** pop-up menu for the first application on the list.

13 Choose the number of the space in which you want to include that application, or choose **Every Space** to include it in all spaces; refer to the thumbnails above to see the numbers of your spaces.

After you make a selection, the space number is shown on the menu for the application, and the space's thumbnail at the top of the window is highlighted.

Note: *To delete spaces, click ⊖ next to Rows or Columns.*

14 Repeat Steps **12** and **13** until you have assigned all the applications to the spaces in which you want them to be available (or to every space to have them available at all times).

Note: *To see the list sorted by space number, click the Space column heading.*

15 On the **To activate Spaces** menu, choose the keyboard shortcut you want to use to activate spaces; the default is Fn + F8.

continued

How many spaces should I use?
You want to keep the number of spaces you use to a manageable number; in most cases, you should use between four and six spaces. If you have too many spaces, it will be cumbersome to work with them; too few and each space may have too many applications in it. Try the default number (four) for starters and adjust over time as you use spaces. Realize that you do not need to add every application you use to a space; just add those that you use most often.

Create and Use Desktop Spaces *(continued)*

Spaces can take a bit of getting used to as they are not familiar to many Mac users. It might take some trial and error to configure your spaces in a way that you get the most benefit from them. The most common problem is having too many spaces or too many applications in one space.

Use these steps to configure your spaces initially, and then over time, you discover which spaces work for you and which do not. Keep tweaking your spaces until they are "just right" for the way you work.

Create and Use Desktop Spaces *(continued)*

16 On the **To switch between spaces** pop-up menu, choose the modifier keys you want to use with the arrow keys to jump to your spaces; the default is `Control`+arrow key.

17 To set the modifier key you use to jump directly to a space by its number, open the **To switch directly to a space** pop-up menu and choose the modifier key you want to use; the default is `Control`+number.

18 Press `⌘`+`Q`.

The System Preferences application quits and you are ready to use your spaces.

USE DESKTOP SPACES

1 Open the applications associated with your spaces.

As you open applications, the Spaces bar appears briefly to indicate to which spaces the applications belong.

2 To display all your spaces, press the Spaces activation key (the default is `Fn`+`F8`).

● The desktop is hidden and the Spaces Manager appears. Here, you see each of the spaces you have configured. Within each space, you see the windows that are open in that space.

3 Click a space to move into it.

The applications associated with that space appear.

4 To jump directly to a space, press the keyboard shortcut for switching directly to a space, which by default is `Control`+*spacenumber*, where *spacenumber* is the number of the space you want to move into.

The applications associated with that space appear.

⑤ To move between spaces without using a spaces number, press the keyboard shortcut for switching between spaces, which by default is **Control** +*arrowkey*, where *arrowkey* is one of the arrow keys on the keyboard.

● The Spaces Manager palette appears. Each box on the palette represents one of your spaces. The box highlighted in white is the space currently being shown on the desktop.

⑥ While holding the **Control** key down, press an arrow key to move to the space you want to enter.

● As you press an arrow key, an arrow appears in the palette to show you in which direction you are moving.

⑦ When the space you want to use is highlighted with the white box, release the **Control** key.

The applications associated with that space appear, and you can work with them.

How can I access Spaces using a menu?
On the Spaces pane of the System Preferences application, check the **Show spaces in menu bar** check box. The Spaces menu becomes available on the menu bar; it is indicated by the number of the space you are currently using. Open the menu and choose the space number you want to work with. That space opens.

What happens when I click the Dock icon for an application that is not part of the space I am using?
If an application is available in only one space, when you open it from any source, such as the Dock or the Finder, you switch into the space with which that application is associated. While you cannot add the Finder to a space, it is associated with the space under which a Finder window is currently open; when you click the Finder's Dock icon, you jump into that space and can use that Finder window or open others as needed.

Use and Configure the Dashboard

The Dashboard offers an easy way to access *widgets*, which are small applications that provide very specific functionality. To use a widget, you activate the Dashboard, which fills the desktop and presents the widgets installed on it. You use the widgets you want and then close the Dashboard again.

Mac OS X includes a number of useful widgets by default, such as Weather, Calculator, Address Book, and Flight Tracker. There is even a widget to help you manage your widgets.

Use and Configure the Dashboard

OPEN THE DASHBOARD

1 Press **F4**.

● The desktop moves into the background and the Dashboard appears, displaying the widgets already on the Dashboard.

● If a widget is informational, such as a weather widget, you can view the information it provides.

2 If the widget needs input, click the widget to make it active.

Many widgets require configuration in order to provide useful information to you.

3 Point to the widget you want to configure.

The Info button (a lowercase *i*) appears.

4 Click the **Info** button (![i]).

Note: Many widgets require an Internet connection.

The widget moves into configuration mode.

5 Use the widget's configuration tools to change its settings.

6 Click **Done**.

The widget returns to its normal mode and reflects the changes you made.

CONFIGURE THE DASHBOARD

1 Open the Dashboard.

2 To change the location of widgets, drag them around the screen.

When you release the trackpad button, the widget is saved in its new location and appears in that spot each time you open the Dashboard.

3 Click the **Add Widget** button.

The Dashboard moves into configuration mode. A bar of available widgets appears at the bottom of the screen, and a Close button is added to each widget.

4 Browse the available widgets by clicking the scroll arrows.

5 To add a widget to the Dashboard, drag it from the bar and place it on the Dashboard.

When you release the trackpad button, the widget is installed on the Dashboard and starts to work.

6 To remove a widget from the Dashboard, click its **Close** button.

The widget is removed from the Dashboard, but remains installed, and so you can add it again later if desired.

TIPS

How can I change the key combination to open the Dashboard?

Open the Exposé pane of the System Preferences application and click the **Exposé** tab. On the Hide and Show pop-up menu, select the key combination you want to use to launch the Dashboard. You can press key combinations while the menu is open to be able to select them. For example, hold the Option and Control keys down to see those keys added to the options on the menu.

How else can I activate the Dashboard?

You can set a hot corner so that when you point to that corner, the Dashboard activates. To do this, open the Exposé pane of the System Preferences application and click the **Exposé** tab. Use the Active Screen Corner pop-up menu to choose **Dashboard** for the hot corner you want to set. When you point to that corner, the Dashboard opens.

continued

While Mac OS X includes a number of widgets, these are by no means all of the widgets that are available to you. There are thousands of other widgets available on the Internet for you to download, install, and add to your Dashboard to expand the functionality available to you there.

Downloading and installing widgets is a snap because Mac OS X recognizes widget files and automatically prompts you to install them as soon as they are downloaded to your MacBook Air.

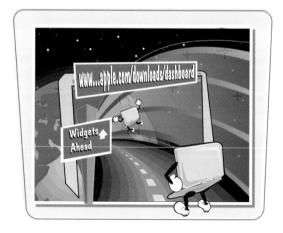

Use and Configure the Dashboard *(continued)*

FIND AND INSTALL MORE WIDGETS ON THE DASHBOARD

① Open the Dashboard, click the large plus sign at the bottom-left corner of the screen, and then click the **Manage Widgets** button.

● The Manage Widgets widget appears.

② Click **More Widgets**.

Your Web browser opens and takes you to the Dashboard Widgets page on the Apple Web site.

③ Use the Web page to browse or search for widgets.

Note: *Details about using Safari to browse the Web are provided in Chapter 11.*

④ When you find a widget you want to install, click its **Download** button.

The widget is downloaded to your MacBook Air. When the process is complete, you are prompted to install the widget.

Note: *If the widget you downloaded does not install automatically, open your Downloads folder to install it.*

⑤ Click **Install**.

The Dashboard opens and you see the widget you are installing.

⑥ Click **Keep**.

The widget is added to the Dashboard.

⑦ Locate the widget on the screen and configure it.

 TIPS

What if I want widgets to show information for more than one location or situation?

You can have as many copies of the same widget on your Dashboard as you want. For example, if you want to track the weather in five locations, add five copies of the Weather widget to your Dashboard and configure one for each area you want to track.

What does the iTunes widget do?

Some applications include a widget that you can use to access that application more quickly and conveniently than opening it directly. For example, the iTunes widget enables you to control content playing in iTunes from the Dashboard. Many other applications have similar widgets that are typically installed with the application; usually you are prompted to install the widget along with the application.

Move to Locations on the Desktop

The Mac desktop provides many ways to get to specific folders that you want to view. Two of the most useful of these are the Sidebar and the Go menu.

Starting from the Sidebar and using the Column view, you can quickly get to any location on the desktop. With the Go menu, you can easily jump to many locations that you commonly visit.

Move to Locations on the Desktop

GO PLACES FROM THE SIDEBAR WITH COLUMN VIEW

① Open a new Finder window.

Note: For information about working with Finder windows, see Chapter 2.

A new Finder window appears.

② Click the **Column View** button (🔲).

③ On the Sidebar, select a starting point such as your Home folder or a disk.

④ Click the first folder whose contents you want to view.

● The contents of that folder appear in the column immediately to the right of the folder you selected.

⑤ Click the next folder you want to move into.

● The contents of that folder appear in the column immediately to the right of the folder you selected.

Note: In Column view, folders have a right-facing arrow at the end of the column; files do not.

⑥ Keep selecting folders until you get to the specific folder or file in which you are interested.

Note: You can always select one of the other views (Icon or List) after you have moved into a folder if you prefer to see a window in one of those views.

GO PLACES WITH THE GO MENU

1 With a Finder window active, open the **Go** menu on the Finder menu bar.

2 Select the location to which you want to move.

● A Finder window opens, showing the location you selected.

TIPS

How can I go places with the keyboard?
The standard folders on the MacBook Air desktop all have keyboard combinations that you can press to jump to them. The following list shows the location and keyboard combination (in parentheses):

Computer (Shift+⌘+C)
Home folder (Shift+⌘+H)
Desktop (Shift+⌘+D)
Network folder (Shift+⌘+K)
iDisk (Shift+⌘+I)
Applications folder (Shift+⌘+A)
Utilities folder (Shift+⌘+U)

How do I make it even easier to move to a folder I use all the time?
Drag the folder onto the right end of the Dock and drop it anywhere on the right side of the dividing line. The folder is installed on the Dock, and you can open it by clicking its icon and choosing **Show in Finder** on the pop-up menu. Or, drag the folder onto the Sidebar so that you can click its icon there to open it on the desktop.

Use Recent Menus

As you work on the desktop, you will probably want to move back to items that you have used recently. Of course, you can always move back to a location in the same way you got there originally, such as by using the Sidebar or Go menu. However, Mac OS X maintains two recent lists, Recent Folders and Recent Items, that you can use to quickly move back to places you have been recently by selecting them on menus.

Use Recent Menus

RETURN TO PREVIOUS FOLDERS

1. With a Finder window active, open the **Go** menu on the Finder menu bar.

2. Choose **Recent Folders**.

3. Select the folder you want to open.

   The folder you selected opens in a Finder window.

RETURN TO PREVIOUS APPLICATIONS, DOCUMENTS, OR SERVERS

1. Open the **Apple** menu (🍎).

2. Choose **Recent Items**.

3. Choose the application, document, or server you want to access.

   The item you selected opens.

Note: To remove all the items from either recent list, you can choose the **Clear Menu** command. The next time you go to an item, it is added to the appropriate menu again.

Create Smart Folders

A *smart folder* is smart because instead of manually placing items within it, you define a set of search criteria, and the items that meet those search criteria are placed within the folder automatically.

For example, you can create a smart folder for a specific project that includes a key phrase that is part of all the file and folder names related to that project. Whenever you create a folder or file whose name includes that phrase, it is included in the project's folder automatically.

Create Smart Folders

1. With the Finder active, choose **File** and then choose **New Smart Folder.**

2. Choose where to search.

   For example, click **This Mac** to search all areas; click **"currentfolder"** to search only that folder; or click **Shared** (if connected to network resources) to search the network.

3. Choose how to search.

   For example, choose **Kind** to search by file type, or choose **Name** to search by filename.

4. Click the **Add Condition** button (⊕).

5. Choose the attribute you want to include.

6. Select the operand.

7. Enter the text or numbers for which you want to search.

   ● As you enter conditions, files and folders that meet those conditions appear in the window.

8. Click **Save**

9. Enter the folder name.

10. Choose a save location.

11. Click **Save**.

    Whenever you open the smart folder, you see all the files and folders that currently meet its criteria.

Rename Files and Folders

You can change the name of files or folders as you need to. Just as when you create them, you can change the names to be just about anything you want, using up to 255 characters.

When you change the name of files, you should usually avoid changing the filename extension (everything after the period in the name) because this extension is an important way that Mac OS X associates documents with applications. However, you can change the part of the name before the period to whatever you want it to be.

Rename Files and Folders

① In a Finder window, select the folder or file whose name you want to change.

② Press **Return**.

● The name becomes highlighted to indicate that you can change it.

Note: *If your user account does not have write permissions for a folder or file, you cannot change its name.*

③ Type the new name of the folder or file.

④ Press **Return**.

The new name is saved.

Note: *Mac OS X uses the filename extension (everything after the period in a filename) to determine which application opens when you open a file. When you change the filename extension, you can change the application with which the file is associated. This can make the file unusable or damage it if the new application is not compatible with the file. Mac OS X warns you so that you do not inadvertently change the filename extension.*

Files and folders take up disk space. You can compress them to reduce the space they consume.

This is most useful when you move these files over a network, especially when you e-mail files as attachments. Not only do compressed files move more quickly, but you can also include all the relevant files in one compressed file to make them easier for the recipient to work with. See Chapter 12 to attach files to e-mail messages.

Compress Files and Folders

COMPRESS FILES OR FOLDERS

1. In a Finder window, select the files and folders you want to include in the compressed file.

Note: Press and hold the ⌘ or **Shift** keys to select multiple items.

2. Press the **Control** key, click the selected items, and select **Compress X Items**, where X is the number of items selected.

   The files and folders are compressed, and a file called Archive.zip is created.

3. Change the name of the Archive.zip file using the steps in the previous task.

Note: Leave the filename extension as .zip or the file might not expand correctly.

EXPAND COMPRESSED FILES

1. In a Finder window, double-click a compressed file.

● The Archive Utility launches and expands the file. It stores the uncompressed files in a folder with the same name as the compressed file.

2. Open the expanded folder to work with the files and folders it contains.

Find Files, Folders, and Other Information

As you use MacBook Air, you create a lot of data in various documents, images, movies, and other kinds of files. You also interact with e-mail, Web pages, and other sources of information. Over time, you might not remember where all this information is. Mac OS X includes tools to help you find the information you need.

You can search for files using the Search tool in Finder windows. You can also use Spotlight on the desktop to search many kinds of information at the same time.

Find Files, Folders, and Other Information

FIND FILES AND FOLDERS WITH FINDER

1. In a Finder window, type the information for which you want to search in the Search bar.

● As you type, the search condition toolbar appears.

2. Choose where the Finder should search.

   For example, click **This Mac** to search all areas; click **"currentfolder"** (where *currentfolder* is the folder you were viewing most recently) to search only that folder; or click **Shared** (if connected to a network resource) to search the network.

3. Choose how the Finder should search.

   For example, click **Contents** to search by file content or **File Name** to search only by filename.

4. To see where a folder or file is located, select it.

● The path to the file or folder is shown at the bottom of the window.

5. To make your search more specific, click the **Add** button (⊞).

   A second search condition bar appears.

6. Configure the search just like when you create a smart folder (see the section, "Create Smart Folders," earlier in this chapter).

● As you add more conditions, the search results become more specific.

FIND INFORMATION WITH SPOTLIGHT

1 Click the **Spotlight** icon located in the upper-right corner of the desktop (🔍 changes to 🔍).

The Spotlight bar appears.

2 Type the information for which you want to search.

● As you type, Spotlight searches MacBook Air to locate information that relates to the text or numbers you entered.

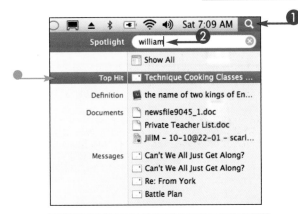

3 Continue typing to make your search more specific.

4 Point to a result to see more information about it.

5 To open one of the found items, click it.

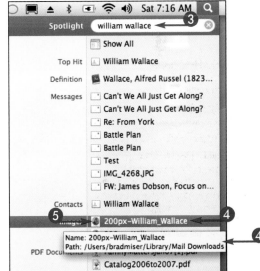

TIPS

How can I save a search so I do not have to reconfigure it each time I want to run it?

Perform a search in a Finder window. When the search works the way you want it to, click the **Save** button. Name the search, choose a save location, and click **Save**. You can run the search again by opening it on the desktop or by clicking it on the Sidebar. A saved search is the same thing as a smart folder.

Smart Folder

How can I use keyboard shortcuts for Spotlight?

You can start a Spotlight search by pressing ⌘+Spacebar. If you click outside the Spotlight window, it closes, but you can easily open it again by pressing ⌘+Spacebar. If you do not like this keyboard shortcut, open the Keyboard Shortcuts tab of the Keyboard & Mouse pane of the System Preferences application. Scroll down until you see the Show Spotlight search field; click its keyboard shortcut and press a new key combination.

When you search with Spotlight, you find a variety of content at the same time. This is good because your searches can easily and quickly expose many different kinds of documents that might be of interest to you. However, if you are not specific when you enter a search term, you might be overwhelmed by the results. Use as specific a search term as you can at first, and make it less specific if you do not find what you want.

You can search for help using the Mac OS X Help system or the help systems provided by third-party applications.

Find Files, Folders, and Other Information *(continued)*

● The item on which you clicked opens and you can work with it.

⑥ To return to the search results, click the **Spotlight** icon again (🔍).

The Spotlight results window appears, and you can view other items in the results or you can change the search criterion.

Note: *To clear a Spotlight search, click the **Clear** button (⊗).*

WILLIAM WALLACE.

CONFIGURE SPOTLIGHT

① Open the System Preferences application.

② Click the **Spotlight** icon.

The Spotlight pane appears.

③ Uncheck the check box for any category of items that you do not want to be included in Spotlight searches.

④ Drag categories up or down the list to change the order in which those categories appear in the Spotlight results window.

⑤ To change the keyboard combination that activates Spotlight, use the **Spotlight menu keyboard shortcut** menu.

⑥ To change the keyboard combination for the Show All command (see the Tip at the end of this section), use the **Spotlight window keyboard shortcut** menu.

7 Click the **Privacy** tab.

● On this tab, you see areas that are not searched when you perform Spotlight searches. Although it is called the Privacy tab, you can use it to exclude an area for any reason, such as to limit the kind of results that you see.

8 Add folders or volumes to the list using the **Add** button (+) or by dragging them from the desktop onto the list.

9 Quit the System Preferences application.

The next time you search with Spotlight, your preferences are used in the search.

FIND HELP

1 While on the desktop, open the **Help** menu on the Finder menu.

The Help Search tool appears.

2 Type the information related to the help you need.

As you type, the Mac Help system is searched.

3 To see where a menu item is, point to it.

● The menu opens and a large pointer points to the menu item.

4 To read a help topic, click it.

● The Help window opens and you see the help topic you selected.

TIPS

What does the Show All result in the Spotlight results window do?

When you click **Show All** in the Spotlight results window or press Option + ⌘ + Spacebar, a Finder window appears configured with the search information you entered in Spotlight, as if you had started the search from the Finder window rather than from Spotlight. Like other Finder searches, you can add search criteria, save the search, and so on.

SHOW ALL

Do all applications use the Mac Help system?

All applications are supposed to provide a Help menu that you can use to get help. Apple applications use the help system provided by Mac OS X so that you can use the same tools to find help in any of these applications. Some non-Apple applications also use the Mac OS X Help system, but others (such as Microsoft Office) implement their own help systems that work a bit differently. No matter what application you happen to be using, start a search for help from its Help menu.

Mac Help

Get Information about Files and Folders

As you learned in Chapter 2, you can choose the specific information you see in some of the views, such as the List view. However, what you see in Finder windows is just some of the information about these items.

To see more detail about any file or folder, you can use the Finder's Get Info command. This command opens the Info window, which provides a lot of detailed information about what you have selected. The information in this window depends on the type of item you selected. For example, you see a different set of information when you select an application file than when you select a document.

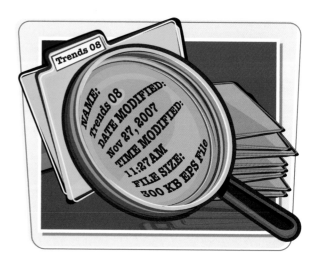

Get Information about Files and Folders

① In a Finder window, select a file or folder you want to get information about.

② Open the **File** menu and choose **Get Info**, or press ⌘ + I.

The Info window appears.

③ Click a section's expansion triangle to see the information it contains (▶ becomes ▼).

Note: In addition to viewing information about a file or folder, you can also use the Info window to make changes to a file or folder. For example, the following steps show you how to change the application that is used to open a file. You can do other tasks as well, such as change the permissions for an item or enter comments for Spotlight searches.

④ Scroll down the window to see all of the sections available for the selected item.

⑤ Expand the **Open with** section.

⑥ On the **Open with** pop-up menu, choose the application in which you want the document to open.

⑦ If you want all documents of the same type to open in that application, click **Change All**.

The next time you open the document, the application you selected is used.

⑧ When you are done viewing or changing information, click ⊙ to close the Info window.

Note: You can leave the Info window open as long as you want, and you can have many Info windows open at the same time, which makes comparing items easy.

TIPS

What are Spotlight Comments?
The Spotlight Comments section appears at the top of the Info window. You can enter text in this field to associate that text with an item. When you search using Spotlight, the information you enter in the Spotlight Comments section is included in the search. For example, you could type a keyword into the Spotlight Comments field for all the files relating to the same project. When you perform a Spotlight search for that keyword, all the files and folders are found based on the keyword you entered.

What does the Sharing & Permissions section do?
This section shows the security settings for the selected item. You see each person or group who has access to the item along with the permissions they have. You can use the controls in this section to change the access people or groups have to the item. First, click the **Lock** icon (🔒) and enter an administrator username and password. Second, use the pop-up menus to change privileges and the **Add** or **Remove** buttons to add or remove people and groups in the list.

Understand Applications

Although every application is different from the others, all applications share fundamental concepts that apply to each of them. Understanding these fundamentals will help you use a wide variety of applications on your MacBook Air.

Applications

The reason computers work so well is that they are very good at following repetitive instructions that adhere to very specific syntax and logic rules. An *application* is a collection of programming statements, more commonly called *code*, that are constructed according to a specific programming language. Applications separate you from the detailed code so that you can control what the application does by interacting with menus and graphical elements of the user interface, instead of having to re-create the lines of code each time you want to do something. Applications are created for many purposes, from running MacBook Air (Mac OS X is a very complex application) to providing the weather at a glance through a simple Dashboard *widget* (a specific kind of application delivered through the Dashboard).

Documents

Most applications, but certainly not all of them, work with documents. In MacBook Air, a document is much more than just a text file; documents can certainly contain text, but they can also be images, e-mails, and songs. Basically, a *document* is the content an application works with. So, for a text processor such as Microsoft Word, a document can include text and graphics. A graphics application, such as Photoshop, uses images as documents. The songs and video stored within iTunes can also be considered documents. If you open or save something with an application, that something can be called a document.

Windows

Chapter 2 talked about the various kinds of windows you see on your MacBook Air. As that chapter mentioned, applications provide windows through which you view documents, or controls and functions when an application does not work with documents (such as a game). An application's windows are whatever you see when you open and use that application. Most applications allow you to have many documents open at the same time, with each appearing in a separate window.

Standard Menus

Applications contain commands that you use to perform actions. For example, when you want to save changes you have made, you use the Save command. Commands are organized into logical collections on menus. When you open a menu, you can see and choose the commands it contains. Mac OS X applications are supposed to support a set of standard menus that have the same or similar commands; these include the *application* menu (where *application* is the name of the application), File, Edit, Window, and Help. These menus also contain a set of standard commands; for example, the application menu always contains the Preferences command. Applications can and usually do have more menus than just the standard menus that are part of Mac OS X design specifications. Some applications, mostly games, do not include standard menus at all.

Application Preferences

Not everyone uses applications in the same way, and everyone has preferences. Because of this, applications include preferences that enable you to configure various aspects of how the application looks and works. You can use preferences to enable or disable functions, change the appearance of the application's windows, and so on. In effect, these commands enable you to tailor the way they work to your preferences, thus the name for this type of command.

Install Applications

To be able to use applications, they must be installed. MacBook Air includes a large number of applications that were installed by Apple, including iTunes, iMovie, and iDVD. You can add many more applications by installing them.

Some applications include an installer program; to install the application, you open the installer and follow the on-screen instructions. Other applications use a drag-and-drop installation method that requires you to drag a folder or file onto your MacBook Air hard drive.

Install Applications

INSTALL APPLICATIONS WITH AN INSTALLER

1. Download the application's installer from the Internet or insert the CD or DVD it came on, and access it through Remote Disc or using the external disc drive on your MacBook Air.

Note: In most cases, the installer starts automatically; if so, skip Step 2.

Note: When you download an installer from the Web, by default, it is stored in the Downloads folder on the Dock. Go there to access the installer.

2. Double-click the application installer's icon to launch it.

   The installer starts running.

3. Read the information on the first screen of the installer and click **Continue**.

4. Continue reading the information and providing the required input, such as clicking **Continue**, to complete the installation process.

   Eventually, you move to the Install screen.

5. Click **Install**.

   You are prompted to authenticate yourself as an administrator.

6. Enter your username.

7. Enter your password.

8. Click **OK**.

   The installer runs and presents progress information in its window. When the process is done, you see the Complete screen.

9. Click **Close** or **Quit**.

   The installer quits and the application is ready for you to use.

INSTALL APPLICATIONS WITH DRAG-AND-DROP

1 Download the application from the Internet or get it from the CD or DVD it came on.

Note: In most cases, the files are provided as a disk image, which usually mounts on MacBook Air automatically. If so, skip Step 2.

2 Double-click the disk image file (its filename ends in .dmg).

The disk image is mounted on MacBook Air.

3 View the files in the disk image; typically, they are organized into a folder and explain what you need to do.

4 Open the **Go** menu and choose **Applications**.

A new Finder window appears, showing the Applications folder.

5 Drag the Applications folder from the disk image window onto the Applications window and release the trackpad button.

The application is copied to and installed in the Applications folder, ready for you to use.

What is the Customize button in the Install window for?

Most installer applications include a Customize button that enables you to customize the application's installation, such as to exclude features or resources you do not need. In most cases, you can ignore this and just perform a standard install. However, if your MacBook Air is very low on disk space, you might want to take a look at the customization options to see if you can skip features or resources you do not need.

Where should I install an application?

In most cases, you should install it in the Applications folder on the MacBook Air startup drive. Most installer applications choose this folder by default, and the instructions with drag-and-drop installations tell you to install there. Keeping your applications in the Applications folder makes them easier for everyone who uses MacBook Air to find, as well as updaters and other programs that need to know the location of applications to run. You can install applications in other locations, but you need to make sure everyone who needs that application has the security to get to the location in which you install it, such as within your Home folder.

Launch and Control Applications

The first step in using an application is to open, or launch, it. There are many ways to do this, and as you use MacBook Air, you will no doubt develop your preferred method.

Once applications are running, there are a number of ways to control them. For example, you open applications by opening documents with which they are associated; you can move between the open applications to jump from one to the other.

Launch and Control Applications

OPEN APPLICATIONS FROM THE DOCK

① Click an application's icon on the Dock.

*Note: The first time you open an application, you see a warning dialog. This is intended to prevent you from unintentionally opening applications that might harm your computer, such as viruses. Click **Allow** to open the application if you are sure it is legitimate.*

The application's icon bounces to show you it is opening, and it is marked with a light-blue dot to show that the application is running.

● When complete, the application's windows appear and it is ready for you to use.

Note: You can also install applications on the Sidebar by dragging their icons there. To open the application from the Sidebar, click its icon.

OPEN APPLICATIONS FROM THE DESKTOP

① Open the **Go** menu and choose **Applications**.

The Applications folder appears in a Finder window.

② Scroll in the window until you see the application you want to open.

③ Double-click the application's icon, or click the icon once to select it, and press ⌘+O.

The application opens and is ready for you to use.

Note: If an application is not installed on the Dock, its icon appears on the right or bottom side of the Dock when it is running. When you quit the application, its icon disappears from the Dock.

OPEN APPLICATIONS FROM DOCUMENTS

1. Find a document in a Finder window.

2. Double-click the document's icon.

   The application with which the document is associated opens, and you see the contents of the document.

Note: Chapter 6 explains how to have applications open automatically when you log in to your user account.

SWITCH APPLICATIONS

1. Open applications as you need to use them; you do not need to close one application to open another one.

2. Press ⌘+Tab.

   The Application Switcher appears. Here you see an icon for each application that is currently running.

● The application with which you are currently working is highlighted in the white box.

3. Click the application you want to move into, or press Tab or Shift+Tab while holding the ⌘ key down until the application you want to use is highlighted, and release the trackpad button.

   The application you selected becomes active, and you can use it.

TIPS

An application does not appear to be doing anything and I see a spinning wheel on the screen.
Occasionally, an application hangs and stops working, even though its windows remain on the screen. Let some time pass to see if the application starts working again. If it does not, open the **Apple** menu and choose **Force Quit**. The Force Quit window appears. Select the application that is having problems (its name will be in red) and click **Force Quit**. Click **Force Quit** again in the resulting dialog. The application is forced to quit. You lose any unsaved changes in the application's open documents, so only do this as a last resort. Restart MacBook Air after normally quitting all other applications.

I have opened a lot of applications and do not want to quit all of them one by one. Is there a faster way?
Yes. Log out of your user account by pressing Shift+⌘+Q and clicking the **Log Out** button. When you log out, all open applications are closed. The next time you log in, no applications are open (unless some are configured to automatically open when you log in).

Save Documents

As you make changes to a document, you need to save those changes to keep them. This sounds simple, and it is, but many people do not regularly save their work. If an application quits before you save changes, you lose all the work you have done. So, get in the habit of saving documents frequently and often.

When you save a document for the first time, you use the Save As command. This is important because you name the document and choose the location in which you save it.

Save Documents

SAVE EXISTING DOCUMENTS

① Open a document and work with it using its associated application.

② Open the **File** menu and choose **Save**, or press ⌘+S.

Note: *The first time you save a document, you use the Save As command instead; see the next step section for details.*

The document is saved in its current state, and the new version replaces the previous version you saved.

SAVE NEW DOCUMENTS

① Open the application with which you want to create a new document.

② Open the **File** menu and choose **New**, where *Document* is the kind of document the application creates, such as a text document, presentation, or image.

● An empty document appears in a new window.

③ Open the **File** menu and choose **Save As**, or press Shift+⌘+S.

Note: *The first time you save a document, you can use the Save or Save As command because they do the same thing. When you want to rename a document or save a new version, you can use the Save As command.*

The Save As dialog appears.

④ Click the **Show Details** button.

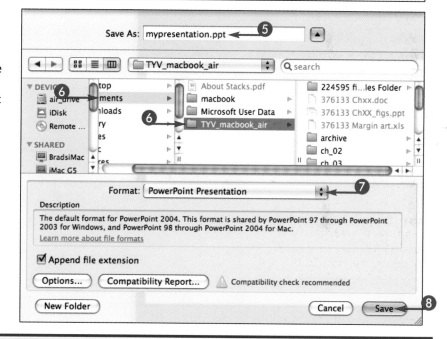

The dialog expands so that you see more details.

⑤ In the Save As field, enter a name for the file; you should leave the filename extension, which is everything after the period, as it is.

⑥ Choose the location in which you want to save the file; this works just like a Finder window in Column view.

⑦ Use the other controls, such as the Format pop-up menu, to change how the file is created.

⑧ Click **Save**.

The document's file is created in the location you set, and you are ready to get to work.

TIPS

Can my documents be saved automatically?
Many applications, such as Microsoft Word, have preference settings that you can configure to save your documents periodically, for example, every five minutes. Open the application's Preferences dialog and look for the Save Preferences. Set them to save frequently. The amount of time that passes without saving your document is the amount of time you have to spend redoing what you have already done if something bad happens, such as an application quitting unexpectedly.

My hard drive crashed. Can I recover my saved document?
It depends on what kind of failure your disk had. In some cases, the documents and other data can be restored. In other cases, you are out of luck. You should always keep important documents backed up so you can recover them if needed. Chapter 17 discusses how to use the Mac OS X Time Machine feature to protect your documents.

Remove Applications

If you no longer use an application, you can remove it from your MacBook Air. However, the storage space an application requires is the only downside of leaving it on your MacBook Air. If you need to free up storage space or you are sure you will never use an application again, you can remove it. Like installing applications, there are two ways to remove an application from MacBook Air: You can use an uninstaller application or drag-and-drop.

If your computer has a lot of available space, you can just leave the application installed in case you ever need it again.

Remove Applications

REMOVE APPLICATIONS WITH AN UNINSTALLER APPLICATION

1 If the application included an uninstaller application, locate it; you can usually find these in the application's folder.

2 Double-click the uninstaller.

The uninstaller application launches.

3 Read the information in the window and click **Continue**.

4 Continue following the on-screen instructions.

● When the uninstallation is complete, you see the completion screen.

Note: *This is sometimes confusing because it says the installation is complete, when it would be more precise to say the uninstallation is complete.*

5 Click **Close** or **Quit**.

REMOVE APPLICATIONS WITH DRAG-AND-DROP

1 Click the desktop so you see the Finder menu bar.

2 Open the **Go** menu and choose **Applications**.

The Applications folder appears in a Finder window.

3 Scroll in the window until you see the application you want to remove.

4 Drag the icon to the Trash; when the Trash icon is highlighted, release the trackpad button.

The application is moved into the Trash. The next time you empty the Trash, it is deleted from your MacBook Air.

TIPS

I want to keep an application that I do not use on my MacBook Air, but documents I open still open in that application. What can I do?

You can stop MacBook Air from opening an application by changing the association between documents and that application. See the task, "Get Information about Files and Folders," in Chapter 4 to learn how to use the Info window to change the application that is associated with documents.

If I remove an application and then decide I need it again, what do I do?

The answer depends on how you obtained the application. If you received it on CD or DVD, you can reinstall it from the original discs (you must also reapply any patches). If you downloaded the application from the Internet, you must have the original files you downloaded to reinstall it; sometimes these continue to be available at the Web site, but sometimes they are not. You should always keep a backup of any software you download from the Internet in case you ever need to reinstall it.

Set Finder Preferences

The Finder is the application that controls the MacBook Air desktop, how files and folders are managed, and many other aspects of the way MacBook Air operates. Like all the other applications you use, Finder has a set of preferences you can configure to change the way it looks and works.

You change Finder preferences using its Preferences command. The resulting dialog has several tabs that you use to configure specific aspects of how the Finder behaves.

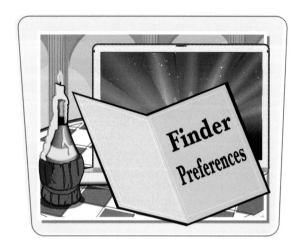

Set Finder Preferences

① Open the **Finder** menu and choose **Preferences**.

The Finder Preferences window appears.

Note: *A faster way to open the preferences for any application, including the Finder, is to press* ⌘ *+* , .

② Click the **General** tab.

③ Check the **Hard disks**, **CDs, DVDs, and iPods**, or **Connected servers** check boxes if you want any of these to show up as icons on the desktop (they are always available within Finder windows).

④ Use the **New Finder windows open** pop-up menu to choose the default location for new Finder windows; choose **Home** to always move to your Home folder, choose **Documents** to move to your Documents folder, choose a volume (such as iDisk) to move there, or choose **Other** and select a start location.

⑤ If you always want folders to open in a new window rather than inside the current one, check the **Always open folders in a new window** check box.

⑥ If you want folders to spring open when you drag icons onto them, check the **Spring-loaded folders and windows** check box, and drag the slider to the left to shorten the time before a folder springs open or to the right to increase the time.

⑦ Click the **Labels** tab.

Note: *You can associate files and folders with labels to help you identify and organize them more easily on the desktop. To do so,* Control *+click a file's or folder's icon and select the color of the label you want to apply.*

⑧ Enter a name for each label in the field next to its color.

Note: *When you apply a label to a file or folder, both the color and name are used, but you do not always see both on the desktop.*

⑨ Click the **Sidebar** tab.

⑩ Check the box next to each item you want to appear in the Sidebar, or uncheck the box next to each item you do not want to appear in the Sidebar.

Note: When you uncheck an item's check box, it is still available in Finder windows; you just do not see its icon on the Sidebar.

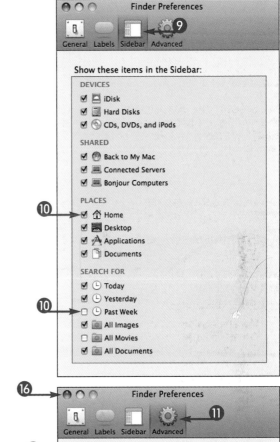

⑪ Click the **Advanced** tab.

⑫ If you always want filename extensions to be shown, check the **Show all file extensions** check box.

⑬ To be warned when you change a filename extension, check the **Show warning before changing an extension** check box.

⑭ If you want to have to confirm emptying the trash, check the **Show warning before emptying the Trash** check box.

⑮ If you want the trash to be emptied securely, making things you delete harder to recover, check the **Empty Trash securely** check box.

⑯ Click the **Close** button (◉).

The Finder Preferences window closes.

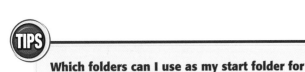

TIPS

Which folders can I use as my start folder for new Finder windows?

The initial location is your Home folder, but you can choose any folder you want. For example, if you keep all of your active projects in a folder, you might want that folder to open by default instead. On the **New Finder windows open** pop-up menu, choose **Other**. In the resulting dialog, move to and select the folder you want to be the default, and then click **Choose**. Each time you open a new Finder window, you move to that folder automatically.

How do I associate labels with folders and files?

Open a Finder window showing the folder or file you want to label. Press ⌘+I. The Info window opens. Expand the General section. Click the label color that you want to apply. The file or folder is marked with that color. You can search for files and folders by their labels; for example, you can create and save a search that automatically finds all folders and files with a specific label. You can also more easily see which files and folders are related because of the label color that is visible in Finder windows.

Explore the System Preferences Application

The System Preferences application is used to configure many different aspects of how MacBook Air looks and works. In fact, most of the personalization you do is through this application.

System Preferences is one application organized in many different panes, with each pane used to configure a specific aspect of MacBook Air. You open the pane you want to use to configure a specific area. For example, you use the Dock pane to configure the Dock, and the Network pane to connect MacBook Air to a network.

OPEN AND USE SYSTEM PREFERENCES

① Open the **Apple** menu and choose **System Preferences**.

The System Preferences application opens and you see all of the panes it offers.

② Click an icon.

The pane associated with that icon appears.

③ Use the controls on the pane to make changes to the way MacBook Air works.

④ When you are done with the pane, click **Show All**.

The open pane closes and you see all the icons again.

SHOW PANES ALPHABETICALLY

1 From the View menu, choose **Organize Alphabetically**.

● The panes are organized alphabetically instead of by category.

SEARCH FOR A PANE

1 To search for a pane, type text in the Search field.

● As you type, panes that meet your search are highlighted.

2 Click the icon you want to use.

TIPS

I cannot make some changes in the System Preferences application, but I can make others. Why?
In order to make changes to various, but not all, settings using the System Preferences application, you must be logged in under an administrator user account or verify that you are an administrator. The easiest way to tell is to look at the Lock icon located in the lower-left corner of a pane. If you do not see the Lock icon, any user can change the pane. If the Lock is "locked," click it to verify that you are an administrator by entering your username and password. If the Lock is "unlocked," you are verified as an administrator and can make changes.

Why do I see a section called Other in my System Preferences application?
Some software you install, especially when it is associated with a hardware device, includes a pane installed on the System Preferences application that you use to configure that software or hardware. All of these additions to the default panes are placed in the Other category.

Change the Desktop's Appearance

Using the Appearance pane, you can configure the color of buttons, menus, and windows along with the color used when something is highlighted to show that it is selected. You can also configure how scrolling in Finder windows works.

While not directly related to appearance, you also use the Appearance pane to determine how many items are stored on Recent menus. You can also control how font smoothing works. *Font smoothing* **makes the edges of large letters and numbers look smoother on the screen – they sometimes can look pixilated or "jaggy."**

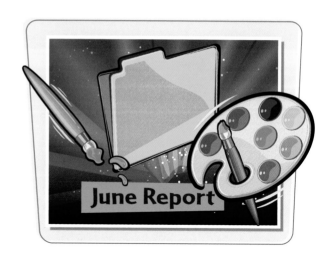

Change the Desktop's Appearance

CHOOSE FINDER COLORS

① Open the System Preferences application and choose the **Appearance** pane.

② On the Appearance pop-up menu, choose **Blue** to see the default button, menu, and window colors.

Note: *For a more subdued color for these items, choose Graphite.*

③ On the **Highlight Color** pop-up menu, choose the color you want to be used to show when a file or folder is selected on the desktop.

④ To create your own highlight color, choose **Other** on the Highlight Color pop-up menu.

The Color Picker appears.

⑤ Click the type of color picker mode you want to use, such as the **Crayon**.

The controls for the color picker mode you selected fill the window.

⑥ Use the controls to configure the color you want to use.

⑦ Click ⬤.

The color you configured is shown on the Highlight Color menu and is used to highlight items on the desktop.

CONFIGURE SCROLL TOOLS

1 Open the System Preferences application and choose the **Appearance** pane.

2 Click the **At top and bottom** radio button if you want scroll arrows to be at the corners of windows; click **Together** if you want them placed together in the lower-right corner of windows.

3 Click **Jump to the next page** if you want to move to the next or previous page when you click above or below the scroll bar; click **Jump to here** if you want to move to a location on the window relative to where you click.

4 If you want scrolling to be smoother when you use a mouse, check the **Use smooth scrolling** check box.

5 If you do not want to be able to minimize a window by double-clicking its title bar, uncheck the **Minimize when double-clicking a window title bar** check box.

SET RECENT ITEMS AND FONT SMOOTHING

1 Open the System Preferences application and choose the **Appearance** pane.

2 On the **Number of Recent Items** pop-up menus, choose the number of items you want to be shown on each of the Recent menus.

Note: *Most applications also have a Recent list; the System Preferences application setting impacts only Mac OS X.*

3 To determine when font smoothing is applied, use the **Font smoothing style** pop-up menu.

4 To determine the point size at which font smoothing is turned off, use the bottom pop-up menu.

Which Color Picker mode is the best?
The Color Picker has different modes that change the way you choose colors. The easiest to use is the Crayon mode because you simply choose colors by clicking a crayon. The other modes offer more control and specificity. For example, you can use the Color Wheel mode to select any color in the spectrum by dragging the intensity bar up or down and then clicking in the wheel to choose a specific color. Other modes offer different tools. To add a custom color to a mode's palette, drag it from the sample box at the top of the window to the palette at the bottom; you can choose your custom color again by clicking it on the palette.

Set a Desktop Picture

As you use MacBook Air, you look at the desktop quite often. So why not look at something you want to see? That is where setting the desktop picture comes in; the desktop picture fills the background on the desktop and you see it behind any windows that are open.

While it is called a desktop picture, you are not limited to pictures. You can use just about any kind of graphic file as a desktop picture.

Set a Desktop Picture

SET A DEFAULT IMAGE AS THE DESKTOP PICTURE

1. Open the System Preferences application and choose the **Desktop & Screen Saver** pane.

2. Click the **Desktop** tab.

   The Desktop picture tools appear.

3. Choose a source of images in the left pane of the window, such as **Apple Images**.

● The images in that source appear in the right pane of the window.

4. Click the image that you want to apply to the desktop.

   That image fills the desktop.

5. To have the image changed automatically, check the **Change picture** check box.

6. On the pop-up menu, choose how often you want the picture to change.

7. If you want images to be selected randomly instead of by the order in which they appear in the source, check the **Random order** check box.

   A new image from the selected source is applied to the desktop according to the timing you selected.

8. If you want the menu bar to be solid so that you cannot see the background through it, uncheck the **Translucent Menu Bar** check box.

SET A PHOTO FROM YOUR IPHOTO LIBRARY AS THE DESKTOP PICTURE

1. Open the System Preferences application and choose the **Desktop & Screen Saver** pane.

2. Click the **Desktop** tab.

3. Scroll down the source list until you see the iPhoto Albums section.

4. Click the source of photos, such as a photo album, containing the images you want to use on the desktop.

● The images in the selected album appear in the right pane of the window.

5. Use the pop-up menu at the top of the window to choose how you want photos to be scaled to the screen; this example chooses the **Fit to Screen** option.

6. Click the **Color** button and use the Color Picker to choose the background color shown behind photos when they do not fill the desktop.

7. To have the image changed automatically, check the **Change picture** check box.

8. On the pop-up menu, choose how often you want the picture to change.

9. If you want images to be selected randomly instead of by the order in which they appear in the source, check the **Random order** check box.

● A new image from the iPhoto album source is applied to the desktop according to the timing you selected.

TIPS

What is the Picture Folder source?

By default, a number of applications store image files in the Pictures folder within your Home folder. If you choose this folder on the source list, you see all the images it contains; you can select images from this source just as you do from one of the other sources.

What if the location of the photos I want to use as the desktop picture does not appear on the source list?

You can choose any folder as a source of desktop pictures by clicking the **Add** button (➕) located at the bottom of the source list. Use the resulting dialog to move to and select the folder containing the images you want. After you click the **Choose** button, that folder appears as a source on the list.

Choose a Screen Saver

A screen saver does two things for you. First, it prevents possible damage to your screen from having the same image on it for a long period of time. Second, and probably more important, it entertains you by displaying images that you choose on the screen. Third, you can require a password to be entered to stop the screen saver, which is a good security measure.

When you are running on battery power, it is better to put MacBook Air to sleep when you are using it instead of showing the screen saver, which uses more power than sleep. The screen saver is more useful when you are running on the power adapter. For more about sleep, see the section "Save Energy."

Choose a Screen Saver

CHOOSE AN APPLE SCREEN SAVER

1 Open the System Preferences application and choose the **Desktop & Screen Saver** pane.

2 Click the **Screen Saver** tab.

3 Click the screen saver you want to use from the list in the Apple section in the left part of the window.

● You see the selected screen saver run in the right pane of the window.

4 Drag the slider to set the amount of idle time that passes before the screen saver activates.

5 If you want the time displayed on the screen saver, click the **Show with clock** check box. If you want a screen saver to be selected at random, check the **Use random screen saver** check box.

6 Click the **Options** button.

The Options sheet appears.

7 Use the tools on the Options sheet to configure the screen saver.

Note: Each screen saver has its own set of options, and so what you see on the Options sheet depends on the screen saver you select.

8 Click **OK** to close the Options sheet.

9 Click **Test**.

You see the screen saver in action.

10 Press a key or drag on the trackpad to stop the screen saver and move back to the System Preferences application.

CREATE YOUR OWN SCREEN SAVER

1. Open the System Preferences application and choose the **Desktop & Screen Saver** pane.

2. Click the **Screen Saver** tab.

3. Scroll down until you see the options in the Pictures section.

4. Click the source of images you want to use in the screen saver, such as **Photos**.

5. If you want the photos to appear as a collage, click the **Collage** button (image).

6. If you want the images displayed in a mosaic, click the **Mosaic** button (image).

● You see the selected images in the screen saver run in the right pane of the window.

7. Drag the slider to set the amount of idle time that passes before the screen saver activates.

8. If you want the time displayed on the screen saver, click the **Show with clock** check box.

9. Click the **Options** button.

The Options sheet appears.

10. Use the tools on the Options sheet to configure the screen saver.

Note: *Each type of screen saver has its own set of options that appear in the Options menu.*

11. Click **OK**.

12. Click **Test**.

You see the screen saver in action.

13. Press a key or drag on the trackpad to stop the screen saver and move back to the System Preferences application.

Why do I never see my screen saver?

The screen saver interacts with the settings on the Energy Saver pane, one of which is the amount of time that passes before the screen darkens to save energy (which also happens to be the best way to save the screen). If that time is less than the screen saver is set for, then you do not see the screen saver before the screen goes dark; you see a warning telling you the screen saver will not activate before the screen goes dark below the time slider on the Screen Saver pane. Reduce the time for the screen saver to be less than the time for the display to be darkened.

Screen Darkens: 10 minutes
Screen Saver: 15 minutes

How can I manually activate the screen saver?

You can set a hot corner so that when you place the pointer in that corner, the screen saver activates. Click the **Hot Corners** button and then choose **Start Screen Saver** on the menu for the corner you want to be hot. When you move the pointer to that corner, the screen saver starts.

Set and Configure the MacBook Air Clock

MacBook Air can help you by keeping track of the time and date for you. Obviously, you can use MacBook Air to see what time it is, but time and date are also important because MacBook Air stamps all the files and folders you use with the time and date they were created and when they were changed. Likewise, e-mails are also time and date stamped. The time and date that are applied to these items are those that are configured on MacBook Air.

There are two basic ways to set MacBook Air's time and date: automatically using a timeserver, or manually. Having MacBook Air set its clock automatically is a good idea so that you can be sure the current time and date are as accurate as possible.

Set and Configure the MacBook Air Clock

CONFIGURE MACBOOK AIR TO SET ITS CLOCK AUTOMATICALLY

1. Open the System Preferences application and click the **Date & Time** icon.

2. Click the **Date & Time** tab.

3. Check the **Set date & time automatically** check box.

4. On the pop-up menu, choose the time server you want to use.

   If you live in the U.S., choose **Apple Americas/U.S.**

5. Click the **Time Zone** tab.

6. Click the time zone you want to set.

● The time zone you select is indicated by the light band on the map and next to the "Time Zone" text.

7. Open the **Closest City** pop-up menu and choose the city closest to your location.

   When MacBook Air is connected to the Internet, it sets the time and date automatically.

CONFIGURE THE MACBOOK AIR CLOCK

① Open the System Preferences application and click the **Date & Time** icon.

② Click the **Clock** tab.

③ If you want to see the clock on the menu bar, check the **Show date and time in menu bar** check box.

④ To see the time in the digital format, click **Digital**; to see it in analog format, click **Analog**.

⑤ If you want to see seconds in the time display, check the **Display the time with seconds** check box.

⑥ To show the AM/PM indicator, check the **Show AM/PM** check box.

⑦ To show the day of the week, check the **Show the day of the week** check box.

⑧ To flash the colon between the hour and minutes at each second, check the **Flash the time separators** check box.

⑨ To use the 24-hour format, check the **Use a 24-hour clock** check box.

⑩ To hear an announcement of the time, check the **Announce the time** check box.

⑪ Use the pop-up menu to choose how often the time should be announced, such as **On the hour**.

⑫ Click **Customize Voice** and use the resulting sheet to select and configure the voice you want MacBook Air to use to announce the time.

TIPS

What if I take MacBook Air to a different time zone?

You can leave MacBook Air in its previous time zone no matter where you are located. Of course, when you are in a different time zone than the one configured on MacBook Air, its time will not match the local time. If that bothers you, you can always change the current time zone using the previous steps.

What if the time and date are not in the right format?

Open the **International** pane of the System Preferences application. Click the **Formats** tab. Choose the region whose time and date format you want to use, or click the **Customize** button for the format you want to change to customize it.

Save Energy

When you first think of saving energy, you might think of lowering your electric bill or reducing the need for electricity. However, MacBook Air uses so little energy that it is unlikely that you can make any difference in either of these areas by changing how MacBook Air uses energy.

However, when you are running MacBook Air on battery power, saving energy is very important because the rate at which MacBook Air consumes battery power determines how long you can work.

Save Energy

① Open the System Preferences application and choose the **Energy Saver** pane.

② Click **Show Details**.

The pane expands so that you see all of its controls.

③ On the Settings for pop-up menu, choose **Battery**.

④ You can choose one of the predefined configurations from the Optimization pop-up menu. For example, to maximize battery life, choose **Better Battery Life**.

The other controls on the pane are adjusted to match the settings you selected. If these are the settings you want to use, you can skip the rest of these steps. To customize the settings, continue to the next step.

⑤ Drag the upper slider to set the idle time after which MacBook Air goes to sleep.

Note: *As soon as you make a change, the setting on the Optimization pop-up menu becomes Custom to show that you are not using a default scheme any more.*

⑥ Drag the lower slider to set the amount of inactive time after which the display darkens.

⑦ To have the hard drives go to sleep when they are not being used, check the **Put the hard disk(s) to sleep when possible** check box.

⑧ Click the **Options** tab for more ways to manage MacBook Air's energy.

⑨ If you want the display to dim slightly after a few moments of idle time, check the **Slightly dim the display when using this power source** check box.

⑩ If you want the screen to be dimmed before it sleeps, check the **Automatically reduce the brightness of the display before display sleep** check box; this gives you some warning before the display goes dark.

⑪ If you want to see the Battery icon in the menu bar, check the **Show battery status in the menu bar** check box.

 TIPS

What about running on the power adapter?
If you choose **Power Adapter** on the Settings for pop-up menu, you can configure energy settings when MacBook Air is running on the power adapter. These can be different from those you use while on battery power. MacBook Air knows when it is on battery power and chooses the appropriate energy options automatically. When you choose Power Adapter, a different set of options appears on the Options tab.

What is the Schedule button for?
If you click the **Schedule** button on the Options tab, you can schedule MacBook Air to automatically start or wake up at a specific time. You can also have it automatically shut down or sleep at a specific time.

Configure the MacBook Air Screen

MacBook Air's screen is what you look at while you use it, and so it is important to know how to configure the screen so it matches your viewing preferences. You can configure the display's resolution, number of colors, and brightness.

Although the physical size of MacBook Air's screen is fixed, the amount of information that it can display (its resolution) is not. That is because each pixel (short for *picture element*) that makes up the display's images can be larger or smaller. When pixels are larger, what is on the screen is shown on a larger, zoomed-in scale. When pixels are smaller, more content is displayed on the screen, but on a smaller, zoomed-out scale.

Configure the MacBook Air Screen

CONFIGURE THE MACBOOK AIR SCREEN ON THE DISPLAYS PANE

① Open the System Preferences application and click the **Displays** icon.

The Displays pane opens.

② Click the **Display** tab.

③ Click a resolution.

● MacBook Air's screen updates to use that resolution. The current resolution is highlighted on the list.

④ Experiment with resolution settings until you choose the highest resolution that is still comfortable for you to see.

⑤ Drag the **Brightness** slider to the right to make the screen brighter, or to the left to make it dimmer.

Note: *If you are running on battery power, you can keep the screen dimmer to lower the amount of power you use, which extends the time you can work.*

⑥ To add a Displays menu to the menu bar, check the **Show displays in menu bar** check box.

⑦ To have the screen brightness adjust automatically based on the lighting conditions where you are using MacBook Air, check the **Automatically adjust brightness as ambient light changes** check box.

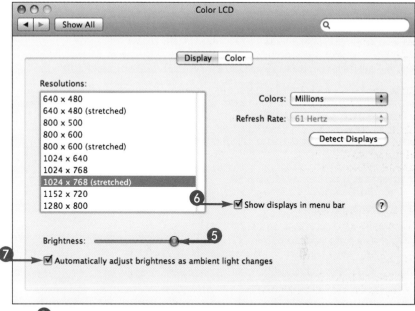

CONFIGURE THE MACBOOK AIR SCREEN ON THE DISPLAYS MENU

① Open the **Displays** menu (▭).

② To change the resolution, select the resolution you want to use on the list of recent resolutions.

③ To set the number of recent resolutions on the menu, choose *number* under **Number of Recent Items**, where *number* is the number of resolutions you want to see on the menu.

④ Choose **Displays Preferences** to open the Displays pane of the System Preferences application.

How else can I set screen brightness?

MacBook Air includes two keys that you can use to change the screen's brightness. Press F1 to lower the brightness or F2 to increase it. These do the same thing as the Brightness slider on the Displays pane. Each time you press one of the keys, an indicator appears on the screen to show you the relative brightness level you have set.

What do the other controls on the Display tab do?

You can use the Colors pop-up menu to set the number of colors displayed on MacBook Air's screen; however, there is not really any reason to use less than Millions of colors (this control is used for older Macs that do not have enough graphics processing power to display millions of colors at all resolutions). The Detect Displays button (and command on the Displays menu) is used when you connect MacBook Air to an external display or projector (see Chapter 9). The Color tab is used to configure a color profile for the display. You will not likely need to do this unless you are doing very precise color printing work, in which case, you can configure a screen profile to match your printer output.

Configure the Keyboard

Obviously, using MacBook Air is a hands-on experience. One of your primary inputs is the keyboard, through which you make commands, add content to documents, send and receive e-mail, and so on. You can configure the keyboard to suit your input preferences.

You use the Keyboard & Mouse pane of the System Preferences application to configure your keyboard. (You can learn how to configure and use the MacBook Air trackpad in Chapter 1.)

Configure the Keyboard

CONFIGURE GENERAL KEYBOARD SETTINGS

① Open the System Preferences application and click the **Keyboard & Mouse** icon.

② Click the **Keyboard** tab.

③ Drag the **Key Repeat Rate** slider to the right to increase the number of times a letter or number repeats while you press a key, or to the left to decrease the rate.

④ Drag the **Delay Until Repeat** slider to the right to increase the amount of time you have to press a key for its letter or number to repeat, or to the left to shorten the time.

⑤ If you do not want to use the built-in functions for the function keys but instead want them to act as normal function keys, check the **Use all F1, F2, etc. keys as standard function keys** check box.

Note: *If you check this box, you press the* Fn *key to use the pre-programmed functions of the function keys, such as* F2 *to brighten the screen.*

⑥ To use the backlight, which illuminates the keys under darkened conditions, check the **Illuminate keyboard in low light conditions** check box.

⑦ Drag the **Turn off when computer is not used for** slider to the left to decrease the amount of time the keys remain illuminated, or to the right to increase the time.

Note: *Keyboard illumination uses power, and so it is better to have it on for a shorter time to maximize battery life.*

⑧ Click the **Modifier Keys** button.

⑨ In the Modifier Keys sheet, use the pop-up menus to choose the key presses associated with the various modifier keys. For example, you can disable the Caps Lock key by choosing **No Action**.

⑩ Click **OK**.

Your changes take effect and the sheet closes.

CONFIGURE KEYBOARD SHORTCUTS

1 In the Keyboard pane, click the **Keyboard Shortcuts** tab.

You see a list of commands and the associated keyboard shortcuts.

2 Uncheck the check box for any listed keyboard shortcut to disable it.

That keyboard shortcut is grayed out in the list and no longer has any effect.

3 Change the keys used for any shortcut by clicking the current shortcut, waiting for it to become highlighted, and pressing the new keyboard combination you want to use.

Note: *If you hover over a keyboard shortcut, a tool tip listing the keys appears. This is helpful because the symbols used in the shortcuts do not appear on the keys, except for the* ⌘ *key.*

4 Add a new keyboard shortcut by clicking ✚.

5 On the Application menu on the New Shortcut sheet, choose the application to which the shortcut applies or choose **All Applications** to have it impact all of them.

6 Type the name of the command in the Menu Title field (you must type the name exactly as it appears on the menu, including a trailing ellipsis).

7 Click in the **Keyboard Shortcut** field and press the key combination you want to use.

8 Click **Add**.

The new shortcut is created and is ready for you to use.

Where do I see the new keyboard shortcuts I have created?

The top of the list of shortcuts on the Keyboard Shortcuts tab shows the default or standard shortcuts that are configured. Scroll down the list until you see the Application Keyboard Shortcuts section. In that section, you see any shortcuts you have added.

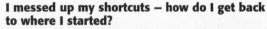

I messed up my shortcuts — how do I get back to where I started?

On the Keyboard Shortcuts tab, click the **Restore Defaults** button to set all keyboard shortcuts as they were when you first started MacBook Air. You lose any changes you have made over time, so if you only want to reset a couple of shortcuts, just change them back to what you want them to be.

Control the MacBook Air Sound

From sound effects to music and movies, sound is an important part of the MacBook Air experience. Additionally, you may want to use sound input for audio and video chats, recording narration for movies, and so on.

The Sound pane of the System Preferences application is your primary stop for managing audio settings on your MacBook Air.

Control the MacBook Air Sound

CONFIGURE SOUND EFFECTS

1. Open the System Preferences application and click the **Sound** icon.

   The Sound pane appears.

2. Click the **Sound Effects** tab.

3. Click a sound on the alert sound list.

   The sound plays.

4. Drag the **Alert volume** slider to make the alert sound louder or quieter.

5. To hear sound effects for system actions, such as when you empty the Trash, check the **Play user interface sound effects** check box.

6. If you want audio feedback when you change the volume level, check the **Play feedback when volume is changed** check box.

7. If you want to hear Front Row's sound effects, check the **Play Front Row sound effects** check box.

Note: When you activate Front Row with its sound effects enabled, you hear sounds for various actions, such as selecting a choice from the on-screen menu.

CONFIGURE SOUND OUT

1. Open the System Preferences application and click the **Sound** icon.

   The Sound pane appears.

2. Click the **Output** tab.

3. Select the output device over which you want MacBook Air to play sound.

Note: If you do not have any external speakers connected to MacBook Air, you have only one choice: Internal Speakers. See Chapter 9 for information about connecting MacBook Air to speakers.

4. Drag the **Balance** slider to set the balance between the left and right speakers.

CONTROL SYSTEM VOLUME

① Open the System Preferences application and click the **Sound** icon.

The Sound pane appears.

② Drag the **Output volume** slider to the right to increase the volume or to the left to decrease it.

③ To mute all sounds, check the **Mute** check box.

④ To configure the Volume menu on the menu bar, check the **Show volume in menu bar** check box.

⑤ To set the volume using the menu, open it and drag the slider up to increase volume or down to decrease it.

CONFIGURE SOUND INPUT

① Open the System Preferences application and click the **Sound** icon.

The Sound pane appears.

② Click the **Input** tab.

③ Select the input device you want to use; for MacBook Air's internal microphone, choose **Internal microphone**.

④ Play the sound you want to input; if you are recording yourself or preparing for an audio chat, begin speaking.

● As MacBook Air receives input, the relative volume of the input is shown on the Input level gauge.

⑤ Drag the **Input volume** slider to the left to reduce the level of input sound or to the right to increase it.

⑥ Keep trying levels until the gauge looks about right; in most cases, the slider should be about 3/4 of the length of the bar.

⑦ If the area you are in is noisy, check the **Use ambient noise reduction** check box.

Create and Configure User Accounts

Mac OS X is a multiuser system. What this means is that you can create user accounts for each person who uses MacBook Air. Each person who uses it then has a unique desktop, folders, files, and preferences so that MacBook Air is tailored specifically to them.

A standard account can access all the MacBook Air's resources, but it cannot perform administrator tasks, such as installing applications; you should use this type for most users. An administrator account allows access to the administration tasks, many of which are discussed in this chapter. (Other types are explained in the tips at the end of this section.)

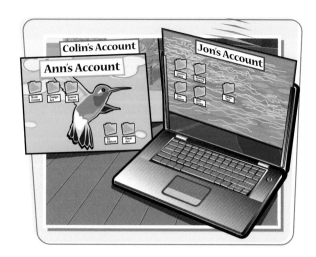

Create and Configure User Accounts

CREATE A USER ACCOUNT

1. Open the System Preferences application and click the **Accounts** icon.

● The Accounts pane appears. In the accounts list on the left side of the window, you see the accounts that currently exist.

Note: *To be able to make changes, you need to click the **Lock** icon ( ) at the bottom of the pane, enter an administrator username and password, and click **OK**. The Lock icon becomes unlocked indicating you can make changes.*

2. Click the **Add** button ( ).

The New Account sheet appears.

3. Choose the type of account on the **New Account** pop-up menu.

Note: *See the tip on the next page to learn about account types.*

4. Enter a full username for the account in the Name field. This can be just about anything you want, but it is usually the person's name.

Mac OS X creates a short username based on what you enter.

5. Edit the short username as needed.

Note: *This name is important because it appears in a number of places, such as the URL to that user's Web site on MacBook Air.*

6. If you know how to enter a password for the user, do so and then skip to Step **11**. Otherwise, go to Step **7**.

7. Alternatively, if you want help creating a password, click the **Key** icon ( ).

The Password Assistant appears.

⑧ Choose a password type from the **Type** pop-up menu.

● Mac OS X generates a password for you. If there are tips related to the type you selected, you see them in the Tips field.

⑨ Drag the **Length** slider to the right to increase, or to the left to decrease, the length of the password.

● As you make changes, the Quality gauge shows you how secure the password is. Green indicates a secure password, yellow is less secure, and red is not secure.

⑩ When you are happy with the password, click back in the New Account sheet while leaving the Password Assistant window open.

⑪ Re-enter the password in the Verify field.

Note: If you did not keep the Password Assistant open, you need to remember the password you configured to be able to type it in.

⑫ If you want users to be able to access a hint when they cannot remember their password, type the hint in the Password Hint field.

⑬ If you want the user's data to be protected with FileVault, check the **Turn on FileVault protection** check box.

⑭ Click **Create Account**.

● The user account is created and appears on the list of accounts.

⑮ Click ⊖ to close the Password Assistant.

⑯ To associate an image with the user account, click the **Image well**.

TIPS

Why can I not make changes on the Accounts pane?

You have to be authenticated as an administrator to be able to create or change other user accounts. You can tell if you are verified by the Lock icon located in the lower-left corner of the pane. If the Lock is closed, you cannot make changes to other accounts on the Accounts pane. To authenticate yourself, click the Lock icon, enter an administrator username and password, and click **OK**. The Lock icon opens and you can make changes.

What types of user accounts are available?

There are six types of user accounts. An *administrator* account has access to all Mac OS X tools and can perform just about any action. A *standard* account can only make changes related to that account. A *managed with parental controls* account enables you to limit the access a user has to various kinds of content. A *sharing only* account can only be used to access shared files. A *group* account is used for configuring access permissions to files and folders. A *root* account has unlimited access to all functions and is used primarily during troubleshooting.

continued

Create and Configure User Accounts *(continued)*

As you create new user accounts, be careful about the kind of account you provide to other people. In most cases, you will want to give other people a standard or managed with parental controls user account so that those people have limited access to MacBook Air's administrative functions.

You should have at least two user accounts. One should be an administrator account (which is the type created when you first started up MacBook Air) that you use regularly. The other should be an administrator account that you create, but do not use so that it remains in the default state. You use this second account during troubleshooting.

Create and Configure User Accounts *(continued)*

⑰ Choose an icon from the pop-up menu and skip to Step **23**.

⑱ Alternatively, choose **Edit Picture**.

If you clicked **Edit Picture**, the Edit Picture sheet appears.

⑲ Drag an image file from the desktop onto the Image well.

Note: *You can select an image from any location by clicking the **Choose** button, moving to the image you want to use, and clicking **Open**.*

● To use a photo as a user account's icon, click the **Camera** icon (📷) and place the subject in front of MacBook Air's iSight camera.

After about three seconds, the image is captured.

⑳ Drag the **Size** slider to the right to zoom in on the image of the user's icon, or to the left to zoom out.

㉑ Drag the selection box until the part of the image you want to use is enclosed in the box.

㉒ Click **Set**.

The image is associated with the user account.

㉓ If the user has a MobileMe account, enter the member name in the MobileMe User Name field.

㉔ If you want the user to be able to administer MacBook Air, check the **Allow user to administer this computer** check box.

㉕ Give the username and password you created to the person who you want to be able to use MacBook Air.

CONFIGURE LOGIN ITEMS FOR A USER ACCOUNT

① Log in under the user's account (you have to be logged into an account to set Login Items for it).

② Open the System Preferences application and click the **Accounts** icon to open the Accounts pane.

③ Click the **Login Items** tab.

④ Drag the items that should open automatically from the desktop onto the pane; you can drag applications, documents, or folders onto the list.

⑤ Check the **Hide** check box for any items you want to be hidden by default.

⑥ Log out of the user's account.

The next time the user logs in, the items you configured open automatically.

TIPS

Do I have to configure a password for a user account?	**What if a user forgets his or her password?**
A user account does not have to have a password. If you leave the Password and Verify fields empty, you see a warning that not providing a password is not secure. If you are sure that is not a problem for you, clear the warning prompt and complete the user creation. The user is able to log in to the MacBook Air without entering a password, which can mean that anyone who has access to the MacBook Air can use it.	Open the Accounts pane, select the user's account on the list, and click **Reset Password**. Use the resulting sheet to configure a new password just as you do when you create an account. The user is then able to log in with the new password.

******

pass word

Protect Users with Parental Controls

The phrase *parental controls* is a bit misleading. Although these can certainly be used to protect children from interactions on the Internet that might not be good for them, you can use the same tools to tailor any user's access to MacBook Air and the Internet.

You can also use Parental Controls to limit access to applications and system functions.

Protect Users with Parental Controls

① Open the System Preferences application and click the **Parental Controls** icon.

② Select the user account for which you want to configure Parental Controls.

③ Click **Enable Parental Controls**.

The Parental Controls tabs appear.

④ Click the System tab.

⑤ To limit the access of the user to specific applications, check the **Only allow selected applications** check box.

⑥ Uncheck the check box for the groups or individual applications you do not want the user to be able to use.

⑦ Use the check boxes at the bottom of the pane to allow or prevent access to system actions.

⑧ Click the **Content** tab.

⑨ To prevent profanity from appearing in the Mac OS X dictionary, check the **Hide profanity in Dictionary** check box.

⑩ To prevent access to adult Web sites automatically, click **Try to limit access to adult websites automatically**.

Note: *Click the Customize button to open the Customize sheet on which you can allow or prevent specific Web sites.*

⑪ To limit access to only specific Web sites, click **Allow access to only these websites**, click the **Add** button (➕), and enter the URLs of the Web sites you want to allow (all other sites are blocked).

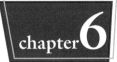

⑫ Click the **Mail & iChat** tab.

⑬ To limit e-mail, check the **Limit Mail** check box.

⑭ To limit chats, check the **Limit iChat** check box.

Note: The e-mail and chat controls work only with Mail and iChat.

⑮ Click ➕.

The Parental Controls sheet appears.

⑯ Configure the Parental Controls sheet for the person with whom you want to allow e-mail or chat interaction.

⑰ Click **Add**.

● The person is added to the allowed list.

⑱ Repeat Steps **14** to **16** for each person with whom you want to allow interaction.

⑲ If you want to receive an e-mail requiring you to grant permission when someone not on the list is involved in an e-mail exchange with the user, check the **Send permission requests to** check box and enter your e-mail address.

 TIPS

What is the Time Limits tab for?
You can use the Time Limits tab to limit the amount of time the user can use MacBook Air. You can configure time on weekdays and weekends. You can also configure "bedtimes" during which the user is unable to access MacBook Air.

What is the Logs tab for?
On the Logs tab, you can view the user's activities, such as Web sites visited, Web sites blocked, and applications used.

Set Login Options

There are a number of ways you can configure the login process for MacBook Air. In the Login window, you can present a list of users so that to log in, a user clicks the username and enters a password. Or, you can present an empty username and password field and the user has to complete both to log in. There are also a number of other ways to configure the Login window by showing or hiding specific buttons. You can also disable or enable Automatic Login.

Fast user switching is another option, which allows multiple people to be logged in to MacBook Air at the same time. Each user can quickly move back into their account because it is left open instead of each user logging out before another logs in.

Set Login Options

CONFIGURE AUTOMATIC LOGIN

① Open the System Preferences application and click the **Accounts** icon.

② Click **Login Options**.

The Login Options pane appears.

③ On the **Automatic login** pop-up menu, choose the name of the user that you want to be automatically logged in.

④ Enter the user's password.

⑤ Click **OK**.

Each time MacBook Air starts, the user you selected is logged in automatically.

CONFIGURE THE LOGIN WINDOW

① Open the Login Options pane.

② To show a list of users in the Login window, click **List of users**; to show empty Name and Password fields, click **Name and password** instead.

③ If you want to be able to restart MacBook Air, put it to sleep, or shut it down from the Login window, check the **Show the Restart, Sleep, and Shut Down buttons** check box.

④ If you want to be able to choose the language layout from the Login window, check the **Show Input menu in login window** check box.

⑤ To show a hint when users forget their password, check the **Show password hints** check box.

⑥ To have MacBook Air read the text in the Login window, check the **User VoiceOver at login window** check box.

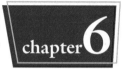

CONFIGURE AND USE FAST USER SWITCHING

1. Open the Login Options pane.

2. Check the **Enable fast user switching** check box.

3. Open the **View as** pop-up menu; then choose **Name** to see the current user's username at the top of the Fast User Switching menu; choose **Short name** to see the user's short name, or choose **Icon** to see a silhouette.

The Fast User Switching menu (👤) appears on the menu bar.

4. Open the **Fast User Switching** menu (👤).

● All the user accounts on MacBook Air are shown. The users that are currently logged in are marked with a check mark.

5. Choose the user to switch to.

6. Enter the user's password.

7. Click **Log In**.

The user is logged in and their desktop appears. The previous user remains logged in; select that user's account on the menu to move back to it.

 TIPS

What happens to running applications when another user logs in using fast user switching?

Because a user does not log out when another one logs in using fast user switching, the applications and processes running under a user account continue to run in the background even while another user is using MacBook Air. As soon as the previous user logs back in, the results of the activity that was ongoing are seen, such as new e-mails, Web pages, and so on.

How I can leave myself logged in so my applications continue to work, but no one else can see or use what I am doing?

On the Fast User Switching menu, choose **Login Window**. The Login window appears, but you remain logged in (you see a check mark next to your username). All applications and processes continue to run in the background. To start using MacBook Air again, choose your user account, enter your password, and click **Login**. You move back to where you left off.

PART

II

Getting Connected

While a standalone MacBook Air is useful, it is not as useful as one connected to a local network and the Internet. Because MacBook Air is made for traveling, you need to know how to keep connected while you are on the move without risking the computer or its data. There are also devices you will want to connect to MacBook Air, such as a hard drive. In this part, you learn how to get and keep MacBook Air connected.

Understand Networking Concepts

The topic of networking is the most technical in this book. MacBook Air and Mac OS X manage most of the details for you, but there are a number of concepts that are helpful to understand as you create your own network.

Network

Simply put, a *network* is two or more computers and other devices connected together using cables or wireless connections. The purpose of a network is to enable the devices on it to communicate with each other. This is done using various *protocols* (which can be thought of as languages) to provide different services. For example, the Transmission Control Protocol/Internet Protocol (TCP/IP) is the basic "language" that devices speak over the Internet. There are other protocols for a variety of services, such as file sharing and printing, but the data for all of these services are communicated over a network. Networks can be large or small, simple or complicated, but they all have the same basic purpose.

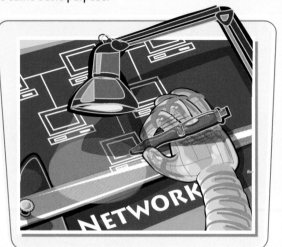

Internet

The Internet is the largest network possible because it literally spans the globe, and millions upon millions of devices and people are connected to it. The Internet makes communication and information available way beyond anything that was possible before it came to be. Many services are available over the Internet, such as e-mail, searching the Web, chats, and file transfers. Connecting MacBook Air to the Internet is just about as important as being able to charge its battery.

Local Network

A *local network*, also known as a local area network or *LAN*, is a network that covers a defined physical space. LANs can be quite large, such as in a business or school, or fairly small, such as in a home. A LAN connects its devices together so they can communicate with one another and also connect to outside networks, most importantly, to the Internet. This chapter focuses on helping you create a small LAN, such as what many people use in their homes. The principles of larger LANs are the same, but the details get much more complicated.

Ethernet

Ethernet is both a physical means of connecting devices together — for example, an Ethernet cable — and the protocol used to communicate over the physical connection. Ethernet can support various communication speeds, and all of them are quite fast. (To connect MacBook Air to other devices using Ethernet, you need to use an Ethernet Adapter; see Chapter 9 for details.) In addition to their speed, Ethernet connections offer other benefits, including simplicity and security. The primary downside to Ethernet is the need for a physical connection between the devices, which can involve a lot of cables.

Wi-Fi Network

Wi-Fi is a general term for a set of wireless communication standards and technologies that are defined in the Institute of Electrical and Electronics Engineers (IEEE) 802.11 specifications. Like Ethernet networks, Wi-Fi enables devices to communicate, but uses radio transmissions instead of physical wires to connect devices. This offers ease of configuration and makes it possible to move around while remaining on a network, which is especially useful for MacBook Air. The downsides of Wi-Fi are that configuration is more difficult and Wi-Fi networks are not as secure as Ethernet networks. Wi-Fi networks are not as fast as Ethernet networks are either. However, the flexibility they provide more than makes up for the slightly more difficult configuration.

AirPort

Apple uses the term *AirPort* for its implementation of Wi-Fi. Like other Macs, every MacBook Air supports AirPort. Apple also offers AirPort base stations that you can use to create your own Wi-Fi networks. Fortunately, AirPort technologies are based on the Wi-Fi standards. As a result, MacBook Air can access any Wi-Fi network, and other kinds of devices that support Wi-Fi can connect to AirPort networks.

Hub/Router/Access Point

All networks need a device that controls the flow of information among the various computers, printers, and other resources on the network. These devices are called hubs, routers, or access points. There are many kinds of these devices, and they all offer different features and benefits. They can support Ethernet, Wi-Fi, or both kinds of networks. Because AirPort Extreme Base Stations offer a lot of nice features and support is built in to Mac OS X, they are the focus of this chapter. However, MacBook Air can be used with other kinds of routers as well. Some of the key features of hubs are the ability to share an Internet connection among many devices and to shield those devices from Internet attacks.

Internet Service Provider

The Internet must be accessed through specific entry points. To do this, you need the services of an Internet Service Provider (ISP). The ISP provides the means that you use to connect your network to the Internet using various technologies, such as cable, Digital Subscriber Line (DSL), or even satellite.

Internet Account

To access the Internet, you need an Internet account with an ISP. The cost of the account varies, depending on the specific ISP you use. Typically, ISPs require you to have only one Internet account for your network, but you are responsible for everything connected to the modem (the device that communicates from your LAN to the ISP) on "your side," while the ISP is responsible for ensuring that the signal to the modem is working. Depending on the type of Internet access you use, you might need a username and password to connect to your account, or it might be based on your physical location (such as with a cable connection).

IP Address

An IP address is the way devices on the Internet are identified. Put another way, to be able to connect to and use the Internet, a device must have an IP address. IP addresses include a set of four numbers with periods between each number, as in 169.455.12.3. In most networks, you do not need to worry about the details of IP addresses because the hub/router uses Dynamic Host Control Protocol (DHCP) to automatically assign addresses to devices as they are needed. You just need to be able to recognize whether or not a device has a valid IP address, which is clear because when you do not have one, you cannot connect to the Internet.

Internet Services and Applications

The reason to connect devices to the Internet is to be able to access the services that are delivered over it. To access these services, you use Internet applications. Obvious examples are Mail for e-mail, and Safari for Web browsing. There are many kinds of services available on the Internet, and many different applications to use each of those services, but you will likely end up using just a few of them. Because Mac OS X includes powerful and easy-to-use Internet applications, they are a good place to start.

Internet Dangers

While the Internet offers amazing capabilities, they do not come without risk. Unfortunately, just like in the physical world, on the Internet, there are many people who want to hurt other people. The dangers of Internet life include the annoying, such as pornography and spam, and the truly dangerous, such as viruses, hacking, or identity theft. Fortunately, with some basic precautions and common sense, you can protect yourself from most Internet dangers relatively easily.

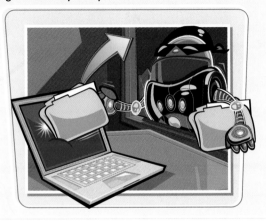

Local Network Services

Similar to the Internet, you can take advantage of services that you can provide over your local network. These include file and printer sharing, local Web sites, and chatting. Configuring and using local network services are pretty straightforward because these services are built in to Mac OS X.

Obtain an Internet Account

In order to connect your network or MacBook Air to the Internet, you must have an Internet account. Different kinds of Internet accounts allow you to connect in different ways. The most common high-speed technologies for homes are cable and DSL. Satellite connections are also available. Before you decide on an Internet account, you should know the options that are available in your location.

If your location has cable TV service, contact the provider to see if Internet access is available and what the cost is. Then locate providers of Internet access through DSL. Choose the type of account and provider that makes the most sense to you.

Obtain an Internet Account

DETERMINE WHAT TYPES OF INTERNET ACCOUNTS ARE AVAILABLE

① If cable service is available to you, contact the cable provider to get information about Internet access, including monthly cost, speed options, and installation or startup costs.

② If you have access to a computer that is connected to the Web, move to dsl.theispguide.com.

③ Use the tools to search for DSL access in your location.

Note: When you contact a potential provider, ask if Macintosh is supported. Although you do not really need formal support because Macs work with standard technologies, Mac support can be a factor when you are choosing a provider.

④ Contact DSL providers that serve your area to get details about their service, including monthly cost, installation costs or startup fees, and length of contract.

Note: Make sure you have potential providers check your actual phone number to ensure that DSL is available. DSL availability in your area does not guarantee service at your specific location.

Note: If cable or DSL is available to you, skip to Step 1 in the next section. Satellite is the best option only when cable or DSL is not available.

⑤ If cable or DSL is not available, access the Web and move to www.dbsinstall.com.

⑥ Follow the links on the DSL provider's Web site to search for satellite providers of Internet access.

CHOOSE, OBTAIN, AND INSTALL AN INTERNET ACCOUNT

1 Compare your options.

If you have only one option for a broadband connection, the choice is made for you and you can skip to Step **3**.

2 If you have a choice between cable and DSL, consider which is best for you based on cost, the provider's reputation for service, and other factors.

Cable offers the fastest optimal performance, but also tends to be more expensive than DSL. Actual performance of cable can vary based on the amount of data flowing to other locations on the same trunk of the cable system you are on. The only technical requirement is that you need a cable outlet near the location of the hub you install for your local network.

● DSL offers steadier performance than cable and tends to be less expensive, but is typically slower. You sometimes have more than one DSL provider from which to choose (unlike cable, which is a localized monopoly). DSL is delivered through a standard phone line, and you probably have phone jacks in more locations, making the installation of a network slightly easier.

3 Contact the provider you want to use to obtain an account and schedule installation.

The provider activates your account, and if you choose to have the provider install the modem, they schedule an appointment with you. Some providers allow a self-install kit to be used. Using a kit is typically straightforward, but it is more work for you and may introduce problems that you need to solve.

Note: *If the provider installs your modem, ask the technician not to install any software on MacBook Air. You do not need any special software to connect to the Internet, and the applications many providers install are really just ways to get you to visit their home pages more frequently.*

TIPS

What about dial-up Internet accounts?
Internet accounts that you access over a standard phone line and dial-up modem are available just about everywhere. Dial-up is very slow and unreliable, and you must connect each time you want Internet access. The speed is so slow that using the Internet requires extreme patience. Broadband connections are available in many areas, which is why they are the focus of this chapter.

If I need an Internet account to connect, why can I use Wi-Fi at public places without an account?
No matter how you connect to the Internet, you are using an Internet account of some sort. In public places, the organization that controls that place can make a wireless network available to you. Through that network, you can access the organization's Internet account. In some cases, you can do this for free. In others, you need to purchase access from the organization providing the network.

Set Up a Local Network

After you have a working Internet connection, you are ready to build a local network. You can include a lot of devices on the network, including both wired and wireless devices. The heart of any network is the hub/router you use.

The best hub choice for most Mac users is an AirPort Extreme Base Station or a Time Capsule, because support for administering AirPort networks is built in to Mac OS X. Also, these base stations shield your network from Internet attacks. The rest of this chapter assumes the use of one of these devices. The steps to install other kinds of hubs are similar. These steps also assume that you have a working Internet connection and modem.

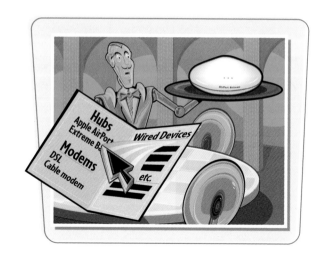

Set Up a Local Network

INSTALL AN AIRPORT EXTREME BASE STATION/TIME CAPSULE

1. Connect the output cable of the modem to the modem (WAN) port on the base station.

2. Connect power to the base station.

3. Start up MacBook Air.

   As long as you have not disabled AirPort, MacBook Air will be able to communicate with the base station wirelessly.

CONFIGURE AN AIRPORT EXTREME BASE STATION/ TIME CAPSULE

1. In the Finder, open the **Go** menu and choose **Applications**.

   The Applications folder opens.

2. Scroll down to the Utilities folder icon.

3. Double-click the **Utilities** folder icon.

Note: The specific screens and options you see in AirPort Utility depend on the type of base station you are configuring and its current status (for example, if it has been configured previously). While the details for your configuration might be different, you follow the same general process as the application leads you through it.

● The Utilities folder opens.

4. Double-click the **AirPort Utility** application.

   The application opens and you see a sheet when AirPort Utility opens.

5. Click **OK**.

*Note: If you see a warning prompt, click **OK**.*

The sheet closes and you see the application window with the base stations connected to MacBook Air displayed on the intro screen.

6 Select the base station you want to configure.

7 Click **Continue**.

Note: *If you are configuring a base station that has already been configured once, you may be prompted to type its password between Steps 6 and 7.*

8 If you are configuring an AirPort Extreme Base Station, skip to Step **10**; if you are configuring a Time Capsule, enter the Time Capsule's name in the Time Capsule Name field.

9 Enter a password in the Time Capsule Password and Verify Password fields.

10 Click **Continue**.

11 Select the **I don't have a wireless network and I want to create one** radio button.

12 Click **Continue**.

continued

There are two ways to configure a base station using the AirPort Utility application. One is to use the guided method as described in these sections. This leads you through each step so that all you have to do is to follow the on-screen instructions.

The other method is manual configuration, which you access by clicking the Manual Setup button in the AirPort Utility application. This provides you more control over the options and also makes configuration faster because you can jump immediately to the areas you want to configure. Some options, such as additional security configurations, are available only in Manual mode.

⑬ Type the name of the wireless network you are creating in the Network Name field.

⑭ Select **WPA/WPA2 Personal**.

Note: The No security option is not recommended because anyone who is in range of your wireless network will be able to access it.

⑮ Type the password for the network you are creating in the two password fields.

⑯ Click **Continue**.

⑰ Select the **I connect to the Internet with a DSL or cable modem using DHCP** option.

*Note: If you connect to the Internet in some other way, choose one of the other options, which you access by clicking the **I do not use DHCP** radio button and clicking **Continue**. The details of those options are beyond the scope of this chapter.*

⑱ Click **Continue**.

A summary screen of the settings you have configured appears.

⑲ Review the settings to make sure they are correct.

⑳ Click **Update**.

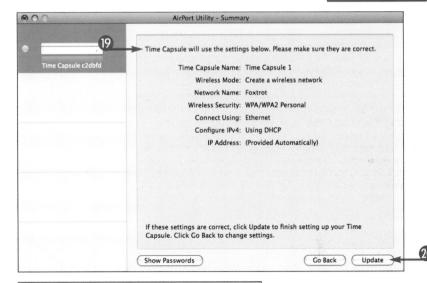

A warning sheet appears.

㉑ Click **Continue**.

The base station is configured and restarts. Once that process is complete, the wireless network is ready for use.

㉒ Press ⌘+Q.

The AirPort Utility application quits.

㉓ If you are connecting the base station to a wired network or to wired devices, connect them using Ethernet cables plugged into the LAN ports on the base station.

TIPS

What is the difference between an Extreme Base Station and an Express Base Station?

The most significant difference is that you cannot have a wired network connected to an Express Base Station because it has only one Ethernet port, which is connected to the modem. Typically, you should use an Extreme Base Station (or Time Capsule) for the primary hub on the network; you can add Express Base Stations to expand the range of the network as needed.

How do I expand the range of my network?

If the Extreme Base Station does not provide sufficient coverage of the area in which you use MacBook Air, you can chain base stations together. Use the AirPort Utility to connect to an Express Base Station and configure it to expand the existing network. You can do this by using the Wireless tab that appears when the AirPort Utility is in manual mode.

Protect a MacBook Air from Internet Attacks

One of the great things about the Internet is that it connects you to an unlimited number of people and organizations. However, all that connectedness opens you up to various kinds of Internet attacks. The worst of these are attempts to steal your identity and to hack into your computers to steal the information they contain or to use them to launch attacks on other computers. You also need to be mindful of the threat from viruses.

Fortunately, while the dangers of these attacks are very real, you can protect yourself with relatively simple techniques. An AirPort Extreme Base Station protects you from most attacks automatically. If you ever connect MacBook Air directly to the modem, such as for troubleshooting, make sure you configure its firewall before doing so.

Protect a MacBook Air from Internet Attacks

CHECK A BASE STATION TO ENSURE IT IS PROTECTING MACBOOK AIR

1 Open the AirPort Utility application.

Note: *See the section "Set Up a Local Network" for details.*

2 Select the base station.

3 Click **Manual Setup**.

The AirPort Utility moves into Manual mode. In this mode, you can make changes to the base station directly, and you can access all possible settings for it.

4 Click the **Internet** button.

5 Click the **NAT** tab.

6 Ensure the **Enable NAT Port Mapping Protocol** check box is checked; if it is, quit the AirPort utility and skip the next step.

7 If the check box is not checked, check it and click **Update**.

When NAT is active, the only IP address exposed to the Internet is the base station's. This shields the devices connected to the Internet through the base station from Internet attacks because devices outside your base station cannot identify the devices on the network; they only see the base station, which cannot be hacked like a computer can.

USE THE MAC OS X FIREWALL TO PROTECT MACBOOK AIR

① Open the System Preferences application and click the **Security** icon.

● The Security pane opens.

② Click the **Firewall** tab.

③ Click **Allow only essential services** to block all incoming connections to MacBook Air, except those it recognizes as legitimate because you have configured MacBook Air to allow them, such as File Sharing or Screen Sharing.

This prevents access to the information on MacBook Air by unknown services, which are often attempts to hack the computer.

PROTECT MACBOOK AIR FROM VIRUSES

① Purchase and install an antivirus application, such as Norton AntiVirus for Macintosh.

② Configure the antivirus application so that it updates its virus definitions and scans MacBook Air automatically (see the instructions for the particular application you use).

TIPS

Do I really need antivirus software?

That depends. Mac OS X is less vulnerable to virus attacks than PCs are. To be as safe from viruses as possible, it is a good idea to install and use antivirus software. However, being smart about how you deal with the Internet can be almost as effective. Never open attachments to e-mail messages unless you are very sure of where they came from, especially if they are Office documents or applications. Download software only from reputable Web sites. In general, be cautious about moving any files onto MacBook Air unless you are very sure of the reliability of the source. Exercising common-sense steps like these offers a good amount of virus protection, but not as much as an antivirus application.

What else can I do with the Manual Setup options?

When you use the Manual Setup options in the AirPort Utility application, you can configure various features of a base station beyond the basics that the guided approach uses. For example, you can change the AirPort network, configure security, configure a printer connected to the base station, and change other, more advanced configuration settings. Once you are comfortable with base station configuration, using the Manual Setup options is easier and faster than the guided approach.

Connect to the Internet with AirPort

The whole point of having a MacBook Air is that you can move around with it. By connecting to an AirPort wireless network, you can connect to the Internet and a local network from any location that is covered by that network.

This section assumes your network uses an AirPort Extreme Base Station. If not, the steps you use to connect to a wireless network might be slightly different.

Connect to the Internet with AirPort

1. Open the System Preferences application.

2. Click the **Network** icon.

● The Network pane appears. In the pane on the left side of the window, you see all the ways you can connect to a network that are currently configured on MacBook Air. When you select a connection to configure it, tools for that type of connection appear in the right part of the window.

3. Click **AirPort**.

4. Click **Turn AirPort On** if it is not on already.

   AirPort services start.

*Note: You might see a window that shows the available networks as soon as you turn AirPort on. Select the network you want to join and click **Join**, or click **Cancel** to follow the rest of these steps.*

5. On the **Network Name** pop-up menu, choose the network you want to join.

6. Type the network's password.

7. Check the **Remember this network** check box.

8. Click **OK**.

   MacBook Air connects to the AirPort network, and you return to the System Preferences application window. The status of the network becomes Connected.

9 Check the **Show AirPort status in menu bar** check box.

10 Click **Apply**.

11 Quit the System Preferences application.

12 Open Safari and move to a Web page.

The Web page opens, showing that MacBook Air is connected to the network and the Internet though AirPort.

If the Web page does not open, troubleshoot the problem.

Note: *See the section "Troubleshoot an Internet Connection," later in this chapter, for information on how to troubleshoot connection problems.*

USE THE AIRPORT MENU

1 Open the **AirPort** menu ().

● You can determine the signal strength of the network by the number of waves at the top of the menu.

More waves mean a stronger and faster connection; one or two waves may result in slow or intermittent performance.

2 Choose another network you want to join by selecting it on the menu.

TIPS

How can I connect directly to another Mac using AirPort?
Open the **AirPort** menu on the Finder menu bar and choose **Create Network**. Name the network, give it a password, and click **OK**. Other Mac users can connect to your network using the same steps you use to connect to a network provided by an AirPort Base Station.

I see only one or two waves and MacBook Air seems to lose its connection. What can I do?
The most likely cause is that MacBook Air is too far away from the base station. The most common solutions are to move MacBook Air closer to the base station so that the signal is stronger or use WDS to add another base station to the network to expand its coverage.

Share Files on a Local Network

Just like services you access over the Internet, you can provide services over a local network. These include sharing files, printers, an Internet connection, Web sites, and iTunes. Any computers that connect to the network, whether they use Ethernet or AirPort, can access any of the services you make available.

File sharing is one of the most useful local network services because you can easily share resources with multiple computers. You can configure MacBook Air to share files with others, and you can access files being shared with you.

Share Files on a Local Network

SHARE FILES WITH OTHERS

1 Open the System Preferences application.

2 Click the **Sharing** icon.

● The Sharing pane appears. In the pane in the left part of the window, you see the services you can provide over a local network. When you select a service, the tools you use to configure it appear in the right part of the window.

3 Type a name for MacBook Air in the Computer Name field.

This is the name others on the network choose to access MacBook Air.

4 Check the **File Sharing** check box.

File sharing starts.

By default, the Public folder within your Home folder is shared on the network.

5 To share specific folders, click the **Add** button (⊞).

6 Select the folder you want to share.

7 Click **Add**.

110

● The folder appears on the Shared Folders list.

⑧ To allow everyone with whom you share files to access the folder, click **Everyone** in the User's list and choose the permission level from the pop-up menu that appears.

Note: See the tip on this page for an explanation of permission levels.

⑨ To configure more users, click ➕ at the bottom of the Users list.

The Select Users tool appears.

⑩ Choose the users for whom you want to configure access on the list.

Note: If the user with whom you want to share files is not on the list, click **New Person** and create a username and password for that person.

⑪ Click **Select**.

The users appear on the Users list.

⑫ Repeat Step **8** to configure the user's access to the shared folder.

⑬ Repeat Steps **5** to **12** to share other folders and configure users to access your shared files.

TIPS

What are the permissions I can assign to folders that I share?

If you select **No Access**, no one else on the network will be able to use an item. Select **Write Only (Drop Box)** to enable people to place items within the shared folder, but not to be able to view or change its contents. When you select **Read Only**, the people with whom you share a folder can view, but not change, its contents. When you select **Read & Write**, people who can access the shared folder can view and change its contents.

When should I use Write Only (Drop Box) access?

This is useful when you need input from other people, but you do not want those people to be able to see each other's input. Suppose you are teaching a class and want your students to place assignments on your computer. You can create a Submission folder and share it with Write Only (Drop Box) access. Your students can then place files in the folder, but they cannot see files that other people have placed there.

continued 111

Share Files on a Local Network *(continued)*

When you connect to a local network, MacBook Air automatically identifies resources on the network that are sharing files. It collects all these resources in the Sharing section of the Sidebar so that you can access them easily.

When you connect to a sharing resource, what you can do with the content of that resource is determined by the permissions that you have been granted for it. For example, if you have Read & Write access, you can use a shared folder just like one you created. If you have Read Only access, you can see its contents, but you cannot change those contents.

Share Files on a Local Network

ACCESS FILES BEING SHARED WITH YOU

1 Move to the Desktop and open a Finder window.

● In the Shared section of the Sidebar, you see all of the computers sharing files on the network.

2 Select the computer whose files you want to access.

● MacBook Air connects to that computer as a guest, and you see the resources to which guest access accounts (Everyone on the Sharing pane) have access.

Note: The Public folder in each user's Home folder is always available to everyone on the network.

3 Click **Connect As**.

4 To connect as a guest, click **Guest** and skip to Step **9**.

5 To connect as a registered user, click **Registered User**.

6 Type the username of the account under which you want to connect.

7 Type the password for the username you typed in Step **6**.

8 Check the **Remember this password in my keychain** check box.

9 Click **Connect**.

MacBook Air connects to the resource under the user account you entered.

● The Finder window that appears shows the resources available to you based on the kind of access the user account you used has.

● The user account under which you are logged in is shown at the top of the window.

⑩ Open a shared resource.

● At the top of the window, you see the Sharing icon to indicate that the resource you are using is stored on a different computer on the network (🖥 changes to 🗂).

⑪ Open folders on the shared resource.

⑫ Double-click files to open them.

⑬ To copy a file or folder from the shared resource onto MacBook Air, drag it from the shared resource folder onto a folder that is stored on MacBook Air.

 TIPS

When are the files that I share available to others?

In order for people to access files you are sharing, MacBook Air must be awake and connected to the network. If it is configured to go to sleep automatically, people lose access to shared files when MacBook Air sleeps. Likewise, if MacBook Air is no longer connected to the network, its files are not available.

Shhhhhh . . .
Do Not Disturb

How can I share files with Windows computers?

Move to the Sharing pane of the System Preferences application and turn File Sharing on by clicking its check box. Click **Options**. In the resulting sheet, select the **Share files and folders using SMB** check box. Select the check box next to each user with whom you want to share files and type the password for that user's account. The user can access the files by typing **smb://*ipaddress*** where *ipaddress* is the current IP address for MacBook Air; this address is shown on the Sharing pane. You can also access files being shared by Windows computers.

Share Screens on a Local Network

With screen sharing, you can control another Mac on your local network just as if you were sitting in front of it. For example, you can log in to a different Mac on your network and run an application like you would if that application was installed on your MacBook Air. This is also useful for helping other users on your network because you can "take over" the other computer to solve problems.

Like file sharing, you must configure screen sharing permissions on each computer to determine who can access this feature.

Share Screens on a Local Network

CONFIGURE SCREEN SHARING ON MACBOOK AIR

① Open the Sharing pane of the System Preferences application.

② Select the **Screen Sharing** service.

● The controls for screen sharing appear.

③ Click **Computer Settings**.

The Computer Settings sheet appears.

④ Check the **Anyone may request permission to control screen** check box if you want to allow anyone who can access your MacBook Air to request to share your screen.

⑤ Check the **VNC viewers may control screen with password** check box and enter a password if you want people using Virtual Network Computing connections to be able to control your MacBook Air.

Note: For a local network, you do not really need to allow this, and so most users should leave this option unchecked.

⑥ Click **OK**.

⑦ In the Allow access for section, click **All users** to allow anyone who can access your MacBook Air over the network to share its screen, or **Only these users** to create a list of user accounts that can share your screen.

Note: To create a user list, click ➕. The User Account sheet appears. Select the user accounts with which you want to share your screen and click **Select**. You return to the Sharing pane and the user accounts you selected are shown on the user list.

⑧ Check the **On** check box for Screen Sharing.

● Screen sharing services start and your MacBook Air becomes available to users on your local network.

SHARE ANOTHER COMPUTER'S SCREEN

① Open a Finder window.

② In the Shared section of the Sidebar, select the Mac whose screen you want to share.

③ Log in under a user account that has permission to share the Mac's screen.

④ Click **Share Screen**.

If you are connected under a user account with screen sharing permissions, the Screen Sharing application starts and you can control the other computer.

If you have to request permission, the other Mac's user has to grant permission for you to share; when he does, the Screen Sharing application opens.

● Within the Screen Sharing application's window, which has the other computer's name as its title, you see the other computer's desktop. When you move your pointer within the window, it is resized according to the resolution of the other computer.

⑤ Within the Screen Sharing window, you can control the shared Mac.

You can use any application or command on the sharing computer as you would if you were sitting in front of it.

TIPS

What happens when someone wants to share my screen?

If you allow anyone to request to share your screen, when someone wants to share your MacBook Pro, you see a permission dialog on your screen. To allow your screen to be shared, click **Share Screen**. The person sharing your screen can then control MacBook Air.

How can I share another computer's screen if that computer is not on my local network?

If you have a MobileMe account, you can also share screens across the Internet. To do this, first set screen sharing permissions. On the MobileMe pane of the System Preferences application, register your MobileMe username and password on each computer among which you want to share screens. Then use the Back To My Mac tab to enable it. You can access any shared services over the Internet like you can on a local network.

Troubleshoot an Internet Connection

You can troubleshoot your Internet connection if you have problems with it. Fortunately, you probably will not need to do this very often. Networks are typically pretty reliable, and once configured correctly, you can usually just keep using them. However, as in the real world, things in the virtual world do not always go according to plan.

Troubleshoot an Internet Connection

DIAGNOSE THE PROBLEM

● An error message appears.

Note: *When you cannot access a Web page, Safari displays the Network Diagnostics button. Click it to start the Diagnostics application.*

1 Determine if the problem is a network issue or related just to one computer by trying the same action on a different computer on the same network.

If the problem occurs, it is a network problem; see the next subsection. If the problem does not occur, it is specific to MacBook Air. Skip to the subsection "Troubleshoot a MacBook Air Problem."

TROUBLESHOOT A NETWORK PROBLEM

1 Check the status lights on the modem.

If the modem appears to be working, move to Step **2**. If not, move to Step **6**.

2 Check the status of the AirPort Base Station.

If the status lights indicate the base station is working, move to Step **3**. If not, move to Step **7**.

3 Disconnect power from the base station and from the modem and wait about 20 seconds.

4 Connect power to the base station and then to the modem.

5 Try the task that you had a problem with.

If it is successful, you are done; if not, continue with the next steps.

6 If the modem's power light is on but the connection light is not, contact the ISP to make sure service is available. It probably is not, in which case you need to wait until service is restored.

7 When you are sure that your Internet service has been restored, remove power from the base station, wait 20 seconds, and connect it again.

8 Try the task that you had a problem with.

The problem should be solved.

TROUBLESHOOT A MACBOOK AIR PROBLEM

1 Open the Network pane of the System Preferences application.

2 Check the status of the various connections.

If the status is Not Connected for a connection, you need to reconfigure that connection using steps shown in the section "Connect to the Internet with AirPort," earlier in this chapter.

3 If the status is Connected, click **Apple** menu ( ), and then click **Restart**.

4 Click **Restart** at the prompt.

5 After MacBook Air restarts, try the activity again.

It is always good to restart when you have a problem; it is easy to do and solves a lot of different issues.

TIPS

When can the Network Diagnostics application help?

Sometimes the Network Diagnostics application can be very helpful because it moves through each phase of troubleshooting to guide you along the way. When it finds a problem, it identifies it and provides some hints about how to solve it. However, it is usually faster to use the steps outlined in this section because they include most of what the application tells you to do.

None of these steps helped. Now what can I do?

While the steps in this section help with many problems, they certainly do not solve all of them. When they do not work, you have a couple of options. First, find a computer that can connect to the Internet and move to www.apple.com/support. Search for the specific problem you are having and use the results you find to solve it. Second, disconnect everything from your network and connect a computer directly to the modem (ensuring the firewall is on first). If the connection works, you know the problem is related to the network; add devices one-by-one, starting with the base station, until you find the source of the problem. If the connection does not work, you need help from your ISP.

Connect to the Internet with Wi-Fi

When you are on the move, there is no reason to be disconnected from the Internet. In most public places, businesses, hotels, restaurants, and other locations, Internet access is readily available through a wireless (Wi-Fi) network connection.

Connecting to the Internet using Wi-Fi is a two-step process. First, you establish the connection between MacBook Air and the network. Second, you register MacBook Air to access the Internet over the network. The second step is required most of the time; especially when you are charged a fee to access the Internet.

Connect to the Internet with Wi-Fi

CONNECT TO A WI-FI NETWORK

Note: When MacBook Air turns on or wakes up, it scans the area for available wireless networks. If it does not find one of your preferred networks (one that you have used before, such as the one in your home), it presents a list of available networks to you.

1 Select the wireless network you want to join.

2 If you will be returning to the location and want to access the network again, check the **Remember this network** check box.

3 Click **Join**.

Note: If the lock icon appears along the right side of the window for a network, it is secured.

4 If the network is secured, enter the network password and click **OK** at the prompt. (Most public networks are not secure, in which case you skip this step.)

MacBook Air joins the network.

5 Open the **AirPort** menu ().

6 Verify that you have connected to the network and that the signal strength is good.

The signal strength is indicated by the number of waves at the top of the menu. You should have at least three waves for best performance.

If you are connected to the network, a check mark appears next to its name.

You are ready to access the Internet over the wireless network.

OBTAIN AND LOG IN TO AN INTERNET ACCOUNT

1 Open Safari and try to go to any Web page.

If the page appears, you do not need an account to use the Wi-Fi network to connect to the Internet, and you can skip the rest of these steps. You should be able to use the Internet as you can when you are connected to your local wireless network.

In most situations, you have to have an account with the network's provider to be able to access the Internet. In this case, you move to the provider's Web page that you use to create and log in to an Internet account.

2 Click the connection link.

Note: *This link goes by different names, such as Create an Account or Access the Internet.*

3 If you do not currently have an account with the provider, skip to Step **6**.

4 If you already have an account with the network's provider, type your username and password.

5 Click the **Go** or **Login** button.

You should see a message confirming that you have Internet access; if so, you can skip the rest of these steps.

Note: *When you connect from a hotel, you usually see a page that enables you to charge the Internet access to your room.*

What does Wi-Fi stand for?
The term Wi-Fi stands for wireless fidelity. It applies to a set of standard protocols and technology that are used to ensure that wireless devices and the software they use are compatible. The technical specifications fall under the Institute of Electrical and Electronics Engineers (IEEE) 802.11 series. The MacBook Air wireless capabilities are Wi-Fi or 802.11 compatible so that you can connect to any network or device that uses these standards (almost every wireless network and device does).

What if there is only an Ethernet connection available?
Some places, such as hotel rooms or meeting rooms, only have an Ethernet connection available. In that situation, you have three options: connect wirelessly through an AirPort Express connected to the Ethernet network, connect using an Ethernet adapter and cable, or connect wirelessly with a broadband wireless card. You can find more information on the first and third methods later in this chapter.

continued

In most cases, an Internet account that you purchase is associated with a time period, such as an hour, day, or month. When the period expires, you have to renew your account. If you travel to multiple places where the same provider offers service, consider purchasing a monthly account because those are less expensive than hourly or daily accounts.

Also, some accounts enable you to access networks from different providers, who have agreed to "share users." When you sign up for an account, check to see which other providers allow you to access the Internet with your account, especially if you are considering a monthly account.

Connect to the Internet with Wi-Fi *(continued)*

6 To obtain an account, click the link to sign up.

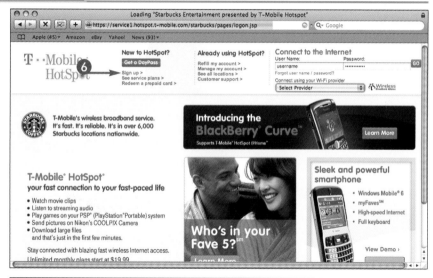

7 Follow the on-screen instructions to create an account.

During the creation process, you select a username and password for your account.

Note: *You can usually choose from a variety of accounts, such as daily, monthly, and so on. Each has specific costs and lengths of commitment. Usually, the longer the account is configured, the less expensive it is per hour of use.*

⑧ Type the username and password you created.

⑨ Click the **Go** or **Login** button.

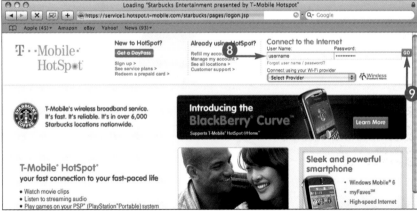

● You should see a page confirming that you are connected.

You can now use your Internet applications, such as Safari, Firefox, Mail, or iChat.

TIPS

Should I use a wireless network if it is not secured?
If you do not need a password to connect to a network, it is not secure. Any wireless device can connect to the network and might be able to intercept data being communicated across that network. In general, you should avoid such networks when you can (most networks in public places are not secure, and so you cannot always avoid them). When you do use an unsecured network, make sure you configure the MacBook Air firewall and other security tools to limit access to your computer over that network. Be especially careful about sending sensitive information that is not protected (especially avoid using a Web site whose address does not start with "https" when you have to provide information to use the site).

What if I cannot see a wireless network?
There are two possibilities. One is that no networks are available, in which case you need to find another option (for example, a broadband wireless card). The other possibility is that the available networks are not broadcasting their identity. If that is the case, you need to know the network name and password before you can join it; when you have this information, choose the **Join Other Network** option on the AirPort menu and enter the information for the network.

Connect to the Internet with an AirPort Express Base Station

An AirPort Express Base Station is a small, portable wireless base station that you can use to easily create your own wireless networks while you are away from your home or office. For example, if you happen to stay in a hotel that only has wired Internet access in its rooms, you can use an AirPort Express Base Station to quickly create a wireless network for MacBook Air.

There are two steps to setting up a temporary wireless network with an AirPort Express Base Station. First, you connect the base station to the wired network. Second, you configure the base station to provide a wireless network.

Connect to the Internet with an AirPort Express Base Station

CONNECT THE BASE STATION TO THE NETWORK

① Using an Ethernet cable, connect the wired network to the Ethernet port on the base station.

② Plug the base station into a power outlet.

● The base station starts up and you see its status light start to flash amber. You are ready to configure the base station to provide an Internet connection.

Note: *The rest of these steps assume that the wired network provides an Internet connection using Dynamic Host Configuration Protocol (DHCP), which is almost always the case in public places (such as hotels).*

CONFIGURE AND ACCESS A WIRELESS NETWORK

③ On the AirPort menu, choose the network being provided by the AirPort Express Base Station.

Note: *If it has been configured before, the base station retains the last network name it provided. If not, the network name starts with "Apple." You must choose the base station's network to connect to it wirelessly to be able to configure it.*

④ Open the AirPort Utility application (located in the Utilities folder within the Applications folder).

⑤ Select the AirPort Express Base Station.

⑥ Click **Continue**.

7 If you are prompted to type the base station's password, do so and click **OK**.

Note: *A base station has a name and password for configuration; these are different than the wireless network's name and password.*

8 Type a name for the base station (different from the network's name).

9 Type the base station's password in both password fields.

10 Click **Continue**.

The first page of the Network Setup screen appears.

11 Select the **I don't have a wireless network and I want to create one** radio button.

12 Click **Continue**.

13 Type a name for the network.

14 Select the **WPA/WPA2 Personal** radio button.

15 Type a network password in both Wireless Password fields.

16 Click **Continue**.

The Internet Setup screen appears.

17 Select the **I use a DSL or cable modem with a static IP address or DHCP** radio button.

18 Click **Continue**.

19 On the Configure IPv4 pop-up menu, choose **Using DHCP**.

20 Click **Continue**.

21 Click **Update**.

22 Click **Continue**.

The base station is updated and restarts. When that process is complete, the status light becomes solid green and you can connect to the Internet through the wireless network.

Do I have to reconfigure the base station when I take it to a new location?
An AirPort Express Base Station uses a profile that saves its configuration. A base station remembers the configuration of the last location in the current profile. As long as each network you connect it to provides access through DHCP, you can simply connect the base station to the new network and it will provide the same wireless network.

How do I create and use profiles?
In the AirPort Utility, select the base station and click **Manual Setup**. At the bottom of the window, use the **Profiles** pop-up menu to select the profile you want to use. To create new profiles, select **Manage Profiles**. You can use up to five profiles.

Connect to the Internet with a Broadband Wireless Modem

If you travel a lot, you should consider a broadband wireless modem, with which you can connect to the Internet at reasonable speeds anywhere within the network's coverage area. National networks provide broad coverage areas, and so you can usually get a connection wherever you are. This can also save money as you use one account and all your access is included in one monthly fee. Most of the large cell phone companies offer this capability.

You do not have to find and sign onto networks in various locations; this makes a broadband wireless modem easy to use because you perform the same steps every time you want to connect.

Connect to the Internet with a Broadband Wireless Modem

OBTAIN A BROADBAND WIRELESS MODEM

1 Explore the major cell phone company Web sites to determine which ones offer a modem you can use; obtaining a broadband wireless modem is a lot like buying a cell phone.

2 Make sure the modem you consider connects using USB.

3 Check the specifications or features to ensure the modem and accompanying software are Mac OS X compatible and to determine the connection speed under ideal conditions.

4 Determine the cost of the modem (many are free when you sign up for an account) and monthly service (typically around $50 per month).

Note: When you compare this cost to the cost of purchasing daily access, you will see that a wireless modem can be the less expensive option if you travel frequently.

5 Check the contract terms; many providers require two-year agreements.

6 Check the coverage area for the provider to make sure it includes the areas you are mostly likely to be in.

You want to be sure you frequent the highest-speed areas of the network.

7 After you have compared your options, choose and purchase the modem that makes the most sense to you.

INSTALL AND CONFIGURE A BROADBAND WIRELESS MODEM

1 Install the software for the broadband wireless modem using the modem's installer application.

Note: *You can probably download the software from the provider's Web site; or you can use the external SuperDrive or Remote Disc to install if from the CD provided with the modem.*

2 Restart MacBook Air.

3 Connect the modem to the USB port on MacBook Air.

4 Launch the modem's setup application.

5 Go through the steps of the setup application until you have finished installing the modem's software and configuring MacBook Air to use the modem.

USE A BROADBAND WIRELESS MODEM TO CONNECT TO THE INTERNET

1 Launch the broadband wireless modem's connection application.

2 Select the connection you want to use.

3 Click **Connect**.

The modem connects to the wireless network and provides you with an Internet connection.

Why am I unable to connect even though I am in my plan's coverage area?
Like cell phones, broadband wireless modems require a signal from a satellite or tower. If you are in a location where such signals are blocked, such as basements or deep in the interior of some buildings, the modem might not be able to receive a signal and you have to find an alternate way to connect. Signal strength can also impact the speed of the connection even if you are able to connect.

Why not use a wireless modem all the time?
If a broadband wireless modem provides sufficient connection speeds in the locations you use MacBook Air the most, you can use it as your primary Internet connection (and so you do not need another account with a cable or DSL provider). However, you will have to share the Internet connection with other devices from MacBook Air, which means that it must be on and awake for other computers to be able to connect. And, the connection speed slows as you share it with more devices. Using a wireless modem as a primary connection is usually only practical for one computer at a time.

Manage Power on MacBook Air

MacBook Air needs power to operate, just like any other electronic device. Because it has an internal battery, you do not need to be connected to an outlet for MacBook Air to run (which is what makes it a mobile computer). One of the most important tasks as you travel with MacBook Air is to manage its power so that you do not run out of power at an inconvenient time.

There are a number of things you can do to manage power on your MacBook Air. First, you can configure MacBook Air to use as little power as possible. Second, you can monitor the MacBook Air power status. Third, you can build a MacBook Air power toolkit.

Manage Power on MacBook Air

CONFIGURE MACBOOK AIR TO MINIMIZE POWER USE

① Use the Energy Saver pane of the System Preferences application to configure MacBook Air so that it uses a minimum amount of power while running on the battery.

Note: See the section "Save Energy" in Chapter 6 for the details.

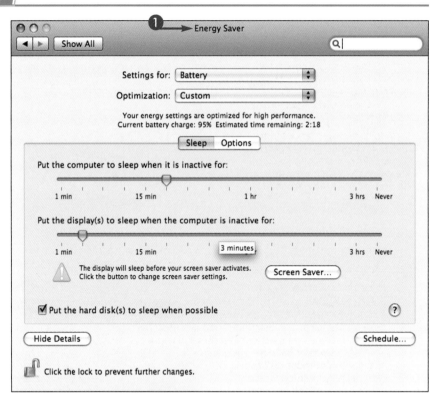

MONITOR THE BATTERY POWER

① Look at the Battery icon (▭) in the menu bar.

As battery power is used, the filled part of the icon shrinks to give you a relative idea of how much battery power remains.

② To access more detailed information, open the Battery menu by clicking the **Battery** icon.

● The amount of operating time you have left is shown at the top of the menu.

③ Click **Show**.

④ Choose how you want battery information to appear. For example, to display an estimate of the time remaining, select **Time**.

The attribute you select appears next to the battery icon on the menu bar so you can monitor your remaining battery time according to your preference.

BUILD A MACBOOK AIR POWER TOOLKIT

① When you travel with MacBook Air, bring its power adapter with you so that you are able to recharge when you can; when possible, work with the power adapter connected to keep your battery fully charged so that you have maximum working time when running on battery power.

② If you frequently travel on long plane flights, purchase an Apple MagSafe Airline Adapter. This enables you to connect MacBook Air to the power outlets provided in some airplanes.

TIPS

What are some other tips to extend my working time on the road?

Put MacBook Air to sleep when you are not using it. When it is sleeping, MacBook Air uses very little power. If you have an iPod, use it to listen to music or watch video instead of iTunes on MacBook Air. iTunes uses significant amounts of power because it requires a lot of disk activity. In general, the more disk activity required to run an application, the faster MacBook Air runs out of power, so be aware of the applications you use; keep only those applications that you are actively using open, to prevent unnecessary activity. Also, turn off AirPort and Bluetooth to save the power they consume. Making your screen dimmer helps too.

How can I determine if my seat on an airplane will have power available?

Many airline Web sites enable you to check the specific kind of plane you will be flying on for flights you have booked or are considering. Often, you can get detailed specifications about the plane you will be on, including whether power ports are available for your seat. Power ports tend to be available on newer, larger planes flying longer routes. Ports are also more likely to be provided for first- or business-class seats. Regional or very old planes seldom have power ports available.

Protect MacBook Air Data with FileVault

When you use MacBook Air while traveling, you incur a higher risk of someone either accessing MacBook Air or stealing it. In either situation, data stored on MacBook Air can be compromised. This can lead to the loss of sensitive information, identity theft, or other harmful outcomes.

The Mac OS X FileVault feature encrypts your data so that it cannot be used without a password. Even if someone does get into your MacBook Air, he cannot access its data without the password, rendering the information stored on your computer unusable.

Protect MacBook Air Data with FileVault

① Open the System Preferences application.

② Click the **Security** icon.

③ Click the **FileVault** tab.

④ Click **Set Master Password**.

The Master Password sheet appears. You use this to create a master password that can be used to reset other users' passwords or to access their data in case they forget their passwords.

⑤ Type a master password in the Master Password and Verify fields.

⑥ Type a password hint in the Hint field.

⑦ Click **OK**.

The sheet closes, the password is set, and you move back to the FileVault tab. The Set Master Password button becomes the Change button to show you that a master password is set.

⑧ Click **Turn On FileVault**.

The password sheet appears.

9 Type the password needed to access the current user's data (this is your user account's password if you are logged in under your user account).

10 Click **OK**.

You move back to the FileVault tab.

11 If you want data to be deleted securely (overwritten so it cannot be recovered from the Trash), check the **Use secure erase** check box.

12 If you want MacBook Air to be even more secure, check the **Use secure virtual memory** check box to encrypt data stored in virtual memory.

13 Click **Turn On FileVault**.

MacBook Air logs you out of the current account and encrypts all the data stored in your Home folder. When the process is complete (expect it to take a long time if you have a lot of data), you can log back in.

Note: *When you are logged in to your user account, your data is available. Make sure you log out whenever you are not using MacBook Air if there is any risk of it being accessed by someone you do not know or trust. Only when you are logged out is your data encrypted with FileVault.*

WARNING: **You are ready to turn on FileVault now. After your files are encrypted, you must enter your login password or the master password to access them. If you forget these passwords, your information will be lost.**

When you turn on FileVault, you will be logged out while FileVault encrypts your home folder, which might take a while. You cannot use your computer while this is occurring.

After you turn on FileVault, you cannot log in to this user account for SMB file sharing or printer sharing.

☐ Use secure erase

☐ Use secure virtual memory

Cancel   Turn On FileVault

TIPS

When I log in and FileVault is on, I do not notice any difference. Is it working?

FileVault protects access to your data from outside your user account. For example, if someone else logs in to MacBook Air, he cannot access your data without entering the FileVault password. When you are logged in under your user account and FileVault is on, you will probably not notice any difference. FileVault is designed to protect data from being accessed outside of your user account. Look at the icon on your Home folder; if it is the Secure icon, FileVault is on.

What happens if I forget my password?

If you do not type the correct password, you cannot access any data that has been encrypted (which is the point, right?). Make sure you choose a password that you can remember, or that you store the password in a secure manner away from MacBook Air. If you forget the required password, you lose access to all the data in your Home folder. You should also create a master FileVault password in case you or other users forget their individual passwords. You can use this password to access all the data on MacBook Air.

Protect MacBook Air with System Security

If MacBook Air is used by other people, or there is some chance it will be, consider adding some extra security to prevent unwanted access to the data stored on the computer.

For example, you can require that a password be entered to wake MacBook Air up or to stop the screen saver. This is good if you sometimes leave MacBook Air running when it is possible for someone else to access it. Without your password, other users cannot access your information even if they can physically access MacBook Air.

Protect MacBook Air with System Security

① Open the System Preferences application.

② Click the **Security** icon.

③ Click the **General** tab.

④ Check **Require password to wake this computer from sleep or screen saver** if you want a password to be required to start using MacBook Air after it goes to sleep or the screen saver activates.

⑤ If you want to prevent automatic login, check the **Disable automatic login** check box.

Note: If you use MacBook Air in unsecured situations, such as in airports or other public locations, you should disable automatic login. If it is enabled, someone can access your data by restarting the computer (by holding the Power key down until MacBook Air shuts off and then pressing it again) to log in to your account.

⑥ If you want to require a password to change any settings through System Preferences, check the **Require password to unlock each System Preferences pane** check box.

⑦ To automatically log out after a specific period of inactivity, check the **Log out after** check box and enter the amount of idle time until you are logged out.

⑧ To make the data stored in virtual memory more secure, check **Use secure virtual memory**.

⑨ If you want to prevent control of MacBook Air with remote control devices, check the **Disable remote control infrared receiver** check box.

⑩ To allow remote control with a specific device only, click **Pair**.

⑪ Hold the remote close to MacBook Air while pressing and holding its **Menu** and **Next** buttons at the same time.

Only that remote can be used to control MacBook Air.

Protect MacBook Air with Its Firewall

When you are using a known network to access the Internet, it should be equipped with its own firewall or Network Address Translation (NAT) protection to prevent computers you do not control from being able to see or access MacBook Air. However, if you are not sure about how much protection a network provides, such as when you are connecting to a network in a public place, you should use the Mac OS X firewall to block attempts to access MacBook Air from the Internet.

You might have to tweak the firewall a bit to be as secure as possible while still allowing you to do what you want.

Protect MacBook Air with Its Firewall

① Open the System Preferences application.

② Click the **Security** icon.

③ Click the **Firewall** tab.

④ To prevent most incoming connections while allowing Mac OS X to automatically allow connections for some applications, click the **Allow only essential services** radio button.

⑤ To allow only specific connections, click the **Set access for specific services and applications** radio button.

⑥ To add applications through which you want to allow incoming connections, click the **Add** button (✚).

⑦ Use the resulting sheet to select the applications or services you want to allow.

● Services and applications that are allowed to have incoming connections are shown on the list.

⑧ Click **Advanced**.

⑨ Check the **Enable Firewall Logging** check box to create a log of incoming connections that were blocked by the firewall.

⑩ To prevent MacBook Air from being detected on a network by services you did not request, such as through Bonjour, check the **Enable Stealth Mode** check box.

⑪ Click **OK**.

Synchronize Files with Other Computers

If you use MacBook Air and another computer, such as an iMac, you should keep documents you work on synchronized on each computer so that changes you make on MacBook Air are reflected on the iMac, and vice versa.

There are several ways to make sure you have the most current version of documents in both locations. If you have MobileMe, you can use your iDisk as the synchronizing mechanism; this is good because the process is mostly automatic. You can also use a smart folder to identify files that have changed recently so that you can synchronize them manually.

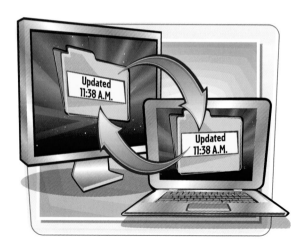

SYNCHRONIZE FILES USING AN IDISK

1. Open the System Preferences application.

2. Open the MobileMe pane.

3. Click the **iDisk** tab.

4. Click **Start**.

   MacBook Air creates a copy of your iDisk on its hard drive.

5. Click the **Automatically** radio button.

MacBook Air synchronizes the version of files on the local iDisk (on your hard drive) with the one stored on the Internet.

6. Save documents that you want to keep in synch on a folder on the iDisk.

7. Perform Steps 1 to 5 to configure your iDisk on each computer that you want to keep in synch.

   Each computer you configure accesses the same version of the files on the iDisk so that you always have the current version on each computer.

Note: *Do not make changes to the same file on different computers at exactly the same time, or the versions will become out of synch.*

SYNCHRONIZE FILES USING A SMART FOLDER

1. Create a smart folder on MacBook Air that uses criteria by which you want to identify files you have changed while traveling with MacBook Air.

Note: See Chapter 4 for the details of creating a smart folder.

2. When you return from a trip, use the smart folder to find all the documents you have changed recently.

3. Copy the changed files from MacBook Air to the computer on which you want to synchronize them.

Note: Configure file sharing to make it easy to copy files between computers (see Chapter 7).

 TIPS

What about synchronization applications?

There are third-party applications that keep files stored in multiple locations in synch. You designate a source folder and a target folder, and then you determine the direction of the synchronization, such as from the target to the source or in both directions. Based on your settings, the application automatically performs the required synchronization. One example is ChronoSynch, available at www. econtechnologies.com.

What do I need to do about backing up files that I change while traveling?

If you configure your iDisk to synchronize automatically and store the files on which you work on your iDisk, your files are automatically backed up as soon as you connect to the Internet. Chapter 17 discusses Time Machine, which enables you to back up information on MacBook Air. As soon as you return to where your backup hard drive is located, connect the hard drive to MacBook Air; the backup process launches immediately so that any changes you made while traveling are protected in the current backup.

Burn CDs and DVDs with the MacBook Air SuperDrive

One of the reasons MacBook Air can be so slim is that it does not have an internal CD/DVD drive. However, you can purchase the MacBook Air SuperDrive to read and write (more commonly referred to as *burning*) DVDs and CDs. A SuperDrive costs about $99 and is simple to use with MacBook Air.

One of the most useful functions of a SuperDrive is to burn your own DVDs and CDs. One method is to create a burn folder and place and organize folders and files within it. You can burn the folder onto a disc to back it up.

Burn CDs and DVDs with the MacBook Air SuperDrive

CONNECT A SUPERDRIVE TO MACBOOK AIR

1. Purchase a MacBook Air SuperDrive.

2. Connect the USB connector on the SuperDrive to the USB port on the MacBook Air.

   The SuperDrive is ready to use.

CREATE AND ORGANIZE A BURN FOLDER

1. Open a Finder window showing the location in which you want to create a burn folder.

2. Open the **File** menu, and select **New Burn Folder**.

● A new burn folder is created; its name, Burn Folder, is highlighted and ready for you to edit.

3. Type a name for the burn folder and press `Return`.

   The new name is saved.

④ Open the burn folder in the Finder window.

● At the top of the window, you see the folder's name.

● You also see the Burn button that indicates it is a burn folder.

⑤ Open a new Finder window so that you have two windows on the desktop.

⑥ In the second window, go to and select the first folders or files you want to burn to a disc.

⑦ Drag the folders or files from the second window onto the burn folder's window.

Aliases, which are pointers to the original folders or file, are created in the burn folder for each file or folder that you move there.

⑧ Organize the files and folders in the burn folder as you want them to be organized on the disc.

Note: *In the burn folder's window, you can create new folders and place the dragged files and folders into them just as you can with other kinds of folders.*

The folder is ready to burn onto a disc.

How else can I use the MacBook Air SuperDrive?
Burning a CD or DVD is only one way to use a SuperDrive. For example, you can also use it to watch DVDs, import audio CDs to iTunes, install software, and copy files. A SuperDrive is a very useful addition to your MacBook Air toolkit, and because it does not require a separate cable or power source and is quite small, it is easy to take with you.

Can I burn to a disc more than once?
When you burn a disc from the Finder using a burn folder, you can only write to that disc one time, and so it is important to arrange the files as you want them in the burn folder before you burn the disc. There are other applications that can append files to a disc in multiple sessions, but it is usually easier just to be careful about when you burn to minimize the number of discs you use. If you use erasable discs, you can use the Disk Utility application to erase a disc and then write to it again (erasing the disc removes all the files on it so that you can start over as if it were a new disc).

continued

There are many reasons to burn files and folders from the Finder to CDs or DVDs, such as to transfer them to someone else or to safeguard copies of important folders and files for future use. A CD or DVD is a great way to archive files so that you can remove them from MacBook Air to save disk space while keeping the files permanently.

You can also store CDs and DVDs that you burn in different locations to keep them secure and prevent the loss of important files from unfortunate events such as theft, fire, or flood.

Burn CDs and DVDs with the MacBook Air SuperDrive *(continued)*

BURN A DISC

1 Open the burn folder that you want to place on a disc.

2 Check the minimum disc size for the folder by looking at the status bar at the bottom of its window.

3 Click **Burn**.

A dialog appears, prompting you to insert a disc.

The dialog also tells you how much disc space you need to burn the disc.

4 Insert a blank CD or DVD.

A confirmation dialog appears.

⑤ Type the name of the disc you are burning.

The default name is the name of the burn folder.

⑥ On the **Burn Speed** pop-up menu, choose the speed at which you want the disc to be burned.

Note: In most cases, leave the setting as Maximum Possible. If the burn process fails, try a slower burn speed.

⑦ Click **Burn**.

The burn process starts and the progress window appears.

Note: You can use MacBook Air for other tasks while the disc is burning.

When the process is complete, the progress window disappears and the disc mounts.

⑧ Open a Finder window.

⑨ Select the disc you burned.

● You see the contents of the disc, which look exactly like the burn folder.

⑩ Click the **Eject** button (⏏) to eject the disc.

You can make copies of the disc by repeating the burn process. When you are done, you can delete the burn folder.

TIPS

What other applications can I use to burn CDs or DVDs?

You can use iTunes to create audio CDs or to back up your iTunes Music Library onto CD or DVD. Using iDVD, you can create DVDs that play in a standard DVD player just like those you might rent or buy. From iPhoto, you can burn photos to disc to archive them or make them easy to share. Each of these applications provides its own burn commands, typically located on the File menu or on the application's toolbar.

How can I create my own application installation discs?

You can use the Disk Utility application to burn disk images onto a CD or DVD; this is especially important when you download applications that you have purchased so that you can reinstall the applications if you ever need to. After you have mounted the disk image by double-clicking its icon, launch Disk Utility and select the disk image you downloaded. Click the **Burn** button and follow the prompts to burn the disk image to a CD or DVD. Should you ever need to install the application again, you can do so from the disc you created.

Expand Storage Space with an External Hard Drive

Your MacBook Air includes a hard drive or a solid-state drive on which you store the operating system, applications, and your own files and folders. Over time, you might run low on available disk space, especially if you do large video or DVD projects. You can connect MacBook Air to an external hard drive to expand the working storage space available to you.

There are two basic steps to preparing an external hard drive to work with MacBook Air. First, you make the connection between the computer and the hard drive. Second, you use the Disk Utility application to format and partition the hard drive.

Expand Storage Space with an External Hard Drive

CONNECT AND POWER AN EXTERNAL HARD DRIVE

1 Connect the hard drive to a power source and turn it on.

You should hear the drive spin up and see its power light.

2 Use a USB cable to connect the hard drive to the MacBook Air USB port.

Note: *Most hard drives include the cable you need to connect to MacBook Air. However, some do not. Check the package information to make sure the cable is included. If it is not, you have to buy a cable separately.*

The hard drive is ready to format and partition.

FORMAT AND PARTITION AN EXTERNAL HARD DRIVE

1 Open the Applications folder, open the Utilities folder, and then double-click the **Disk Utility** application.

● When Disk Utility opens, you see all available disks in the left pane.

② Select the external hard disk.

③ Click the **Partition** tab.

● You see the number of partitions in which the disk is currently organized; a new disk has one partition.

④ On the **Volume Scheme** pop-up menu, choose the number of partitions you want to create on the disk.

● The space on the disk is grouped into the number of partitions you selected. Each partition is named "Untitled *X*," where *X* is a sequential number.

What kind of external hard drive works with MacBook Air?

MacBook Air supports any external hard drive that supports USB 2.0, and you want to get the largest drive you can afford. For backing up data, the hard drive should be at least twice as large as the disk in MacBook Air; for example, if your MacBook Air has an 80GB hard drive, the external hard drive should be at least 160GB. You can also use hard drives that are Mac- or Windows-compatible. If a hard drive is formatted for Windows, you should reformat and partition it before using it (any software that comes with it probably will not run on MacBook Air, but you do not need it anyway).

What is the difference between a hard drive and a solid-state drive?

A hard drive uses a spinning magnetic disk on which data is written and from which it is read. A solid-state drive uses solid-state electronics to store information (some solid-state drives use flash memory like an iPhone does). The benefits of a solid-state drive are that it is small and has no moving parts, which means that it is more reliable and durable than a traditional hard drive. However, solid-state drives are also more expensive than traditional hard drives, and the present technology does not allow solid-state drives to be as large as hard drives.

Although being able to access more storage space is useful for current projects and documents, it is even more important for backing up the information you have stored on MacBook Air.

With an external hard drive, you can use the Mac OS X Time Machine feature to back up your important data. Should something happen to this data on MacBook Air or to the MacBook Air itself, you can easily recover the data from the external drive so that you do not lose important information or your investment in iTunes content or applications. For more information about Time Machine, see Chapter 17.

Expand Storage Space with an External Hard Drive *(continued)*

⑤ Select the top partition.

● Its information is shown in the Volume Information section.

⑥ Type a name for the partition in the Name field.

⑦ On the **Format** pop-up menu, choose **Mac OS Extended (Journaled)**.

⑧ Enter the size of the first partition in the Size field and press **Return**.

Note: *You can also change the size of partitions by dragging the resize handle located in the horizontal bar between the partitions in the Volume Scheme box.*

The partition is named and sized.

⑨ Select the next partition.

⑩ Repeat Steps **6** to **8** to name, format, and size the partition.

⑪ Repeat Steps **9** and **10** until you have configured each partition.

Note: *The total size of the partitions equals the usable size of the hard disk.*

⑫ Click **Apply**.

The partition warning appears.

Note: *When you partition a disk, all the data it contains is erased, so make sure you do not need its data before continuing.*

⑬ Click **Partition**.

Disk Utility partitions the drive according to your settings, and the Time Machine dialog appears.

⑭ Click **Cancel** in the Time Machine dialog.

Note: *See Chapter 17 for information about configuring Time Machine.*

⑮ Quit Disk Utility.

Partition Disk

Partitioning this disk will permanently erase all the data from the disk.

The following volumes will be erased:
"Valiant"
"Alternate_Startup"

The following volumes will be added:
"Book Projects"
"Work Projects"

Are you sure you wish to partition the disk "WDC WD25 00JB-00EVA0 Media"?

⑬

Cancel   Partition

⑯ Open a Finder window.

● You see the partitions on the external drive, and they are ready to be used just like the MacBook Air internal hard drive.

Note: *Before disconnecting a hard drive from MacBook Air, click the **Eject** button (⏏) next to its icon in the Sidebar or press the ⏏ key and wait for the disk icon to disappear from the Sidebar. Disconnecting a drive without ejecting it first can damage its data.*

TIPS

Why can I not partition a new hard drive?

Some Windows hard drives come in a format that is incompatible with the Mac operating system, and when you try to partition them, the process fails while displaying an error message that is not all that helpful. Before you click the **Apply** button on the Partition tab of the Disk Utility application, click the **Options** button. On the resulting sheet, click **GUID Partition Table** and then click **OK**. The sheet closes. Continue with the rest of the steps as described. This reformats the drive so that it is compatible with MacBook Air.

What is a partition and how many should I create on my external hard disk?

Partitions are logical volumes on a hard disk, which means that they behave as if each partition is its own hard disk, even though they are actually on the same physical disk. You can create partitions for various purposes, such as to organize data. In most cases, you should limit the partitions on one disk to one or two so that you do not end up with a lot of partitions that are too small to be usable.

Connect and Use an External Display

You can never have too much screen space to work with. In addition to making your document windows larger so that you can see more of their contents, more screen space helps you work efficiently because you can have more windows open so you can use them at the same time.

To add screen space to MacBook Air, you can connect an external display.

Connect and Use an External Display

CONNECT THE REQUIRED ADAPTER TO THE EXTERNAL DISPLAY

1. Select the Micro-DVI adapter that is appropriate for the display you are using.

Note: *Micro-DVI to VGA and Micro-DVI to DVI adapters are included with MacBook Air.*

2. Plug the small end of the adapter into the Micro-DVI port on your MacBook Air.

3. Connect the other end of the adapter to the cable connected to the VGA or DVI input port on the display.

4. Connect the display to a power source, and power it up.

CONFIGURE THE EXTERNAL DISPLAY

1. Open the System Preferences application and click the **Displays** icon.

   A Displays pane opens on the MacBook Air display and on the external display.

2. Click the **Arrangement** tab on the Displays pane on the MacBook Air screen.

- You see an icon representation of each display.

3. Drag the external display's icon to match the physical location of the display compared to MacBook Air (on its left or right side).

4. If you want the external display to be the main display, drag the menu bar from the MacBook Air display's icon onto the external display's icon.

5. If you want the displays to show the same information, check the **Mirror Displays** check box and skip the rest of these steps.

⑥ Select the **Displays** pane from the System Preferences on the external display.

⑦ Click the **Display** tab.

⑧ Choose the resolution for the external display by selecting it on the list of available resolutions.

⑨ If the **Refresh Rate** pop-up menu appears, choose the highest rate available.

⑩ Use the other controls to configure the external display.

⑪ Click the **Color** tab.

⑫ Select the color profile for the display you are using.

⑬ Quit the System Preferences application.

You now can use the external display. When video mirroring is off, the two displays act as a single, large desktop area. When video mirroring is on, you see the same information on both screens.

TIPS

What kind of external display should I get for MacBook Air?

MacBook Air supports many different displays and resolutions. The two most important considerations are size and cost. Larger displays are better because they give you more working space. They also tend to be more expensive, although that depends on the specific brand you choose. Be wary of very inexpensive displays because they tend to have poor image quality. In most cases, if you choose a display from a reputable manufacturer, such as Apple (the Apple displays are extremely high quality, but are also on the expensive end of the scale) or ViewSonic, any display you get will work well for you.

Can I use a projector with MacBook Air?

Yes. You connect and use a projector in the same way as an external display. When you use a projector, you typically want to turn display mirroring on (by checking the **Mirror Displays** check box in the Arrangement tab) so that the audience sees the same information that appears on the MacBook Air screen.

Connect and Use a Bluetooth Mouse

You might find that the MacBook Air trackpad works really well for you and that you never want to use anything else; or, you might prefer a mouse when you are working with MacBook Air in one place. It is mostly a matter of personal preference.

If you do want to use a mouse, a Bluetooth mouse is a good option because it has no wires and therefore does not take up the precious USB port on your MacBook Air.

Connect and Use a Bluetooth Mouse

① Insert batteries into the mouse and turn it on.

② Place the mouse in discovery mode.

Note: See the documentation for the specific mouse you use to see how this is done.

③ Open the System Preferences application and click the **Bluetooth** icon.

The Bluetooth pane appears.

● If you have configured Bluetooth previously, you see the devices that you have connected to in the left pane of the window.

If you have not configured Bluetooth previously, you see an empty pane with the Set Up New Device button in its center.

④ Check the **On** check box to turn Bluetooth power on.

⑤ Check the **Discoverable** check box so that other Bluetooth devices can find MacBook Air.

⑥ Check the **Show Bluetooth status in the menu bar** check box to enable the Bluetooth menu so that you can control Bluetooth from the desktop.

⑦ Click the **Add** button (⊞), or the **Set Up New Device** button.

The Bluetooth Setup Assistant appears.

⑧ Click **Continue**.

⑨ Select the **Mouse** radio button.

⑩ Click **Continue**.

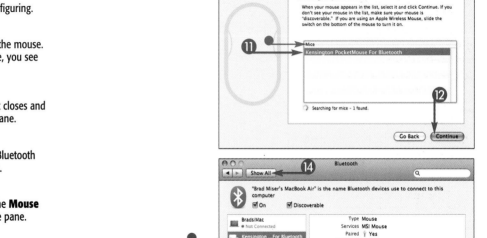

● MacBook Air searches for mice with which it can communicate. These appear on the list of available devices.

⑪ Select the mouse you are configuring.

⑫ Click **Continue**.

MacBook Air pairs itself with the mouse. When the process is complete, you see the Conclusion screen.

⑬ Click **Quit**.

The Bluetooth Setup Assistant closes and you return to the Bluetooth pane.

● The mouse is shown on the Bluetooth tab and you can start using it.

⑭ Click **Show All**.

⑮ Configure the mouse using the **Mouse** tab of the Keyboard & Mouse pane.

The mouse is ready for use.

TIPS

What about other kinds of mice?
You can use any mouse with MacBook Air, whether it is a Bluetooth mouse or not. To use a wired mouse, simply plug its USB cable into the MacBook Air USB port. To use a non-Bluetooth wireless mouse, connect its receiver to the USB port. Regardless of how you connect a mouse to MacBook Air, you can use the Mouse tab of the Keyboard & Mouse pane of the System Preferences application to configure it.

What is the best kind of Bluetooth mouse?
Choosing a mouse is a personal decision in that one person's favorite mouse might be unusable to someone else. The most important consideration when choosing a mouse is the comfort of the mouse in your hand. If possible, you should try using a mouse before buying it. Next, consider the number of controls, buttons, and other features a mouse offers. At the least, a mouse should have two buttons and a scroll wheel. Some devices have more controls; for example, the Apple Mighty Mouse enables you to click a left or right button by pressing one side or the other, scroll horizontally and vertically using its scroll ball, and program buttons on the side for specific actions.

Connect and Use External Speakers

MacBook Air has speakers, but their sound quality is somewhat less than spectacular. With iTunes, DVD Player, and all the other great applications for which sound is an important element, you should consider using external speakers when you use MacBook Air in only one location.

You can use a variety of speakers with MacBook Air as long as they are powered (also called computer) speakers. Some speaker sets have two speakers (left and right), while others have three (left, right, and sub-woofer).

Connect and Use External Speakers

1 Connect the speaker input to the audio/headphones out port on the right side of MacBook Air.

2 Make the connections between the speakers, such as between the left and right speaker and the sub-woofer.

3 Power up the speakers.

4 Open the System Preferences application and click the **Sound** icon.

The Sound pane appears.

5 Click the **Output** tab.

6 Select the speakers you want to use for sound output.

This option appears as Headphones even when you attach a set of speakers.

Note: *You can also connect any pair of analog headphones to the MacBook Air audio port, which is a great way to enjoy good sound quality on the move.*

7 If controls for the speakers appear, use them to improve the sound.

For example, you might be able to set a balance level and system volume level.

⑧ Play sound with an application such as iTunes.

Note: *For more information about iTunes, see Chapter 18.*

⑨ Use the application's controls to set the specific volume level.

⑩ Adjust the volume level and other settings using the speaker system's controls.

TIPS

Does MacBook Air support digital audio?
In its present incarnation, MacBook Air supports only analog audio, which means that you cannot enjoy surround sound when you watch DVDs. However, you might be so amazed at the sound quality provided by a three-speaker set that "going analog" does not bother you all that much.

ANALOG ONLY

What kind of speakers should I get?
The speakers you should get depend on how important sound quality is to you, how much money you want to spend, and whether you want the speakers to be portable. A nice three-speaker set can deliver reasonable sound quality for a modest price. If you want to have better sound when you move around with MacBook Air, consider purchasing a portable speaker system. Many of these are available for iPods. As long as they have an auxiliary input, you can connect MacBook Air to them.

Connect To and Use a USB Hub

Many devices use USB to connect to a computer. Examples of these include external hard drives, mice, iPhones, iPods, digital cameras, and printers. MacBook Air has only a single USB port, and so you are only able to connect one device to it at a time, which can be inconvenient.

For situations in which you want to connect multiple USB devices to MacBook Air at the same time, you can use an external USB hub. You connect the hub to MacBook Air and then connect USB devices to the ports on the hub. MacBook Air can access these devices just as if they are connected to its USB port.

Connect To and Use a USB Hub

OBTAIN AN EXTERNAL USB HUB

1. Visit your favorite retailer.

2. Look for a hub with the number of ports matching or exceeding the number of devices you want to have connected at the same time.

Note: *You should also consider whether the hub gets its power from MacBook Air or requires an external power source. An external power source is a nuisance because you have to carry it with you, but a self-powered hub uses power from MacBook Air, which shortens life when operating on battery power.*

3. Purchase a hub.

INSTALL A USB HUB

1. Connect the input port on the hub to the MacBook Air USB port.

2. Connect the hub to a power source, if required.

3. Connect USB devices to the hub.

   The devices are ready to use.

Connect To and Use Ethernet Devices

MacBook Air is designed to be wireless when it comes to connecting to many devices, most importantly, local networks and the Internet. However, Ethernet, which is a wired technology, does offer some benefits over wireless connections. Ethernet is faster, and so achieves the best network performance. Ethernet is also more secure than wireless because you have to be physically connected to a network to access it.

To connect to a network or devices (such as a printer) with Ethernet, you need to use a USB to Ethernet adapter. Use an Ethernet cable to connect the adapter to an AirPort Base Station or other Ethernet device.

Connect To and Use Ethernet Devices

OBTAIN A USB ETHERNET ADAPTER

① Locate and purchase an Apple USB Ethernet Adapter, which is not included with MacBook Air.

CONNECT MACBOOK AIR TO ETHERNET DEVICES

① Plug the Ethernet adapter into the MacBook Air USB port (or into a USB hub connected to that port).

② Connect an Ethernet cable to the adapter.

③ Connect the other end of the cable to an Ethernet device, such as an AirPort Extreme Base Station.

④ Configure the Ethernet connection using the appropriate pane of the System Preferences application.

You can use the Network pane to configure an Ethernet network connection.

Synchronize MacBook Air with an iPhone

In addition to its amazing cell phone features, the iPhone offers iPod functionality along with calendars, contacts, e-mail, and Web browsing.

Some of the information you use on iPhone can come from MacBook Air. For example, if you use iCal to manage your calendar, you can synchronize your calendar on iPhone so that changes you make in iCal are reflected on the iPhone, and vice versa. You can also synchronize your e-mail accounts, contacts from Address Book, and even your Safari bookmarks.

Synchronize MacBook Air with an iPhone

① Connect your iPhone to your MacBook Air using its USB cable.

The iPhone is mounted on your MacBook Air, iTunes opens, and you see the iPhone in the Devices section of the iTunes Source list.

② Select your **iPhone**.

③ Click the **Info** tab.

④ Check the **Sync Address Book contacts** check box.

⑤ To synchronize all contacts, click the **All contacts** radio button, or to synchronize just specific groups, click the **Selected groups** radio button and check the check box for each group you want to synchronize.

⑥ To add contacts that you create on your iPhone to a specific group in Address Book, click the **Put new contacts created on this iPhone into the group** check box and choose the group on the pop-up menu.

⑦ In the Calendars section, check the **Sync iCal calendars** check box.

⑧ To synchronize all of your calendars, click the **All calendars** radio button, or if you want to synchronize only specific calendars, click the **Selected calendars** radio button and check the check box for each calendar you want to synchronize.

⑨ To exclude older events from the synchronization, check the **Do not sync events older than** check box and enter the number of days in the field.

⑩ Choose the calendar onto which events created on the iPhone should be placed.

11 Scroll down to the Mail Accounts and Web Browser sections.

12 To move your e-mail accounts to your iPhone, check the **Sync selected Mail accounts** check box.

Note: *For information about e-mail, see Chapter 12.*

13 Check the check box for each account you want to synchronize.

14 To synchronize your Web bookmarks, check the **Sync Safari bookmarks** check box.

15 Scroll down to the Advanced section.

16 Check the box for the information you want to be replaced on your iPhone when you synchronize.

17 Click **Apply**.

The next time you synchronize, the information you configured is moved between your MacBook Air and iPhone.

TIPS

Can I synchronize MacBook Air with other kinds of cell phones?

If your cell phone supports Bluetooth, you can synchronize its information with MacBook Air wirelessly. In most cases, you can at least synchronize contacts. With other devices, you might be able to move calendar and other information from MacBook Air to the cell phone, and vice versa; it depends on the specific phone that you use. Some devices require a third-party application to fully synchronize.

How do I do synchronize with a Bluetooth cell phone?

To synchronize with a Bluetooth cell phone, you must pair it with MacBook Air. You do this like other Bluetooth devices using the Bluetooth Setup Assistant (see the section "Connect and Use a Bluetooth Mouse," earlier in this chapter) except that you choose the Mobile phone button instead of the Mouse button. Once paired, you can choose the information that you synchronize between the two devices. Although not as easy and powerful as synchronizing with iPhone, it does enable you to share some information between the two devices.

Enjoying the Internet

MacBook Air is ideal for taking advantage of all the Internet has to offer. Mac OS X includes great applications for working with the Web: you can send, receive, and organize e-mail; you can text, audio, and even video chat; and using MobileMe, you can make the Internet an integrated extension of your MacBook Air desktop. With its built-in wireless capabilities, you can take advantage of all these great tools almost anywhere you and your MacBook Air happen to be.

A MobileMe account gives you access to a number of useful services and online applications that you can use as much as you want. Because your MobileMe account is integrated with MacBook Air, you can consider MobileMe to be an extension of your MacBook Air desktop on the Internet.

MobileMe Account

To use MobileMe, you must have a MobileMe account. You can obtain an account from the MacBook Air desktop or by using Safari. A MobileMe account includes, by default, 20GB of storage space on Apple servers, an e-mail account, space for online galleries of your photos, and more. You can also purchase a family account that provides several different user accounts under a single MobileMe account (for distinct e-mail addresses and iDisks). At the time of this writing, the cost of an individual MobileMe account is $99 per year, while the cost of a family account is $149 per year. You can also upgrade accounts by adding disk space.

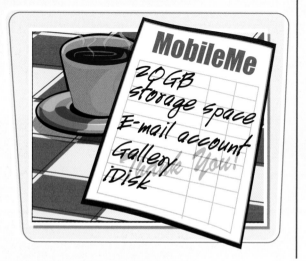

iDisk

One of the best features of MobileMe is iDisk, which is a virtual disk that you access on Apple servers. Your account includes 20GB of disk space (you can purchase more if you need it) that you can use just like the MacBook Air internal drive. The iDisk is also where you store the files you use to build your Gallery sites and where your MobileMe e-mail is stored. You can access your iDisk directly from the MacBook Air desktop, from the iDisk application on the MobileMe Web site, and from any other computer you use, including Windows computers.

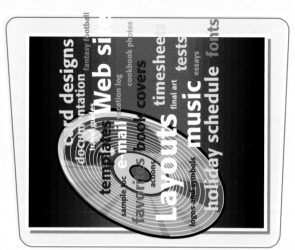

MobileMe E-mail

Another great feature of MobileMe is that you get an e-mail account, with an e-mail address that is *yourmacusername@me.com*, where *yourmacusername* is the name of your MobileMe user account. You can send and receive e-mail from your MobileMe account just like you do from other e-mail accounts that you may have, from an e-mail application such as Mail or directly from the MobileMe Web site. You can also create e-mail aliases that enable you to use multiple addresses at the same time.

Gallery

Using the Gallery, you can easily display photos on the Web. You can upload photos directly to the Gallery from your desktop, or you can publish a Gallery directly from iPhoto. You can organize your online galleries in different photo albums; once an album is on the gallery, people can use the album's link to view its photos within a Web browser.

Synchronization

If you have more than one Mac, such as a MacBook Air and an iMac, or an iPhone, you probably want to be able to access certain information from all your devices, such as your e-mail, calendars, and contacts. Using MobileMe, you can synchronize Macs and iPhones so that changes you make to information on one device are copied to the others automatically or on your command. This makes it easy to ensure that you have access to information you need from any Mac you happen to be using as well as from your iPhone.

Obtain and Configure a MobileMe Account

Because MobileMe is integrated into Mac OS X, you can obtain a MobileMe account right from the MacBook Air desktop. When you do, you move to the Apple Web site, where you provide the information required to create your account.

After you have created your account, you configure MacBook Air (and your other computers and iPhone) to access MobileMe, and all its services are ready for you to use.

Obtain and Configure a MobileMe Account

① Click the **Apple** menu (◆) and then select **System Preferences**.

The System Preferences application opens.

② Click the **MobileMe** icon.

The MobileMe pane appears.

③ Click **Learn More**.

Safari opens and moves to the MobileMe Web site.

The Login dialog appears.

④ Click **sign up for a free trial**.

The first page of a two-step form appears.

⑤ Fill out the information on this page.

Note: *Be thoughtful about what you choose as your member name; in addition to using this to log in to MobileMe, it becomes part of your e-mail address. You cannot change this name after you have created an account.*

⑥ Click **Continue**.

⑦ In a similar way, complete the second page of the form.

The Welcome to MobileMe screen appears, and provides information that you need to use your MobileMe account.

8 Move back to the MobileMe tab of the System Preferences application by clicking its icon on the Dock.

9 Type your member name.

10 Type your password.

11 Click **Sign In**.

● Your account information is configured on MacBook Air, and the MobileMe pane updates to show that you have configured MobileMe. You can now access MobileMe services from the desktop or from the MobileMe Web site.

TIPS

What happens when my trial period expires?
You can use your MobileMe account for 60 days at no cost to you. If you do not cancel the account prior to the end of the trial period, your account is converted into a full account and is available to you for one year (you have the option to renew the account on yearly basis). You only need to take action to cancel the account if you do not want it past the trial period.

Are MobileMe services available outside the United States?
Yes. You can create and use a MobileMe account from many different countries. The rates charged for a MobileMe account vary from country to country, but the MobileMe services that you can access are similar.

Use an iDisk

iDisk is a volume of disk space on the Apple servers that you can access through your MobileMe membership. iDisk is built into Mac OS X so that after you configure MacBook Air for MobileMe, it appears on your desktop just like other hard drives that you use. You can also access your iDisk using the iDisk application on the MobileMe Web site.

By default, iDisk has a number of folders on it, such as Public, My Documents, and Sites. Some folders, such as Public, are used to store files that you want other people to be able to access. You can use these folders or create your own and then store documents and other files in them.

CONFIGURE IDISK

1. Open the MobileMe pane of the System Preferences application and click the **iDisk** tab.

● The iDisk Usage gauge shows how much of your iDisk space you are currently using.

2. If you want other people to be able to store files in your iDisk's Public folder, select the **Read and Write** radio button.

3. To put a password on your Public folder, check the **Password-protect your public folder** check box; if you do not want to protect your Public folder with a password, skip to Step **7**.

4. Type the password for the folder in the Password field.

5. Confirm the password by typing it again in the Confirm field.

6. Click **OK**.

The sheet closes and your password is set.

If you only want to access your iDisk over the Internet, skip to Step **10**.

⑦ If you want to keep a copy of iDisk on MacBook Air so that you can access it even when you are not connected to the Internet, click **Start**.

⑧ To update your copy of iDisk automatically, click the **Automatically** radio button.

⑨ If you want to manually update iDisk, click the **Manually** radio button.

⑩ Press ⌘+Q to quit the System Preferences application.

USE IDISK

① Open a Finder window and click the **iDisk** icon.

Note: You can also move to your iDisk by choosing **Go**, clicking **iDisk**, and then clicking **MyiDisk**.

● The contents of your iDisk appear.

If you chose to keep a copy of iDisk on MacBook Air, all of its data is copied to MacBook Air.

Note: If you choose to keep a copy of iDisk on MacBook Air and select the Manually option, you can click the **Sync** button ( ) next to the iDisk icon to synchronize the two versions of iDisk.

How do I access my iDisk from a Windows PC?
To access your iDisk from a Windows computer, open the MobileMe Preferences control panel (you must have installed the latest version of iTunes for this to be available) and sign into your MobileMe account on the PC. Open a desktop window. From the Tools menu, choose **Map Network Drive**. Choose the drive letter for your iDisk. In the Folder box, type **http://idisk.me.com/membername**, where *membername* is your MobileMe username. Click the different username link. Enter your MobileMe username and password and click **OK**. Click **Finish**. You can access the iDisk by using the drive letter you assigned to it.

Can I use iDisk to back up my files?
You can use your iDisk to store any files, including backups. Even better, you can download Apple's Backup application from the Software folder on your iDisk and use it to automatically back up files to folders on your iDisk. Backing up to iDisk is useful because the files are stored independently of your computer, and even your location, for maximum protection. Because they are stored online, you can access your backups from any computer that can access your iDisk.

Use MobileMe Webmail

You can access your MobileMe e-mail in an e-mail application, such as Mail. You can learn how to use Mail to access your MobileMe e-mail in Chapter 12.

You can also access MobileMe e-mail from any computer through the Web. This makes MobileMe e-mail very convenient because as long as you are using a computer with Internet access, your MobileMe e-mail is not far away.

Use MobileMe Webmail

1 Open a Web browser and move to www.me.com.

The MobileMe Login dialog appears.

2 Type your MobileMe member name if needed.

3 Type your password.

4 Check the **Keep me logged in for two weeks** check box if you want to remain logged in to your account.

5 Click **Log In**.

You move to the MobileMe application Web site.

6 Click the **Mail** icon.

The MobileMe Mail Web application appears.

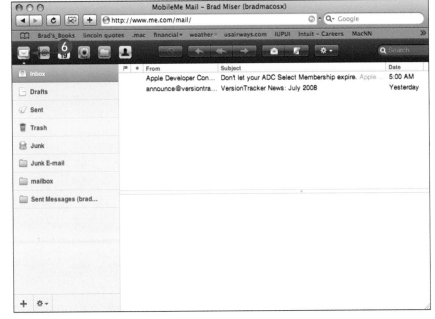

7 Click an e-mail to read it.

● The message appears in the lower pane of the window.

8 To reply to a message, click the **Reply** button (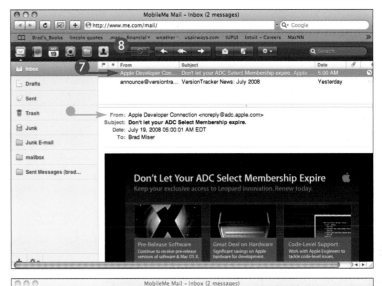) and type your reply.

9 To create a new message, click the **New Message** icon ( ).

● The New Message window appears.

10 Address the message, type the subject, and type the message.

11 Click the **Send** button ( ).

The e-mail is sent.

Note: Most of the tools available on the MobileMe Mail Web application work just like they do in the Mac OS X Mail application (see Chapter 12 for details).

How do I access my MobileMe e-mail in Mail?

Mail is designed to work with MobileMe e-mail accounts. When you configure MacBook Air to access MobileMe services, your MobileMe e-mail account is available immediately, and you can set it up with just a couple of clicks. See Chapter 12 for more information.

Do I have to use Mail or the MobileMe Web site to access my MobileMe e-mail?

No, you can access MobileMe e-mail as you can any other e-mail account. When you sign up for MobileMe, information appears for the servers that you need to configure to access MobileMe e-mail. You can use this information to set up your MobileMe e-mail in any e-mail application, such as Entourage on the Mac or Eudora on Windows.

Create an Online Photo Gallery

With a MobileMe account and iPhoto, you can quickly and easily publish photos to the Web, where they are viewable in any Web browser. You can also allow people to download photos from the gallery to their computers.

Use iPhoto to create a photo album and then publish it as a gallery. Then, you can visit the gallery from your MobileMe account or via any Web browser.

USE IPHOTO TO PUBLISH A GALLERY

① In iPhoto, create a photo album.

Note: For help with iPhoto, see Chapter 19.

② Add the photos you want to publish to the album.

③ With the album selected, click the **Web Gallery** button.

The Gallery sheet appears.

④ On the Album Viewable by pop-up menu, choose **Everyone** to make the gallery available to everyone who visits its site, **Only Me** to limit access to the site to you, or **Edit Names and Passwords** to identify specific people who can access the site.

Note: If you choose Names and Passwords, a sheet appears. Use the sheet to create usernames and passwords and then select the galleries those users will be able to access.

⑤ To allow visitors to be able to download photos, check the **Downloading of photos or entire album** check box.

⑥ To permit people to upload photos via the Web, check the **Uploading of photos via web browser** check box.

⑦ To allow viewers to add photos via e-mail, check the **Adding of photos via email** check box.

⑧ To display titles on the gallery, check the **Photo titles** check box.

⑨ If you checked the check box in Step **7**, check the **Email address for uploading photos** check box to display the e-mail address on the gallery page.

⑩ Click **Publish**.

iPhoto publishes the photo album to the Web.

VISITING A GALLERY FROM YOUR MOBILEME SITE

1. If you are not already logged in to your MobileMe page, then log in.

2. Click the **Gallery** button.

   The Gallery application opens.

3. Select the album you want to view.

- The images in the album appear.

- The gallery's URL is shown in the upper-right corner of the window.

VISITING A GALLERY FROM A WEB BROWSER

1. Using a Web browser, move to the gallery's URL.

- The gallery appears in the Web browser window.

2. View images in the gallery.

3. Use the controls to change how the photos are displayed, download photos, and so on.

TIPS

How do I enable others to view my photos?

Move to the gallery in a Web browser. Click the **Tell a Friend** button. Complete the resulting sheet by typing your e-mail address, the person's e-mail address, a message, and other options. When you send the message, it includes a link on which the person can click to move to the gallery. If you require a username and password to view the gallery, make sure you tell the recipient that information or he will not be able to view the gallery.

How does uploading via e-mail work?

If you allow photos to be uploaded via e-mail, an upload e-mail address is created for the gallery. People can send e-mail messages containing photos to be uploaded to this address. The images they send are automatically added to the gallery, so be careful about who you provide this address to if you want to control the photos in the gallery.

Synchronize Information among Multiple Macs

If you have more than one Mac, you can use MobileMe to keep a variety of information synchronized on each Mac. For example, you can make sure you have the same set of contacts in Address Book on each computer or to ensure that all your favorite bookmarks are available when you need them.

To get started, you need to configure each computer to be part of the synchronization process. MacBook Air then ensures that it is synchronized automatically, or you can perform synchronizations manually.

Synchronize Information among Multiple Macs

① Open the MobileMe pane of the System Preferences application and click the **Sync** tab.

② Check the **Synchronize with MobileMe** check box.

③ On the pop-up menu, select how you want synchronizations to occur.

You can choose **Manually** to synchronize manually; choose a time, such as **Every Hour**, to synchronize at those times; or choose **Automatically** to have synchronizations performed automatically.

④ Check the check box next to each item you want to include in the synchronization.

⑤ Click **Sync Now**.

The information you selected is copied onto MobileMe.

If some of the information already exists, an alert appears.

⑥ On the pop-up menu, choose how you want data to be synchronized.

You can choose **Merge all data** if you want the data on MobileMe to be merged with the information on MacBook Air. Choose **Replace data on computer** to replace the information on MacBook Air with information stored on MobileMe. Choose **Replace all data on MobileMe** to have the information on MacBook Air copied to MobileMe to replace the information stored there.

⑦ Click **Sync**.

The synchronization process begins.

As changes are made to data, you are alerted about what is going to be done.

⑧ Click the **Sync** button to allow the synchronization to continue.

This example shows the **Sync Contacts** button.

⑨ Repeat Step **8** at each prompt.

The time and date of the last synchronization appear at the bottom of the Sync tab when the process is complete.

TIPS

Where is synchronized information stored, and can I access it from the Web?

All the information you synchronized through MobileMe is stored on your iDisk. You can access it from the Web by clicking the appropriate links on the MobileMe Web page. For example, to access your contact information, click the **Address Book** Web application icon.

Can I include documents in synchronizations?

No. MobileMe synchronization only works with specific information. However, if you save documents onto your iDisk and set synchronization to occur automatically, any documents you save are available on each computer that is configured to access your MobileMe account. You can also manually copy documents to your iDisk and then copy them from the iDisk onto each computer if you prefer.

Explore Safari

Safari is an elegant application, meaning that it offers a lot of functionality and is a pleasure to use at the same time. As soon as you open it, Safari is configured for easy use, and you can set various preferences to tailor the way it works for you.

SAFARI IN BROWSE MODE

● **Back**

Moves back to the previous page

● **Forward**

Moves forward to the next page

● **Refresh or Stop Loading**

Refresh (C) gets the current version of the page, or stops loading (X) a page.

● **Create Web widget**

Enables you to capture part of a Web page and put it on the Dashboard

● **Add Bookmark**

Saves the current location as a bookmark

● **Address bar**

Shows the current Web address (Uniform Resource Locator, or URL)

● **Search bar**

Enter information here to search for it via Google

● **Bookmarks bar**

The Bookmarks bar provides quick access to your favorite bookmarks. At the end of the bar, click **More Bookmarks** (≫) to show bookmarks that do not fit on the Bookmarks bar

● **Tabs**

You can open each Web page in its own tab

● **Web page**

Provides access to the information and tools on the Web page

● **Status bar**

Shows the current status of Safari activity

● **Title**

Shows the title of the Web page being displayed

SAFARI IN BOOKMARKS MODE

● **Bookmarks mode button**

Click this button ( ) to toggle between Browse and Bookmarks mode

● **Collections**

Special groups of bookmarks, such as those on the Bookmarks bar

● **Selected source**

Select a source of bookmarks to see them on the list

● **Bookmarks**

Shows individual bookmarks and folders containing bookmarks

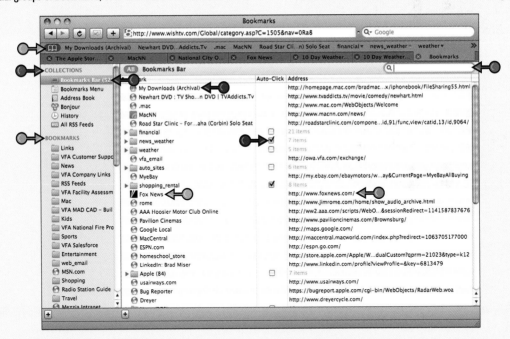

● **List of bookmarks in selected source**

Shows the bookmarks and folders of bookmarks in the selected source

● **Search tools**

Enables you to search for bookmarks

● **Bookmark name**

A descriptive name that you can assign to bookmarks

● **Address**

The URL to which the bookmark points

● **Auto-click check box**

Enables you to open all the bookmarks in a folder with one click

Move to Web Sites

The most basic task when you use the Web is to move to the Web site in which you are interested and then navigate within that site's pages. There are a number of ways to do this, and you will probably use all of them as you explore the Web.

Moving to a Web site by entering its URL address is the most flexible method, and is the one you can always use. For most sites that you use regularly, you need to type the URL only once. After that, you can move back to it with a bookmark or by using the Safari History list.

MOVE TO A WEB SITE BY ENTERING A URL

① Launch Safari by clicking its icon on the Dock.

Safari opens and you move to the current home page.

② Type the address of a Web site.

While a full Web address begins with either "http://" or "https://", you do not need to type either of these prefixes because Safari automatically adds them to any address that you type. If the address begins with "www", you do not need to type the "www" part, either. For example, to move to, you just need to type **apple.com**.

As you type in the Address bar, Safari tries to match what you type with a site you have visited previously and shows you the matches on a list under the Address bar. You can click an address on the list to move to it.

③ When you finish typing the address, press **Return**.

● Safari moves to the address and you see its content.

MOVE TO WEB SITES WITH A BOOKMARK

1 To use a bookmark on the Bookmarks bar, click the bookmark.

2 To access a bookmark that is stored on the Bookmarks menu, open the **Bookmarks** menu.

3 Select the bookmark you want to use.

4 To move to any bookmark you have saved using Safari's Bookmarks mode, click **Show All Bookmarks**.

TIPS

How can I use bookmarks that I have saved on one computer on all my Macs?

If you use more than one Mac, you are likely to create different bookmarks as you surf the Web on each computer. Re-creating those bookmarks on each Mac can be a nuisance. Fortunately, if you use MobileMe, you do not have to. You can synchronize the bookmarks on each Mac you use so that whether you use MacBook Air or a different Mac, you always have the same set of bookmarks available to you. See Chapter 10 for detailed information about using MobileMe synchronization.

How do I know specifically where a bookmark points?

Because you can name a bookmark anything you would like, and you usually use an abbreviated name when you add a bookmark to the Bookmarks bar, you might not remember where a bookmark points. To see a bookmark's address, point to the bookmark on the Bookmarks bar without clicking it. After a second or two, the full address for the bookmark appears.

continued

As you move to Web addresses, a new page opens, which is also what happens when you click a link that points to a different address (on the same Web site or elsewhere). As you navigate through pages, you create a "chain" of pages that you can move back and forward through. You can do this because Safari "remembers" each page as you move through it, and each page is temporarily stored on MacBook Air.

You can also move to Web pages from outside Safari by clicking hyperlinks in documents, such as e-mail and text documents. When you click a Web link, Mac OS X recognizes it as an address and opens it in your default Web browser.

Move to Web Sites *(continued)*

● The Web site is replaced by the Bookmarks window, which means that Safari is in Bookmarks mode.

❺ Choose a location in which to save the bookmark.

❻ If the selected source includes folders, click their expansion triangles to view the bookmarks they contain (▶ changes to ▼).

❼ Double-click the bookmark you want to use.

Whichever method you used to access a bookmark, once you click it, its Web page fills the Safari window.

MOVE TO WEB SITES USING HISTORY

❶ Open the **History** menu.

In the fourth section of the menu, you see a list of Web pages you have visited most recently.

❷ If the page to which you want to return is on the list, select it.

❸ If the site is not on the list, select the folder for the time period in which you visited it.

❹ Select the site you want to visit on the resulting menu.

The site you selected opens.

MOVE TO WEB SITES USING A LINK

① Click a link in an e-mail or other document.

Safari opens and moves to the Web site.

MOVE THROUGH WEB PAGES

① Click a link to move to Web pages.

② Click the **Back** button (◀) to move to a previous page.

③ Click the **Forward** button (▶) to move to a later page in the current "chain" of pages you have been browsing.

What does the http that Safari adds to the front of URLs stand for?

The http prefix stands for Hyper Text Transfer Protocol, and is the basic *protocol*, or language, that Web pages employ. There are other protocols you can access with Safari, such as FTP (File Transfer Protocol), in which case the URL starts with ftp: instead of http:. The vast majority of sites that you will visit with Safari use http, and so Safari assumes that this is the kind of site you want. To move to a different kind of site, you have to add that prefix at the beginning of the URL, such as ftp://.

What is https?

A lot of Web sites deal with information that needs to be protected, such as bank accounts and credit cards. These sites use Secure Socket Layer (SSL) technology to encrypt and therefore protect the data being sent between the Web page and Safari. These sites use the https protocol (Hyper Text Transfer Protocol Secure). You typically do not have to add https at the beginning of addresses to move to them; when you reach the part of the site that is secure, https is employed automatically.

Search the Web

One of the most useful things to do on the Web is to search for information, and one of the best search engines is Google. Google searching is built into Safari to make Web searches fast and easy.

You can perform a Google search by using the Safari built-in Search tool. Of course, you can also move directly to the Google Search page by entering the URL, google.com, in the Address bar and pressing Return **, but it is easier and faster to use the Safari Search tool.**

Search the Web

① Type the information for which you want to search in the Search bar.

② Press Return.

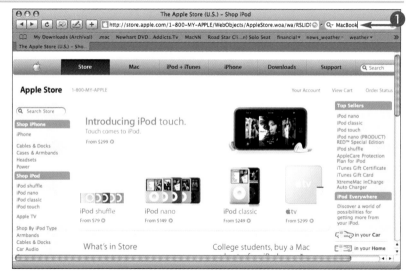

The search is performed and you see the Google results page.

③ Click a link to visit one of the search results.

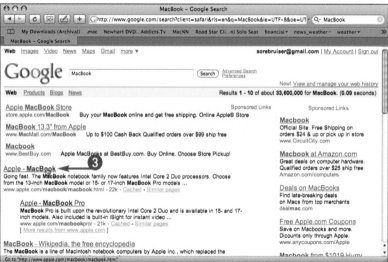

That Web page appears.

● View and use the Web page.

④ Click the **SnapBack** button ().

You return to the search results page.

⑤ Scroll the page to explore other results.

Note: *When you get to the bottom of a search results page, you see how many pages are in the results. Click* **Next** *to move to the next page of results, or click a page's number to jump to it.*

TIPS

How can I repeat a previous search?
Safari remembers the most recent searches you have performed. To repeat a search, click the magnifying glass icon (🔍) in the Search bar and choose the search that you want to repeat on the list that appears.

Can I use any search page with Safari, or do I have to use Google?
You can use any search page by moving to its URL. For example, to search with Yahoo!, type **yahoo.com**. The search page appears and you can use its tool to search the Web. When you use the Safari Search bar, you search using Google only.

Download Files

There are all kinds of great files that you can download from the Web. These include applications that you can run on MacBook Air (in fact, many applications you obtain are downloaded from the Web), images, PDF documents, and so on.

After you download a file, how you use it depends on the kind of file it is. Most applications are provided in a disk image file (with the filename extension .dmg), which mounts automatically. Some files, such as PDF documents, are downloaded as they are. Other files are archived so that you need to uncompress them before you use them.

DOWNLOAD FILES FROM THE WEB

① Move to a file that you want to download.

② Click the file's download link or button.

● The file begins to download, and the Downloads window appears.

③ Monitor the progress of the download.

Note: *You do not really have to monitor a file download because it downloads in the background. You can continue to do other things as files download.*

When the download is complete, the file is ready for you to use.

USE DISK IMAGES YOU HAVE DOWNLOADED

1. Open a Finder window.

2. Choose the disk image that you downloaded.

   The contents of the disk image are shown just like a hard drive or other volume you select.

3. Run the application installer, or install it with drag-and-drop (see Chapter 5 for details).

USE DOCUMENT FILES YOU HAVE DOWNLOADED

1. Open the **Downloads** folder, which is located in your Home folder.

Note: The Downloads folder has a default stack on the Dock. This contains the icon of the most recent file you have downloaded. Click the icon, and it expands to show the contents of the folder; click an icon to use it, or click **More in Finder** to open the folder in a Finder window.

2. Find the downloaded document you want to use.

3. Double-click the document to open it.

   It opens using the application with which it is associated.

Note: When you download a group of files that have been compressed using the ZIP format, they are uncompressed for you automatically. Instead of a single file, you see a folder with the zip file's name. Open that folder to see the files it contains.

 TIPS

What is a SIT file?

These are files compressed with an older scheme first introduced by an application called StuffIt. When Mac OS X was introduced, support for the Windows standard compression (file extension .zip) was built into the OS, and so most files you encounter these days are compressed as ZIP files. However, there are a few older files that might have .sit as their filename extension. If you come across one of these, you need to download and install the free StuffIt Expander application (do a Web search and you will find it) to be able to open SIT files.

What about FTP?

Some sites use FTP to provide files for you to download. The primary benefit of an FTP site is that files are usually downloaded faster than they are through HTTP. You can access FTP sites in Safari (their URLs start with ftp:// instead of http://), or you can use an FTP application, such as Fetch. Most FTP sites require you to have a username and password to be able to download files.

Browse the Web with Tabs

Often, you will want to have several Web sites open at the same time. Opening each of these in its own window works, but it can result in screen clutter.

The tabs in Safari enable you to open as many Web pages at a time as you want, while keeping all those pages in one window so that you do not clutter up your desktop. Moving to a page is as simple as clicking its tab.

CONFIGURE SAFARI TO USE TABS

1 Press ⌘+,.

The Safari Preferences window opens.

2 Click the **Tabs** tab.

3 Check the top check box if you want to be able to press the ⌘ key when you click a link to open a Web page in a new tab.

4 Check the middle check box if you want to move to new tabs and windows when they are created.

5 Check the bottom check box if you want to confirm closing a window when it has multiple tabs open.

6 Review the keyboard shortcuts shown at the bottom of the window; these reflect the check boxes that you have checked or unchecked.

7 Close the Preferences window.

OPEN AND USE TABS

1 Open a Safari window and move to a Web page.

2 Press ⌘+T.

A new tab appears.

3 Open a Web page in the new tab using any of the techniques you learned earlier in this chapter.

● The Web page fills the tab.

4 To open a link in a new tab, press and hold the ⌘ key while you click the link.

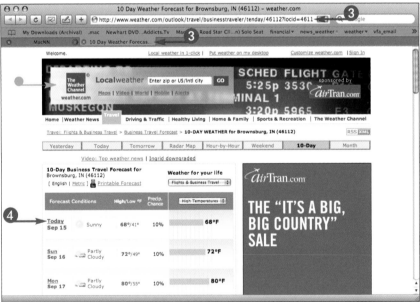

● A new tab opens and displays the destination page of the link.

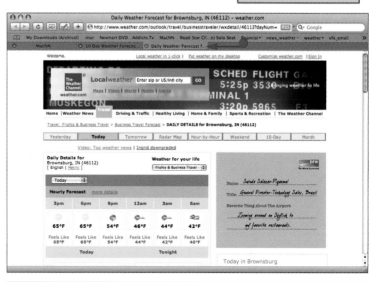

⑥ To move to a tab, click it.

The tab's Web page appears.

⑦ To close a tab, click its **Close** button ().

The tab disappears.

TIPS

How can I move through open tabs with the keyboard?
Press ⌘+} to move to the next tab, or press ⌘+{ to move to the previous tab.

When should I open more windows instead of tabs?
Tabs are great because you can have many pages open in the same window. However, you can see only one page at a time. If you open multiple windows instead (press ⌘ +N), you can arrange the windows so that you can see multiple windows at the same time. To convert a tab into a window, move to it, click the **Window** menu, and then click **Move Tab to New Window**.

Set and Organize Bookmarks

By default, Safari includes a number of bookmarks that you can use, but as you explore the Web, there will be a lot of sites that you visit regularly. You can create bookmarks for each of these sites so that it is simple to get back to them.

Because you are likely to end up with many bookmarks, you need tools to keep them organized. Safari also helps with that.

CREATE BOOKMARKS

1 Move to a Web page that you want to bookmark.

2 Press ⌘ + D.

You can also open the **Bookmarks** menu and then select **Add Bookmark,** or you can click the **Add** button (➕).

● The Bookmark sheet appears.

3 Name the bookmark.

4 Open the pop-up menu.

5 Choose the location in which you want to store the bookmark.

● The location you selected appears in the pop-up menu.

6 Click **Add**.

The bookmark is created in the location you selected. You can move back to the site at any time by choosing the new bookmark.

ORGANIZE BOOKMARKS

1 Press **Option**+**⌘**+**B**, or choose **Show All Bookmarks** from the Bookmarks menu.

Safari opens the Bookmarks window.

2 To create a new folder for bookmarks, click the **Add** button (➕).

Type a name for the bookmark, and choose where to keep it.

Online Banking

financial

Cancel   Add

How do I store bookmarks on the Bookmarks bar?
The Bookmarks bar is a convenient way to access bookmarks because it appears at the top of the Safari window so that you can move to a bookmark just by clicking its button on the bar. To add a bookmark to the bar, choose **Bookmarks Bar** on the pop-up menu on the New Bookmark sheet. When you add the bookmark, it is placed on the left edge of the bar, becoming the first bookmark on the bar.

How do I change the location of a bookmark on the Bookmarks bar?
The contents and organization of the Bookmarks bar are determined by the contents of the Bookmarks Bar collection. To move a bookmark toward the left side of the Bookmarks bar, drag its icon up the list of bookmarks that appears when you select the Bookmarks Bar collection. Drag a bookmark down the list to move it to the right on the Bookmarks bar.

continued

In addition to making it much easier to move to Web sites, using bookmarks also reduces the chance for errors when you type a URL. Sometimes these errors are merely annoying, while at other times, they can lead you to places on the Web where you would rather not be.

Over time, you are likely to create many bookmarks. You can use the techniques in this section to keep them organized. Place the bookmarks you use most often on the Bookmarks bar or on the Bookmarks menu so that you can get to them easily. Use folders to create sets of bookmarks related to specific topics or purposes, such as finances or news.

● A new untitled folder appears. The bookmarks list is empty because there are not any bookmarks in the folder.

③ Type a name for the folder.

④ Press **Return**.

⑤ Select the location containing bookmarks you want to move into the folder.

⑥ Drag a bookmark from its current location onto the folder that you want to contain it; when that folder is highlighted in blue, release the trackpad button.

⑦ Repeat Steps **5** and **6** to place more bookmarks in the folder.

8 Select the folder you created.

The bookmarks you placed in it appear on the list.

9 To create a folder within the selected folder, click ⊞.

10 Name the new folder and press **Return**.

11 Drag bookmarks onto the nested folder to place them in it.

12 Drag bookmarks and folders up and down in the folder to change the order in which they appear.

13 To add the bookmarks you use most frequently to the Bookmarks bar or Bookmarks menu, select **Bookmarks Bar** or **Bookmarks Menu**.

14 Drag bookmarks onto the list.

15 Organize the contents of the Bookmarks bar or Bookmarks menu just like other locations.

Note: To delete a bookmark or a folder of bookmarks, select what you want to delete and press **Delete**.

When should I bookmark a site?

It is best not to think of bookmarks as permanent things. Although there are some pages that you use over long periods of time and for which you will definitely want to have bookmarks, there are others that are useful only in the short term. For example, if you are researching a product, you might find several sites that provide useful information. Bookmark these sites as you go so that you can get back to the ones you need. When you are done, just delete the bookmarks you created to prevent Safari from becoming cluttered with bookmarks you no longer use.

Can I change the order in which folders are shown in the Bookmarks window?

Yes. To reorder folders in the Bookmarks section of the Source pane, drag them up or down until they are in the order you want.

Open Several Web Pages at the Same Time

Using tabs, you know you can have many Web pages open at the same time, which is useful. However, opening one tab after another takes longer than it needs to. And who needs that? It would be nice if there were a way to open a lot of pages at the same time.

Fortunately, Safari allows you to do this. By using bookmarks, folders, and tabs, you can configure any collection of Web pages to open with a single click. First, prepare the folder containing bookmarks for the pages you want to open. Second, open those pages.

PREPARE A ONE-CLICK BOOKMARK FOLDER

1. Set bookmarks for the pages you want to open.

2. Choose **Show All Bookmarks** under the Bookmarks menu.

   Safari moves into Bookmark mode.

3. Create a folder for the group of pages you want to open at the same time.

4. Add the bookmarks you want to open to the folder you created in Step 3.

5. Drag the bookmarks up or down the list so they are in the order in which you want them to open.

The bookmark at the top of the list becomes the first tab in the Safari window, the next one down is the second tab, and so on.

6. Select the **Bookmarks Bar** collection.

7. Drag the folder you created in Step 3 onto the bookmark list in the order in which you want it to appear on the Bookmarks bar (the top of the window represents the left end of the bar).

8. Check the **Auto-Click** check box.

● The folder you created appears on the Bookmarks bar. At the right side of its name on the Bookmarks bar, you see a box, which indicates it is an auto-click folder.

OPEN A LOT OF PAGES WITH A CLICK

1 When you want to open all the bookmarks in the Auto-Click folder, click it on the Bookmarks bar.

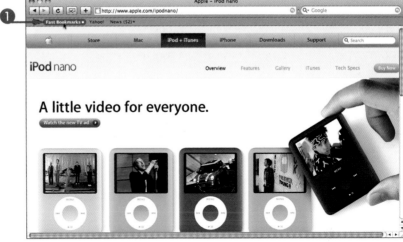

● Each bookmark in the folder opens in its own tab.

Can I also put other folders on the Bookmarks bar?
You can place any folder of bookmarks on the Bookmarks bar. When you do, the folder becomes a menu showing the bookmarks it contains (immediately to the right of its name, you see a downward-pointing triangle to indicate this). Click the folder and it opens, showing you the bookmarks it contains. Select a bookmark to open it, or choose **Open in Tabs** to open all the bookmarks, each on its own tab.

What if I do not want to open all the bookmarks in an Auto-Click folder at the same time?
Click the bookmark's name on the Bookmarks bar and hold the trackpad button down. A menu appears, showing you each of the bookmarks in the folder. Choose a bookmark to move to it.

Watch Movies on the Web

Movies are common on the Web. From trailers for the latest Hollywood productions to instructional videos, commercials, and other video content, there is a lot to watch. You can use Safari to view many of these movies through its embedded QuickTime player.

① Move to a site containing a movie you want to watch.

For example, most movie Web sites have previews for you to watch.

② Click the size of the movie you want to watch.

Larger movies look better, but require more bandwidth to download.

Note: *If you are using a broadband connection, you can usually choose the largest size.*

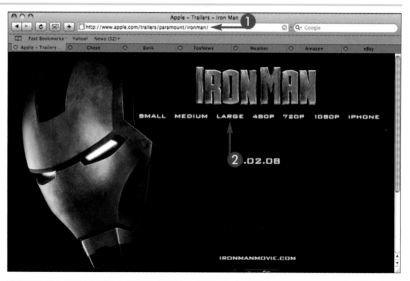

● The movie opens, starts to download, and begins to play.

③ Use the **Volume** menu (🔊) to change the volume.

④ Click **Pause** (⏸) to pause it.

⑤ Drag the playhead to the right to scan forward, or to the left to scan backward.

Note: *The shaded part of the timeline bar indicates how much of the movie has downloaded; you can watch only that part. If the connection slows down for some reason, the movie may stop; just restart it when more of the movie has downloaded.*

Use AutoFill to Quickly Complete Web Forms

As you use the Web, you will probably need to complete forms, such as when you are registering for an account on a Web site or when you are doing some online shopping. Many of these forms require the same basic set of information, including your name, address, and telephone number. Using the Safari AutoFill feature, you can complete this basic information with a single click.

AutoFill can also remember usernames and passwords that you use to log in to Web sites so that you do not have to retype this information each time you want to access your account on a site.

Use AutoFill to Quickly Complete Web Forms

CONFIGURE AUTOFILL INFORMATION

1. Press ⌘+,.

   The Safari Preferences window opens.

2. Click the **AutoFill** tab.

3. To complete forms using the information on your card in Address Book, check the **Using info from my Address Book card** check box.

Note: *Your card is automatically populated with the information you entered when you registered your MacBook Air. You can also edit your card by clicking the Edit button and then using Address Book. See Chapter 14 for information about Address Book.*

4. To have Safari remember usernames and passwords for Web sites you access, check the **User names and passwords** check box.

5. To have Safari remember information for other forms, check the **Other forms** check box.

6. Close the Preferences window.

USE AUTOFILL INFORMATION

1. Move to a Web site that requires your information.

2. Click **Edit** and then click **AutoFill Form** (or press Shift + ⌘ + A).

● Safari completes as much information as it can, based on the form and the contents of your Address Book card. The fields it completes are highlighted in yellow.

3. Manually complete or edit any of the fields that AutoFill did not correctly fill in.

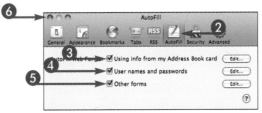

Create Your Own Web Widget

Chapter 3 explained how to use the Dashboard to access widgets that perform various functions. You can create your own widgets from any Web page and then access the widgets you create on the Dashboard.

When you create a widget, you capture part of a Web page. Because pages are constructed in different ways, the part of the page you capture may or may not work the way you expect. The only way to know is to try it. Fortunately, creating widgets is easy, and so you will not have wasted much time if it does not work the way you expect.

Create Your Own Web Widget

① Move to a Web site containing information that you want to have on a widget.

② Click the **Open this page in Dashboard** button (⊠).

● The widget toolbar appears, and part of the page is selected; the rest of the page is grayed out.

③ Drag over the section of the page that you want to be a widget.

④ Drag the handles on the selection box to fine-tune the selection area.

Note: *Safari tries to capture functional blocks on a page. If a section of a page is selected automatically when you click it, you should use that section "as is" for best results.*

⑤ Click **Add**.

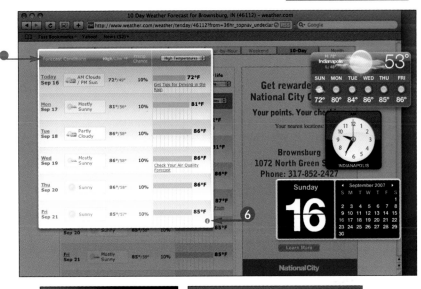

- A widget is created, the Dashboard opens, and you see the new widget.

⑥ Click the **Info** button ( ).

The widget moves into configure mode.

⑦ Choose a theme for the widget.

⑧ If the widget contains audio, check the **Only play audio in Dashboard** check box if you want that audio to only play when the Dashboard is open.

⑨ To adjust the area captured in the widget, click **Edit** and proceed to Step **10**; otherwise, click **Done** and skip Steps **10** and **11**.

⑩ Resize the widget using its resize handle.

⑪ Click **Done**.

You see the new widget with the theme and size you selected. You can manage widgets that you create (such as by changing locations on the Dashboard) just like the other widgets.

Note: See Chapter 3 for more details about widgets.

Note: When you click a link on a Web page widget, the page that link points to opens in Safari or another default Web browser.

What happens if the Web page I captured changes?
If the Web page you have captured is reorganized, your widget may also change. When you capture a widget, you capture it based on the area you select on the page. If the content in that area changes, your widget also changes. In that case, you need to re-create or edit the widget based on the new page layout.

I captured the login section of a Web page, but when I enter my username and password and then click Login, nothing happens. Why?
Sometimes the underlying code related to a button is not physically in the area of the button that you capture as a widget. When that area is separated from the button on a widget, that button in the widget does not work. You can try capturing other parts of the page or just use AutoFill to make it easier to log in.

Save or E-mail Web Pages

As you explore the Web, you will probably find Web pages that you want to view again. Because the Web is always changing, there is no guarantee that a page you are viewing now will exist a day from now, or even five minutes from now. If you want to make sure you can view a page again in the future, you can save it on MacBook Air.

Some pages that you encounter are worth sharing. You can easily send links to Web pages to others, or you can even send the contents of a Web page in an e-mail.

SAVE WEB PAGES

① Move to a Web page you want to save.

Note: Any receipts or account information that you see on a Web page are good candidates for saving.

② Open the **File** menu, and then select **Save As**.

● The Save sheet appears.

③ Enter a name for the Web page.

④ Choose the location in which you want to save it.

⑤ Choose **Web Archive** on the Format pop-up menu.

⑥ Click **Save**.

The page is saved in the location you specified. You can view it again later by double-clicking its icon; the page opens in Safari.

Note: A page that you save is a copy of what it was at the time you viewed it. To see the current version, you need to return to it on the Web.

E-MAIL A LINK TO A WEB PAGE

① Move to a Web page you want to share.

② Open the **File** menu, and then select **Mail Link to This Page**.

A new e-mail message is created, and a link to the page is added to the body of the message.

③ Add recipients.

④ Edit the subject, and add comments to the body of the message.

Note: *Do not change the link that was pasted into the e-mail message or it might not work.*

⑤ Send the message.

When the recipient receives the message, they can click the link to view the page.

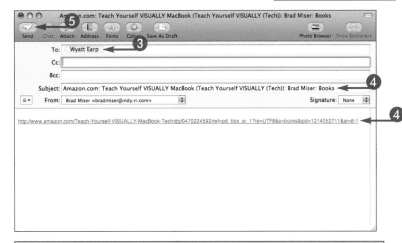

E-MAIL THE CONTENTS OF A WEB PAGE

① Move to a Web page you want to share.

② Click **File**, and then click **Mail Contents of This Page**.

A new message is created, and the content of the page is pasted into the body.

③ Complete the message by adding recipients, editing the subject, and adding comments.

④ Send the message.

When the recipient receives the message, she can view the page in it.

Note: *To be able to view a page in an e-mail, the recipient's e-mail application must be capable of displaying HTML messages.*

 TIPS

How do I tell if I am viewing a page saved on MacBook Air or one on the Web?

Look at the URL. If it starts with file://, you are viewing a saved Web page. If it starts with http://, you are viewing a live page on the Web.

Should I send a link or content?

When you are viewing a Web site that does not change frequently or that uses direct URLs to the resource you are viewing, sending a link is better because it reduces the size of the e-mail. However, if you want to make sure your recipients see what you intend them to, send the content instead.

Set Safari Preferences

Safari includes a number of preferences that you can set to change the way it looks and works. You set other Safari preferences similarly to the Tab and AutoFill preferences. (For more information, see the sections "Use AutoFill to Quickly Complete Web Forms" and "Browse the Web with Tabs.")

You can also move to Web pages from outside Safari by clicking hyperlinks in various documents with which you work, such as e-mail and text documents. When you click a Web link, Mac OS X recognizes it as an address and opens that address in your default Web browser.

① Press ⌘+,.

The Safari Preferences window opens.

② Click the **General** tab.

③ On the **New windows open with** pop-up menu, choose the page you want to open automatically when you open a new Safari window.

④ Type the URL for your home page, or click **Set to Current Page** to make the page you are currently viewing your home page.

Note: If you want your home page to be empty, delete the contents of the Home page field.

⑤ Use these settings to specify how Safari handles history items, downloads, and links.

⑥ Click the **Appearance** tab.

⑦ To change the standard font used on Web pages, click the top **Select** button and choose the font you want to use.

8 Click the **Bookmarks** tab.

9 If you want to see links in cards in your Address Book as an option on the Bookmarks bar, check the upper **Include Address Book** check box.

10 If you want the bookmarks on the Bookmarks bar to also be available on the Bookmarks menu, check the **Include Bookmarks Bar** check box.

11 To include the Address Book and Bonjour collections in the Bookmarks window, check their respective check boxes.

12 Click the **Security** tab.

13 Use the three top check boxes to enable plug-ins, Java, and JavaScript. If you disable any of these features, many Web sites will not work properly.

14 Check the **Block pop-up windows** check box to prevent Web pages from opening pop-up windows.

15 If you want to tightly control information that Web sites store on and access from MacBook Air, click **Never**.

*Note: If you prevent all cookies from being accepted, some Web sites will not work correctly, and no Web sites will "remember" you. You should never choose the **Always** option because it exposes you to security risks from sites you do not visit or do not intend to visit.*

16 Close the Preferences window.

What are RSS preferences?

RSS is a format designed to deliver information in RSS feeds that change frequently, such as news. You can view RSS pages in Safari; these pages are more efficient to view because you can control how much information you see, and you can collect information from different sources on the same page. The RSS preferences enable you to control how Safari works with RSS. For example, you can set Safari to check for updates periodically.

What are Advanced preferences?

Advanced preferences enable you to set universal access features such as minimum font size and enabling Web page navigation with the Tab key. You can also choose a default style sheet and configure a proxy server if you use one.

Explore Firefox

While Safari is the Mac OS X default Web browser, as well as one of the best browsers available for any type of computer, it certainly is not the only one available. Firefox is an alternate Web browser that many Mac users find to be better in some respects (such as speed and compatibility with more Web sites) than Safari.

Because Firefox is free, there is really no reason not to give it a try to see which you prefer. Of course, you do not really have to have a preference, as you can use both browsers if you want to.

DOWNLOAD AND INSTALL FIREFOX

① Launch Safari and type **firefox.com** in the Address bar.

You see the Firefox home page.

② Click the **Download** link.

Firefox downloads to MacBook Air. When the application's file has downloaded, you see its license screen.

③ Click **Accept** (assuming you accept the license terms, of course).

● The Firefox disk image is mounted on your desktop, and a Finder window appears showing the Firefox application file.

④ Drag the **Firefox** file to the Applications folder.

The application is installed.

⑤ Click the **Eject** button (⏏) for the Firefox disk image.

The image is unmounted.

⑥ Delete the disk image file that you downloaded.

Note: Step 6 is optional, but it saves some space. You can always download the installer again should you ever need it.

BROWSE THE WEB WITH FIREFOX

1. Open the **Applications** folder.

2. Launch Firefox.

3. Click **Open** in the security warning prompt that appears.

● The Import Wizard appears.

4. Leave the **Safari** radio button selected.

5. Click **Continue**.

6. On the Home Page Selection window, choose **Firefox Start**.

   This setting uses a special Firefox page as your home page.

7. Click **Continue**.

   After a few seconds, that screen disappears and you move into Firefox. You are prompted to set Firefox as your default browser.

8. Uncheck the **Always perform this check when starting Firefox** check box.

9. If you want to make Firefox your default browser, click **Yes**; if not, click **No**.

10. Review the first run tab and close it when you are done.

Note: You only need to perform Steps 3 to 10 the first time you launch Firefox.

● You see your home page in Firefox.

11. Browse the Web.

   While they are different applications, there are enough similarities between Safari and Firefox that you will not have any trouble learning to use Firefox if you know how to use Safari. Because you imported your bookmarks, they are available in Firefox just as they are in Safari.

 TIPS

Can I use both browsers?
Yes, and you can even use them at the same time. If you run into a Web page that does not work properly in one browser, try it in the other. If it works there, add it as a bookmark and use that browser when you want to access that specific page.

How do I set my default Web browser?
As you work with both browsers, one will probably emerge as your favorite. To make that your default browser, open the **General** tab of the Safari Preferences window and choose your preferred browser on the **Default Web Browser** pop-up menu. Any Web links you click open in that browser automatically.

Explore Mail

Mail includes many useful features, and it wraps those features in an interface that makes sense and is easy to use. Mail provides all the capabilities that you want in an e-mail application so that you can work with e-mail efficiently and effectively.

● **Mail icon**

The Mail Dock icon enables you to launch the Mail application and also shows you how many new messages you have

● **Toolbar**

Contains tools you can use to work with e-mail

● **Inbox**

Contains mailboxes for each e-mail account

● **Account Mailboxes**

Contain e-mail for various accounts that you have configured in Mail

● **Account Mailbox Folders**

Organize e-mail in different states, such as Sent or Draft, for each account

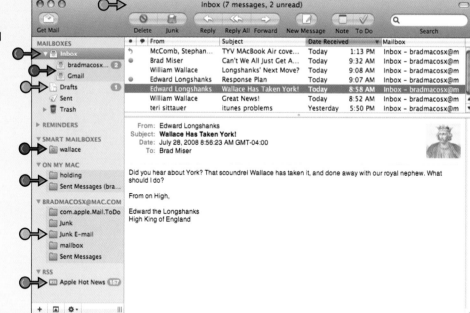

● **Smart Mailboxes**

Automatically organize e-mail based on criteria that you define

● **Mailboxes**

Folders in which you can store and organize e-mail

● **Online e-mail Accounts**

Shows the folders used by your online accounts (such as IMAP accounts)

● **RSS**

Shows RSS feeds that you are managing in Mail

Selected source

The source of e-mails with which you want to work, such as those you have received in a specific account

Message pane

Shows the messages in the selected source

Read/Unread

A blue dot indicates a message that you have not read

From

The name of the person who sent the message to you

Subject	Date	Sort column	Sort direction	Selected message
The subject of the message	The date and time on which you received the message	The column highlighted in blue is the one used to sort the message list	The triangle indicates the direction in which the list is sorted	To read a message, you select it; the selected message is highlighted in blue.

Reading pane

Displays the selected message

Message details

Who the message is from, the subject of the message, when it was sent, and who the other recipients are

Sender's image

Shows the image associated with the sender in Address Book

Body

The message's text

Attachments

Shows files attached to the message and enables you to save or view them

Set Up E-mail Accounts

Before you can work with e-mail, you must obtain one or more e-mail accounts and configure Mail to access them.

The details of configuring an e-mail account depend on the type of account it is; for example, configuring a MobileMe account is slightly different from configuring an account you have received from your Internet service provider (ISP). However, in all cases, you enter the configuration details for each type of e-mail account in the appropriate fields in Mail.

① Launch Mail.

② Press ⌘+⌐.

The Mail Preferences window opens.

③ Click the Accounts tab.

④ Click the **Add Account** button (➕).

The Add Account sheet appears.

⑤ Type the full name for the account.

⑥ Type the e-mail address for the account.

⑦ Type the password for the account.

⑧ Uncheck the **Automatically set up account** check box and click **Continue**.

⑨ Choose the type of account on the **Account Type** pop-up menu.

Note: *You should choose the type of account based on the information you received when you obtained the account. For example, if you are configuring an account from your ISP, its details tell you what kind of account it is. Some are more obvious, such as a MobileMe account.*

⑩ Type a description of the account in the Description field.

⑪ Type the incoming mail server's address in the Incoming Mail Server field.

Note: *You are provided with the configuration details, such as incoming and outgoing servers, when you obtain an e-mail account.*

⑫ Type your username (usually everything before the "@" in the e-mail address) in the User Name field.

⑬ Type the password for the account and click **Continue**.

Mail checks the information by accessing the account using the information you provided.

⑭ Type a description for the account.

⑮ Type the outgoing mail server address.

⑯ If you leave **Use only this server** unchecked, you can send mail using another account's outgoing mail server.

⑰ If the account uses authentication (some do not), check the **Use Authentication** check box and complete Step **18**; if not, skip to Step **19**.

⑱ Type the username and password for the outgoing mail server.

⑲ Click **Continue**.

Mail checks the information by accessing the account using the information you provided. The Summary screen appears.

⑳ Check the **Take account online** check box.

㉑ Click **Create**.

● The Account appears on the Accounts list and is ready to use.

㉒ Close the Preferences dialog.

 TIPS

A MobileMe e-mail account was already set up when I launched Mail; how did that happen?

When you configure a MobileMe account, either during the initial MacBook Air setup or on the MobileMe pane of the System Preferences application, the MobileMe e-mail account is set up in Mail automatically. See Chapter 10 for more information about MobileMe online services.

Where can I get free e-mail accounts?

You can obtain a GMail account at www.google.com. You can also get a free e-mail account at www.yahoo.com. It is a good idea to have at least two e-mail accounts so that you can use one to guard against spam. For more information, see the section "Avoid Spam."

Read and Reply to E-mail

One of the reasons to use e-mail is, of course, to read it. Mail makes it easy to do that. You can read e-mail in the Reading pane, as described in the following steps, or you can double-click a message to open it in its own window.

You can also easily reply to e-mail that you receive to start or continue an e-mail conversation, also called a *thread*.

READ E-MAIL

1 Select the **Inbox**.

Note: *You can also select a specific e-mail account to read e-mail that you have received only for that account.*

2 Select the message you want to read.

The message you select appears in the Reading pane.

3 Read the message.

Note: *After you have viewed a message in the Reading pane, its blue dot disappears so that you know you have read it. The number of new messages is also reduced by one on the Mail icon and next to each mailbox.*

4 If the message is too long to fit into the current window, press Spacebar to scroll down in the message.

5 To open a message in its own window, double-click it.

The message appears in a new, separate window.

6 Read the message in its window.

Note: *You can use the buttons in the window to mark the e-mail as junk, or reply to it just as when you read messages from the Mail window, which is discussed next.*

7 Close the message when you are done.

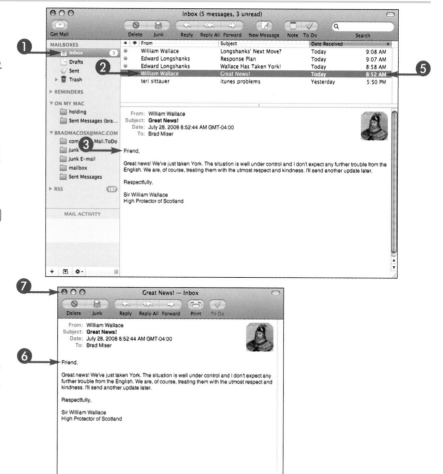

REPLY TO E-MAIL

1 Open a message.

2 Click the **Reply** button ().

● If more than one person is listed in the From or Cc fields and you want to reply to everyone listed, click the **Reply All** button ( ) instead.

● A new message appears, addressed to the sender of the message (and all recipients if you clicked **Reply All**).

● "Re:" is added to the beginning of the subject to show that the message is a reply.

● The contents of the original message are pasted into the body in blue and marked with a vertical line to show it is quoted text.

3 Type your reply.

4 Click the **Send** button ( ).

The window closes, the e-mail is sent, and you hear the sent mail sound effect.

TIPS

How do I delete a message I do not want to keep?

Select the message and click the **Delete** button ( ) on the toolbar. The message is removed from the Message list and placed in the appropriate Trash folder. How long it remains there depends on the trash settings for that e-mail account. You can recover a message by opening the Trash folder and moving a deleted message back into an Inbox.

Can I add more recipients to a reply?

Yes, you can add more addresses to a reply e-mail to include other recipients. In fact, all the tools that are available to you when you create a new e-mail message are also available when you reply to messages. For more information, see the section "Send E-mail."

When you want to communicate with someone, you can use the Mail New Message tool to create and send e-mail. You can send a message to as many people as you want.

People who are the primary recipients should be in the To field. People who are receiving a message for their information only should be in the Cc field. People who should be invisible to other people who receive the message should be included in the Bcc field.

Send E-mail

① Click the **New Message** button ( ) on the toolbar.

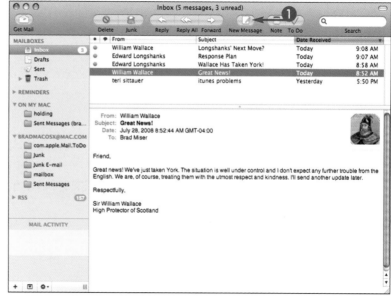

The New Message window appears.

② Type the name or e-mail address of the first recipient in the To field.

Note: *As you type, Mail attempts to match a previously used e-mail address or an address in Address Book to what you type.*

③ Press .

④ Type another e-mail address.

⑤ Click in the **Cc** field or press Tab to move there, and type e-mail addresses of people who should receive a copy of the message.

⑥ Type the subject of the message in the Subject field.

⑦ On the **From** pop-up menu, choose the e-mail address from which you want to send the message.

Note: *In addition to identifying you, the From address determines the address replies to which your message will be sent.*

⑧ Type the message in the body.

Note: *You can use the Fonts and Colors buttons to format new messages.*

● As you type, Mail checks your spelling. Misspelled words are underlined in red.

⑨ To correct a misspelled word, point to the underlined word and **Control**+click it.

⑩ Choose the correct spelling on the list.

Note: *If the word is spelled correctly and you want to add it to the dictionary so that it is not flagged as a mistake in the future, choose **Learn Spelling**.*

⑪ Review your message and make sure it is ready to be sent.

Note: *You can save draft versions of messages by clicking the **Save As Draft** button (□). You can continue working on it later by selecting the Drafts folder and then opening the message.*

⑫ Click **Send** ().

The window closes, the message is sent, and you hear the sent message sound effect.

Note: *Once you send a message, you cannot retrieve it, so make sure you are comfortable with it before you click the **Send** button.*

TIPS

How do I avoid having to type e-mail addresses?
You can store e-mail addresses in Address Book so that you can type an e-mail address by typing a person's name, which is usually much easier to remember. As you type an e-mail address, Mail searches e-mail that you have sent, e-mail that you have received, and cards in Address Book to identify e-mail addresses for you. You can select one of these to easily address a message.

From where else can I start a new e-mail message?
When you are using a Mac OS X application, such as Address Book, and you see an e-mail address, you can almost always send an e-mail to that address by **Control**+clicking it and choosing **Send Email** on the contextual menu. A new message to that address is created in Mail, and you can then complete and send it. You can send photos using e-mail in iPhoto by choosing the photos you want to send and clicking the **Email** button (▣).

Work with Files Attached to E-mail

In addition to communicating information, e-mail is a great way to send files to other people, and for people to send files to you. Files can be documents, photos, and even applications.

In Mail, some file attachments, particularly photos, can be displayed within an e-mail message. In all cases, you can save attachments to the MacBook Air hard drive for your use.

Work with Files Attached to E-mail

① Select a message containing attachments.

● The Attachments section appears below the To field.

② Click the expansion triangle to see the attachments to the message.

③ Scroll the message to see the attachments in the body of the message.

● To preview the attachments, click **Quick Look**. The Quick Look viewer appears and you see the contents of the attachments.

● If the attachment can be displayed in the message (most images can be), then you can view it in the body.

④ Click **Save**, and press and hold the trackpad button.

⑤ Choose **Save All** to save all of the attachments, or choose a specific attachment to save it.

If you selected **Save All**, the Save sheet appears. If you selected an attachment, it is saved to your Downloads folder and you can skip Steps **6** and **7**.

⑥ Choose the location in which you want to save the attachments.

⑦ Click **Save**.

The attachments are saved in the location you selected, and you can use them just like files you have created.

Attach Files to E-mail

You can attach files to e-mail messages that you send in order to make those files available to other people. You can attach any file to a message and, assuming the recipient has a compatible application, anyone who receives the message can use the files that you attach.

When you attach files to a message, the size of the e-mail increases by the size of those files. If you attach only one or two small files, you can attach them "as is." However, to attach many or large files, you should compress them and send the compressed file as an attachment instead. See Chapter 4 for more information about file compression.

Attach Files to E-mail

1 Create a new e-mail message by clicking **New Message** ( ) in the Mail toolbar.

● A window appears for you to compose your message in.

2 Compose the message by addressing it, and typing the body.

3 Click **Attach** ( ).

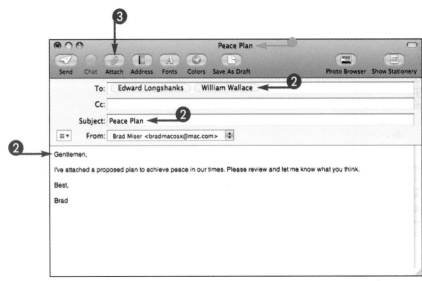

The Attach File sheet appears.

Note: You can also attach files to a message by dragging them from the desktop onto the New Message window.

4 Move to and select the files you want to attach.

Note: You can select multiple files to attach by holding the ⌘ key down while you click each file.

5 Click **Choose File**.

The files you selected are attached to the message.

6 Send the message.

When the recipients receive the message, they can work with the attachments you included.

Organize
E-mail

As you use Mail, you are likely to end up with a lot of e-mail messages. Mail provides two great ways to keep your e-mail organized: Mailboxes and Smart Mailboxes. Mailboxes are like folders in the Finder. Smart Mailboxes automatically organize e-mail based on rules that you create.

However, one of the best ways to keep your e-mail organized is to delete messages that you do not need, which is probably most of those that you receive. The fewer messages you keep, the fewer you have to organize.

ORGANIZE E-MAIL IN MAILBOXES

1 Click ➕ in Mail.

2 Select **New Mailbox**.

The New Mailbox pop-up menu appears.

3 On the Location pop-up menu, choose **On My Mac**.

This setting stores e-mail on MacBook Air rather than on the mail server.

4 Type a name for the mailbox.

5 Click **OK**.

- The mailbox appears in the On My Mac section of the Mailboxes pane.

6 Drag messages from the Messages pane onto the mailbox you created.

The message is moved into the mailbox.

ORGANIZE E-MAIL WITH SMART MAILBOXES

1 Click ➕ in Mail.

2 Select **New Smart Mailbox**.

The New Smart Mailbox sheet appears.

3 Name the new Smart Mailbox.

4 On the **Contains** pop-up menu, choose **messages**.

5 On the **that match** pop-up menu, choose **all**.

You can choose **any** if you want a message to be included if it matches any of the conditions.

6 Use the pop-up menus and fields to create a condition for the messages that you want to be included.

7 To add another condition, click the **Add** button (➕) and use the pop-up menus and fields to configure the condition.

Note: To remove a condition, click its **Remove** button (➖).

8 Click **OK**.

The mailbox is created and any messages that meet its conditions appear in it automatically.

TIPS

How do I change how messages are listed on the Messages list?

Just click the column heading, such as **From**, to sort the list by that column. To change the direction in which messages are listed, click the triangle in the current sort column. You can also drag the right edge of columns to change their width.

SORT MESSAGE LIST

I have received a message saying that I am over my mail storage quota. What do I do?

E-mail can be stored in two locations. One is on the mail server associated with the e-mail account. The other is on MacBook Air. Most e-mail accounts have a limit on how much e-mail you can store on the server. When you reach this limit, you can no longer receive or send e-mail with that account. To prevent e-mail server storage overload, store e-mail in mailboxes on MacBook Air. You should also check account settings to make sure mail is not being stored on the server unintentionally (see the section "Set Mail Preferences," later in this chapter).

Search E-mail

As you accumulate messages, you may want to be able to find messages that contain information or attachments you need. You can use the Mail Search tool to quickly find important messages.

One of the best ways to be able to find e-mail is to keep it organized. A little time spent organizing e-mail earlier prevents some of the effort to find it later. For more information, see the previous section, "Organize E-mail."

Search E-mail

① Type the information for which you want to search in the Search bar.

● As you type, Mail presents messages that meet your search in the lower pane.

Note: *By default, the messages are sorted by rank, which is how Mail determines how relevant the messages are to your search term.*

② To read a message, select it.

● The message opens in the Reading pane that appears at the bottom of the window.

③ To search in all mailboxes, click **All Mailboxes**, or to search in only the selected mailbox, click the button to the right of the All Mailboxes button, which is labeled with the name of the selected folder or Inbox.

④ Click the button to indicate what part of the messages you want to search.

For example, to search for messages by sender, click **From**.

● The results are refined, based on the choices you made.

⑤ To read a found message, click it.

⑥ To save a search as a Smart Mailbox so that you can run it again, click **Save**.

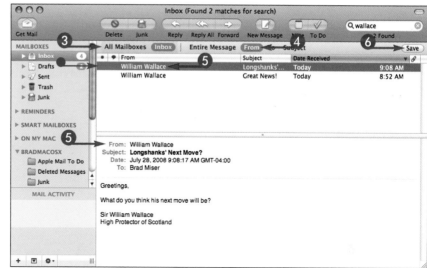

The Smart Mailbox sheet appears.

⑦ Configure and save the Smart Mailbox.

Note: For more information on configuring a Smart Mailbox, see the section "Organize E-mail."

You can repeat the search at any time by selecting its folder in the Smart Mailboxes section of the Mailbox pane.

Do I have to be using Mail to search e-mail?

The Mac OS X Spotlight feature enables you to search for information on MacBook Air no matter where that information is found, including files, folders, and e-mail. If you are sure the information you need is in an e-mail, search in Mail. If not, use Spotlight instead. To learn how to use Spotlight, see Chapter 4.

Can I have the same e-mail in more than one mailbox?

An e-mail can exist in only one mailbox in the same location, such as the mailboxes stored on MacBook Air. (Of course, you can make copies of messages and place the copies in different locations.) Because Smart Mailboxes do not actually contain the messages (a Smart Mailbox makes pointers to the actual e-mail messages), e-mail messages can be included in many Smart Mailboxes at the same time.

Avoid Spam

One of the perils of receiving e-mail is spam. Spam is annoying at best, with messages that stream into your Inbox with advertising in which you have no interest. At worst, spam contains offensive or dangerous messages that promise all kinds of rewards for just a few simple actions (usually an attempt at identity theft).

Notice that the title of this section is "Avoid Spam," as opposed to "Eliminate Spam" or "Prevent Spam." Unfortunately, spam is part of receiving e-mail, and the best you can do is to minimize your exposure to it as much as possible.

1. Press ⌘+,.

   The Mail Preferences window appears.

2. Click the **Junk Mail** tab.

3. Check the **Enable junk mail filtering** check box.

4. Click **Mark as junk mail, but leave it in my Inbox** if you want Mail to highlight junk e-mail, but not do anything else with it.

5. Click **Move it to the Junk mailbox** if you want Mail to move spam to the Junk mailbox.

6. Click **Perform custom actions (Click Advanced to configure)** if you want to define what Mail does using a mail rule.

   If you select this option, use the Advanced button and sheet to configure the rules that Mail should apply to junk mail.

   Note: For more information about rules, see the section "Create E-mail Rules."

7. Check the check boxes to specify e-mails that are exempt from junk mail filtering.

   For example, if the sender of a message is someone in your Address Book, it is highly unlikely that the message is junk, and so you should check the top check box in this section.

8. Close the Preferences window.

   As you receive e-mail, Mail takes the action that you selected when you receive e-mail that it identifies as junk.

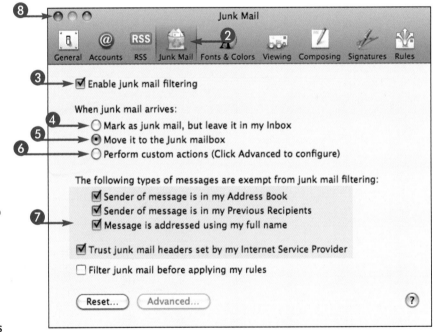

Note: *The remaining steps assume that you selected the option wherein Mail moves junk messages to the Junk folder. If you selected a different option, the details will be different.*

9 Click the **Junk** folder.

● The contents of the Junk filter, which are all the messages that Mail has classified as junk, appear.

10 Select and review each message.

11 If a message is junk, do nothing; the message stays in your Junk folder.

12 If a message is not junk, click **Not Junk**.

The message moves back to your Inbox and is no longer marked as junk.

Over time, Mail learns from your actions and gets better at identifying junk mail.

13 Click to delete junk messages.

Note: *Consider using a sacrificial e-mail address when you participate in activities, such as posting to an online forum, that are likely to get you spammed, while you use your permanent addresses in safe situations. If the sacrificial e-mail address gets spammed, you can just stop using it and obtain another one. Free e-mail accounts are ideal for sacrificial e-mail addresses. For more information, see the section "Set Up E-mail Accounts."*

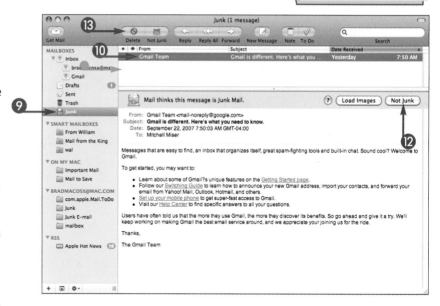

TIPS

I have received an important message saying my account is going to be closed unless I update its information. What should I do?

One effective spam technique that criminals use is to model their spam e-mails so that they look just like e-mail from legitimate companies; examples include eBay and online banks. They usually mention that your account is out of date or compromised, and that you need to provide information to correct the situation. These messages are always spam and you should never respond to them. Legitimate companies never ask you to update information through e-mail requests. If you do respond and provide the requested information, your identity will be stolen.

How can I tell if a message is legitimate or spam?

Just by looking at an e-mail, there is no way to tell whether it is authentic because many criminals make their e-mails look like they are from legitimate organizations. However, most of these e-mails include a link to take you someplace, usually your account so that you can verify some information, which really means that they are trying to steal information from you. Point to these links (**do not click!**), and the URL pops up. You will see that the first part of the URL has nothing to do with the real company, which is a dead giveaway that it is an attempt to steal your identity.

Create and Use E-mail Signatures

It is good practice to include a signature at the end of your e-mails to make your communication more personal or to provide important information, such as your phone number or Web site address. You can even advertise in your signature.

You can configure Mail to make adding signatures easier and faster. You can create many different signatures and easily use the one that is most appropriate for a specific e-mail message that you send. You can also have a signature inserted into new messages automatically.

Create and Use E-mail Signatures

CREATE SIGNATURES

① Press ⌘+,.

② Click the **Signatures** tab.

③ Click **All Signatures**.

④ Click ➕.

A new signature is created and its name appears in the center column, ready to be edited.

⑤ Type a name for the signature and press **Return**.

When a signature is selected in the center column, its contents appear in the far-right column.

⑥ With the signature selected, type the content of the signature in the right column.

Your signature can be any text you want, arranged as you want it to be.

⑦ If you use the default font for your messages, check the **Always match my default message font** check box so that the signature uses that font.

⑧ If you use standard quoting (where your reply is always above the quoted message), check the **Place signature above quoted text** check box.

⑨ Repeat Steps **3** to **6** to create as many signatures as you want.

⑩ Drag signatures from the center column onto the e-mail accounts with which you want to use them in the left column.

The number of signatures available for each account is shown under the account name.

⑪ Click an e-mail account.

⑫ Choose the default signature for the account on the **Choose Signature** pop-up menu.

Whenever you send an e-mail from the account, the default signature is pasted in automatically.

⑬ Close the Preferences window.

USE SIGNATURES

① Create a new message.

● If you configured a default signature for the e-mail account, it is pasted in the new message.

② To change the signature, choose the signature on the **Signature** pop-up menu.

Note: *If you do not select a default signature for an account, you can choose a signature on the menu to add it to a message. The signatures available on this menu are those that you added to the account on the Signatures tab.*

What are the other choices on the Choose Signature pop-up menu on the Signatures tab?

If you choose **At Random** on the **Choose Signature** pop-up menu, Mail selects a signature randomly each time you create a message. If you choose **In Sequential Order**, Mail selects the first signature on the list for the first message, the next one for the second message, and so on.

Can I put images or links in my signature?

Yes. To add an image (for example, a scanned version of your written signature) to a signature, drag the image file from the desktop onto the right pane of the Signature tab. You can also add links to a signature by typing the URL in the signature block or by copying and pasting it in.

Create E-mail Rules

If you find yourself doing the same tasks with certain kinds of e-mail, you can probably configure Mail to do those tasks for you automatically by configuring rules, which are automatic actions that Mail performs for you.

To determine whether you can create a rule, you need to be able to define the conditions under which one or more actions should be taken, and the actions you want to happen every time those conditions are met. In the following steps, you learn how to create a rule to automatically file e-mails from specific people in a folder and to alert you that they have arrived. You can configure other rules similarly.

Create E-mail Rules

① Press ⌘+.

② Click the **Rules** tab.

The center pane shows the configured rules. By default, you see a rule for e-mail from Apple.

Note: For a rule to be active, its check box must be checked. You can disable a rule by unchecking its check box.

③ Click **Add Rule**.

The New Rule sheet appears.

④ Name the rule.

⑤ Choose **any** on the pop-up menu if only one condition has to be true for the rule to apply, or **all** if all of the conditions have to be true for the rule to apply.

⑥ Select the attribute for the first condition on the left pop-up menu.

The default value is **From**.

⑦ Choose the operand for the condition on the center pop-up menu, such as **Contains**.

⑧ Type the condition value in the box.

⑨ Click ⊕.

⑩ Repeat Steps **6** to **8** to configure the new condition.

*Note: To remove a condition, click its **Remove** button (⊖).*

⑪ Repeat Steps **9** and **10** to add and configure more conditions.

12 On the top-left Action pop-up menu, choose the action you want to happen when the conditions are met.

13 On the top-right Action pop-up menu, choose the result of the action, such as a location or a sound.

14 To add another action, click ⊕.

15 Repeat Steps **12** and **13** to configure the new action.

16 Repeat Steps **14** and **15** to add and configure more actions.

17 Click **OK**.

The rule is created and appears on the list of rules on the Rules tab.

A confirmation message appears.

18 If you want the rule to be applied to the messages currently in your Inbox, click **Apply**; if not, click **Don't Apply**.

The rule is created and appears on the list of rules. When messages are received that meet the rule's conditions, whatever actions it includes are performed automatically.

What are some examples of useful actions that are available for rules?

Move Message moves e-mail messages to specific locations, such as mailboxes that you have created on MacBook Air or even the Trash. Forward Message can be useful when you always want to forward messages to another address in specific situations. If you usually reply to a specific person's e-mail, Reply to Message can be useful.

How do I know a rule is working?

To test the actions of a specific rule, select a message to which the rule should apply, open the **Message** menu, and then select **Apply Rules**. If the actions you expect happen, then the rule is working. If they do not, then something is wrong with the rule and you need to edit it to fix the problem. You should also select a message to which the rule should not apply and do the same thing. If the actions happen, then the rule is not configured correctly.

Set Mail Preferences

This chapter has discussed a number of Mail Preferences tools already, but there are several more that you should explore as you use Mail.

The two most important of these are the General and Accounts preferences. You use the General tab to set general Mail preferences, such as sound effects, where attachments are stored, and what location to include in searches; you use the Accounts tab to set preferences for specific e-mail accounts.

Set Mail Preferences

SET GENERAL PREFERENCES

1. Press ⌘+,.
2. Click the **General** tab.
3. On the **Check for new mail** pop-up menu, choose how often you want Mail to check for new messages.
4. On the **New mail sound** pop-up menu, choose the sound you want to hear when you receive new messages.
5. If you do not want to hear sounds for other actions, uncheck the **Play sounds for other mail actions** check box.
6. On the **Dock unread count** pop-up menu, choose the mailbox for which you want the number of unread messages to be displayed on the Dock icon for Mail.
7. On the Downloads folder pop-up menu, choose the folder in which attachments should be stored by default.
8. Use the search check boxes to configure specific areas that should be included in searches.

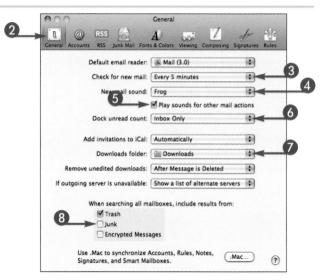

SET ACCOUNT PREFERENCES

1. Press ⌘+,.
2. Click the **Accounts** tab.
3. Select the account you want to configure.
4. Click the **Account Information** tab.
5. Make any changes to the account's configuration, such as changing the incoming mail server password.

6 Click the **Mailbox Behaviors** tab.

7 Use the check boxes and pop-up menus to configure where messages are stored.

Note: If you choose to store messages on the server, those messages count against your total storage space for e-mail. Over time, you may use all or most of your allotted space, which could prevent you from sending or receiving e-mail. Use the delete pop-up menus to configure Mail so that messages stored on the server are deleted periodically.

8 Click the **Advanced** tab.

9 To disable an account, uncheck the **Enable this account** check box.

10 To include the account when Mail checks for e-mail, check the **Include when automatically checking for new mail** check box.

11 To store all messages and their attachments on MacBook Air so that you can access them even when you are not connected to the Internet, choose **All messages and their attachments** on the upper pop-up menu.

What are Viewing preferences?
There are a number of options on the Viewing tab that determine how messages appear. You can set how much detail is shown in the message headers. You can also configure mail to show the status of chat buddies, have unread messages bolded, disable images stored outside of an HTML message, disable smart addresses (so that e-mail addresses are always shown instead of names), and select the color used to show e-mail threads.

What are Composing preferences?
These preferences impact how Mail works when you create messages. For example, you can choose the format of messages, such as Plain or Rich Text. You can also configure spell checking and automatically Cc yourself on your messages. There are also a number of options related to how e-mail that you create is addressed and how e-mails to which you reply are formatted.

Explore iChat

Like the other "i" applications, iChat is both powerful and easy to use. Its interface is simple and elegant, but packs all the features that you need to have great text, audio, and video chats.

After you have done some quick configuration of iChat, you can use it to communicate with people all over the world in any format you choose. It can even help when you have problems because you can use iChat to share the desktop of your MacBook Air.

Text chat window

Text conversations appear in their own window

Who you are texting with

At the top of the window, you see who you are texting with

What the other person is saying to you

On the left side of the window, you see text from the other person involved in the conversation

What you have said

On the right side of the window, you see your contributions to the conversation

Text box

When you want to add to the conversation, enter text in the text box

Emoticon menu

You can add emoticons to a conversation by selecting them on the menu

Audio Chat window

When you audio chat with people, you see a visual representation of the sounds you hear

How many people are involved

At the top of the window, you see how many people are participating

Each person participating

Participants in the conversation have their own sound bar so that you can see when they speak

Your volume level

The bottom bar represents how loud your speech is

Add button

Click this button to add more people to the conversation

Mute button

Click this button to mute your sound

Volume slider

Use this slider to set the volume level of a conversation

● **Video chat window**

Shows each of the people you are video conferencing with

● **Participant windows**

Each participant gets his own window for the chat

● **Your window**

During a video chat, you see yourself as the other participants see you

● **Effects**

You can use the Effects tools to apply a variety of interesting effects to the video

● **Add**

You can add up to three other people in a video conference

● **Mute**

Click the **Mute** button to block sound from your end

● **Full-screen**

When you click this button, the video conference fills the desktop

● **Shared screen**

You can use iChat to view and control another person's computer

● **Your computer**

When you are sharing a desktop, you see a preview of your desktop; click it to move back to your computer.

● **Shared applications**

When someone shares a screen with you, you can work with applications and documents on their computer just as if you were seated in front of it

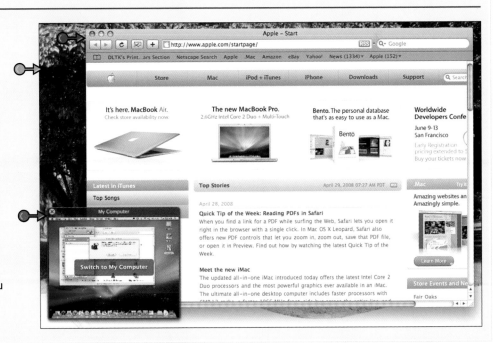

Configure an iChat Account

Before you start chatting, you need to do some basic configuration of iChat, such as setting up the chat accounts that you are going to use, and setting volume levels for the microphone.

The first time you start iChat, its Setup Assistant guides you each step of the way. You can also configure iChat using its Preferences.

Configure an iChat Account

① Launch iChat by clicking its icon on the Dock or by double-clicking its icon in the Applications folder.

The first time you launch iChat, the Setup Assistant runs.

② Read the information in the first screen.

③ Click **Continue**.

④ From the **Account Type** pop-up menu, choose the type of account you want to use to chat.

Note: You can use a MobileMe, America Online Instant Messenger (AIM), Jabber, or Google Talk account with iChat. You need a MobileMe account or an AIM account to be able to video chat.

⑤ Type a member, screen, or username for your account.

⑥ Type the password for your account.

Note: If you do not have a chat account, click the **Get an iChat Account** button and follow the on-screen instructions.

⑦ Click **Continue**.

If you use a MobileMe account, you see the Encrypted iChat screen.

⑧ If you want your chats with other MobileMe users to be encrypted for better security, check the **Enable iChat encryption** check box.

⑨ Click **Continue**.

⑩ Click **Done**.

iChat opens, you see your Buddy lists, and you are ready to start chatting.

TIPS

Do I have to use the Assistant to configure iChat?
No. You can configure all aspects of iChat using its Preferences dialog (press ⌘+,). For example, you can use the Accounts pane to configure your chat accounts, and the Messages pane to configure the format of text chats.

What kind of Internet connection do I need to audio and video chat?
Audio and video chats require broadband Internet connections. As long as you can connect through a Wi-Fi, DSL, cable, or T1 connection, you can chat with audio and video. Prepare to be amazed at the quality of both audio and video chatting.

Chat with Text

Text chatting is a great way to have almost real-time conversations with other people while not consuming all of your and their attention throughout the conversation. Text messaging is a great way to communicate short messages in the format of a conversation.

iChat enables you to text message other people (called buddies) easily and quickly.

ADD A BUDDY

1. Launch iChat.

2. Expand the Buddies list and the Offline list.

   If the person with whom you want to chat is not on either list, continue with the following steps.

   Note: *A buddy that appears on the Offline list is unavailable for chatting.*

3. At the bottom of the AIM Buddy list, click the **Add** button (➕).

4. Choose **Add Buddy**.

   The Add Buddy sheet appears.

5. Choose the type of account on the **Account Name** pop-up menu.

6. Type the person's e-mail address in the Account Name field.

7. On the Add to Group pop-up menu, choose **Buddies**.

8. Type the buddy's name in the appropriate name fields.

9. Click the **Show Address Book** button (▲).

   The sheet expands to show a mini Address Book.

10. If the person is in your Address Book, select his card to associate the buddy with the address card.

11. Click **Add**.

    The person is added to your Buddy list.

START A TEXT CHAT

1 Launch iChat.

2 Select the buddy with whom you want to chat.

3 Click the **Text Chat** button (A).

● A new text chat window appears.

4 Type your message.

5 Press Return.

Your message is sent and is added to the message log at the top of the window next to your icon.

● You see the person's response in the message window next to their icon.

6 Read the reply.

7 Type your response.

8 To add an emoticon to it, choose one on the pop-up menu.

9 Press Return.

Your response is sent and added to the conversation.

Note: Because text chatting is supposed to be fast and simple, you can expect to see misspellings and shorthand in chats.

What happens when someone starts a chat with me?

When someone wants to chat with you, a new message window appears in iChat and you see the message that has been sent to you. Click the message; the window expands to show the response field. To decline the chat, click the **Decline** button. To block all attempts to chat, click the **Block** button. To accept the chat, type your response and click **Accept**. Chat just like when you start a chat session.

What is the Bonjour list?

You can use iChat and the Mac OS X Bonjour networking function to text, audio, and video chat on your local network. When people on your local network sign in to chat, they appear on your Bonjour list. You can chat with them just like chatting over the Internet, except the conversation never leaves the local network. This is really useful if you have several Macs in the same area because you can communicate with everyone on your network easily.

Chat with Audio

Text chatting is great, but being able to talk to someone can be even better. Of course, you can always use the phone, but that can be expensive. Using an iChat audio chat, you can have conversations with one or more people at the same time at no cost to you.

Before you start talking, take a moment to set up your MacBook Air microphone. Then you can talk whenever you want.

CHECK THE MICROPHONE

1 Press ⌘+,.

The iChat Preferences dialog opens.

2 Click the **Audio/Video** tab.

3 On the **Microphone** pop-up menu, choose **Internal microphone**.

4 Speak normally.

● As you speak, the level indicator just above the pop-up menu measures the relative input volume. When you speak normally, the gauge should register toward the right end of the bar while remaining green (if it becomes red, the input level is too high). If the level needs to be adjusted, perform Steps **6** to **10**.

5 Open the System Preferences application and click the **Sound** icon.

6 In the Sound window, click the **Input** tab.

7 Drag the **Input volume** slider to the right to increase the level of sound input, or to the left to decrease it.

8 If you are in a noisy environment, check the **Use ambient noise reduction** check box.

9 Speak normally.

● Use the Input level gauge to measure the level of sound. Like the gauge in iChat, the bars should move toward the right end of the gauge without going all the way to the end.

10 Adjust the Input volume until the gauge looks right.

AUDIO CHAT

1 On the Buddy or Bonjour list, select the buddy with whom you want to chat.

Note: If the Audio Chat button does not become active when you select a buddy, the buddy is not capable of audio chatting with you.

2 Click the **Audio Chat** button (image).

● The Audio Chat window opens and iChat attempts to connect to the buddy you selected. If the person is available and accepts your chat request, you are connected and the audio chat begins.

3 Speak to the person and listen as you would on a telephone.

4 To change the volume, drag the slider to the left to decrease the volume level, or to the right to increase it.

5 To mute your side of the conversation, click the **Mute** button (image); click it again to unmute it.

6 To add another person to the chat, click the **Add** button (image) and choose the buddy you want to add.

● Once the second person accepts, all three of you are able to hear each other.

7 Keep adding people and chatting.

8 When you are done, close the chat window.

 TIPS

What if I do not want to chat in any form?

To prevent any chat requests from popping up, you need to quit iChat. If you want to show your status to others, open the **Status** pop-up menu that is just below your name at the top of the Buddy and Bonjour list windows. Choose the status you want them to see on their Buddy lists. Choose **Offline** if you do not want to chat. To chat again, choose **Available** on the menu. No matter what status you choose, you see windows pop up when someone tries to chat with you. You can just ignore those windows or decline the chats if you do not want to chat.

Are audio chats basically free phone calls?

Yes. If you already have an account that supports audio and video chats, there is no additional charge for the chats. In effect, you can make free phone calls and have free video conferences with anyone with whom you can chat, no matter where the person is located in the world.

Chat with Video

With the rise of iChat, iSight cameras, and broadband Internet connections, video conferencing became simple and easy to do (well, at least it is easy if you use a Mac).

With MacBook Air and an Internet connection, you can see people while you talk to them. This is the next best thing to being there in person, and you do not have to go anywhere.

Chat with Video

CHECK THE CAMERA

1. Click the **Camera** icon () next to your name at the top of the Buddy or Bonjour lists.

   The My Built-in iSight window opens.

2. Move MacBook Air or yourself until the image is what you want others to see.

*Note: Click the **Preferences** button to open the Audio/Video pane of the iChat Preferences dialog.*

3. Resize the window by dragging its resize handle.

4. When you are satisfied with the view, close the window.

VIDEO CHAT

1. On the Buddy or Bonjour list, select the buddy with whom you want to chat.

2. Click the **Video Chat** button ().

● The video chat window opens. When the person accepts your chat invitation, you can talk to her and see her image in the window.

● The inset preview window shows you what the other person is seeing in their chat window.

❸ Drag the preview window so that it is where you want it to be on the screen.

❹ To apply special effects to the image, click the **Effects** button.

The Effects pane opens and you can use its tools.

Note: *For more information about effects, see the next section, "Add Effects and Backgrounds to Video Chats."*

❺ To mute your end of the conversation, click the **Mute** button (🎤); click it again to unmute it.

❻ To make the window fill the desktop, click the **Fill Screen** button (🔲).

❼ To add another person to the conversation, click the **Add** button (➕).

● When the person accepts your invitation, a third video window appears and you see the second person.

You can talk to and see the other people, and they can see and talk to each other.

❽ When you are done, close the window.

TIPS

How many people can I have in a video or audio conference at the same time?
You can have up to four participants (including yourself) in a single video conference. You can have up to ten people (including yourself) in an audio conference at the same time.

Is iChat compatible with other kinds of video conference systems?
To use iChat for video conferences, all participants must be using iChat or the latest version of AOL Instant Messenger for Windows (do not expect the same quality for Windows users that you experience with Mac users).

Add Effects and Backgrounds to Video Chats

Having a video chat is both an effective way to communicate with other people, and a lot of fun. There are ways to make it even more fun.

You can apply special effects to the images being shown during a video chat, and you can apply background images or movies to video chats to make them more interesting.

1. Start a video chat.
2. Click the **Effects** button.

   The Effects pane appears.
3. Scroll to the left or right in the Video Effects palette to browse the default effects, image backgrounds, and video backgrounds.

4. Click the effect, image, or video that you want to apply.

   If you select an effect, it is applied to your image immediately, and you can skip the next two steps.
5. If you selected an image or video background, move out of the camera view at the prompt.
6. When the prompt disappears, move back into the picture.

   ● To the other participants, it looks as if you are actually in front of the background image or video.

Present Online with iChat Theater

There are times when you want to share documents with other people while you talk about the documents. The obvious case is a presentation that you want to use to convey information to others, but there are times when you want to "talk" through a document to explain it to someone, such as when you are collaborating with someone on it.

You can use iChat to present documents to other people over the Internet. When you present a document, the other people see the document, as well as see and hear you through a video chat.

Present Online with iChat Theater

① Open the **File** menu and then select **Share a File With iChat Theater**.

The Share with iChat Theater dialog appears.

② Move to and select the document (such as a presentation) that you want to share.

③ Click **Share**.

The document is prepared, and you see a message stating that iChat Theater is ready to begin.

④ Select the buddy with whom you want to share the document.

⑤ Start a video chat.

● When the buddy accepts your invitation, you see the Video Chat window.

● You also see a window showing the document you are sharing.

● In the lower-left corner of the window, you see a preview window showing the buddy with whom you are chatting.

⑥ Move through the document and speak to deliver your message to the audience.

Note: *If you share a presentation created with Apple's Keynote software, you can use the Keynote controls to present the document.*

⑦ When you are done, close the Video Chat window.

Share Desktops during Chats

You can share your desktop with other Macs so that the people with whom you are chatting can see and control what happens on your computer. When you share someone else's screen, you can see and control his computer as if you were sitting in front of it. Sharing screens is a great way to collaborate on projects or to share information.

Screen sharing is especially useful when troubleshooting problems. The person who is having a problem can share his desktop with the person helping so that the helper can see what is happening, which is much easier than trying to describe a problem. The helper can also take control of the computer to actually solve the problem.

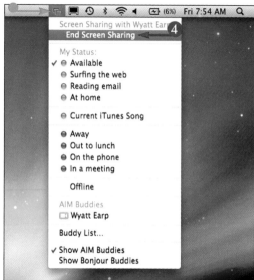

SHARE YOUR DESKTOP

Note: *Screen Sharing must be enabled on the Sharing pane of the System Preferences application for it to work within iChat. See Chapter 7 to learn how to configure it.*

1. On the Buddy or Bonjour list, select the buddy with whom you want to share your desktop.

2. Click the **Share Desktop** button (⊟).

3. Click **Share My Screen with *buddyname***, where *buddyname* is the name of the buddy you selected.

● When the buddy accepts your invitation, the Sharing status indicator appears (⊟) at the top of the iChat menu on the toolbar.

The buddy with whom you are sharing your screen can now use your MacBook Air. Do not be surprised when the pointer moves and commands are activated without you doing anything.

While screens are being shared, you can audio chat. It is a good practice for the person controlling the computer to explain what they are doing as they do it.

4. To end screen sharing, open the iChat menu and choose **End Screen Sharing**.

The sharing connection ends and your computer returns to your control.

SHARE A DESKTOP BELONGING TO SOMEONE ELSE

① On the Buddy or Bonjour list, select the buddy whose desktop you want to share.

② Click the **Share Desktop** button ().

③ Click **Ask to Share *buddyname*'s Screen**, where *buddyname* is the name of the buddy you selected.

iChat sends a share request to the buddy. When he responds, you see two windows on your screen.

● One window is the buddy's desktop, which is the larger window by default.

● The other window is a preview of your desktop, which is labeled My Computer.

Note: *You can move the preview window around the screen if it blocks the part of the shared desktop that you want to see.*

④ You can work with the buddy's computer just as if you were sitting in front of it.

⑤ To move back to your desktop, click in the My Computer window.

The two windows flip-flop so that your desktop is now the larger window.

⑥ When you are done sharing, click the **Close** button on the My Computer window.

TIPS

What happens when someone wants to share his screen with me?

You receive a screen-sharing invitation in iChat. When you click the invitation, you have the following options: Accept to start screen sharing, Decline to prevent it, or Text Reply to send back a text message. If you choose to share the person's screen, you are able to see and control the other person's computer.

What if I want to share a Mac screen that is on the same local network as my MacBook Air?

Open the Sharing pane of the System Preferences application and check the **Screen Sharing** check box to turn it on. Use the Allow Access For tool to configure share permissions for specific user accounts or for all users. On a different Mac on the local network, select the computer whose screen you want to share. Click **Connect** and log in under a user account that has permission to share the screen. Once you are logged in, click **Share Screen**.

Taking Care of Business

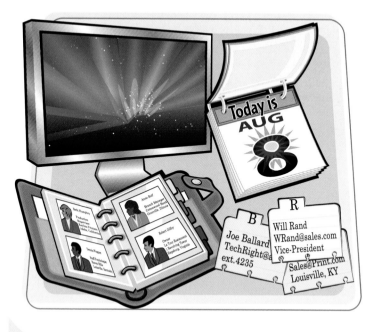

Address Book is very useful for organizing and viewing contact information, as well as sending e-mail, visiting Web sites, and printing envelopes. iCal is a calendar program that offers its own useful features, such as publishing and subscribing to online calendars. Printing is definitely part of taking care of business, and Mac OS X also has you covered there, whether you want to print on paper or electronically. And MacBook Air takes care of business as long as you take care of it, by maintaining it and your data, and troubleshooting problems.

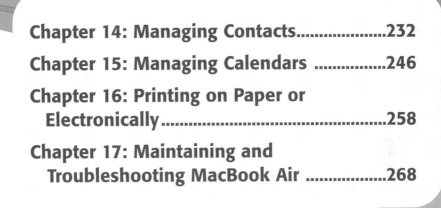

Address Book is both powerful and easy to use. You can quickly build your contact information and then use that information in many ways.

Open Address Book by clicking its Dock icon, which is a book with the @ symbol on its cover, or by double-clicking its icon in the Applications folder.

● **Toolbar**

Includes the View buttons, Action pop-up menu, and Pair button

● **Group Pane**

Shows groups you are using to organize contact information

● **Name Pane**

Lists each contact in Address Book

● **Search Tool**

Enables you to search for contacts

● **Selected Group**

The highlight indicates the group currently selected

● **Selected Card**

The highlight shows the card selected in the Name pane whose information is displayed in the Card pane

● **Card Pane**

Shows the detailed information for the card selected in the Name pane

● **Add Group**

Enables you to create groups

● **Add Card**

Enables you to add cards

● **Edit**

Use this button to change the information on the card being displayed. When the button is blue, you are in Edit mode; when it is black, you are in View mode.

Before you start using Address Book, check out a few important concepts to help you master your contacts quickly and easily.

Cards

Each contact is represented by a card. Like Rolodex cards of old, Address Book cards contain contact information. Unlike physical cards, Address Book cards are virtual cards, or *vCards*, making them flexible because you can store a variety of information on each card; you can also store different information for various contacts.

Contact Information

Each card in Address Book can hold an unlimited number of physical addresses, phone numbers, e-mail addresses, dates, notes, URLs, and so on. Because vCards are flexible, you do not have to include each kind of information for every contact; you include only the information that is appropriate for each specific contact. Address Book displays only fields that have data in them so that your cards are not cluttered up with a lot of empty fields.

Groups

Groups are collections of cards. They are useful because you can do something once with a group and the action affects all the cards in that group. For example, you can create a group containing family members whom you regularly e-mail. Then, you can address a message to the one group instead of addressing each person individually.

Smart Groups

Smart groups are also collections of cards, but unlike regular groups, you do not have to manually add cards to a smart group. Instead, you define criteria for the cards you want to be included in the smart group, and Address Book automatically adds the appropriate cards for you. For example, suppose you want a group for everyone with the same last name; you can simply create a smart group with that criterion, and Address Book adds all the people with that last name to the group automatically.

Address Book Actions

In addition to using information stored on cards indirectly — for example, looking at a phone number to dial it — you can use some data to perform an action by Control+clicking the information and choosing an action. Some of the most useful actions are sending e-mails, visiting Web sites, and dialing a phone number.

Add a Contact Manually

Before you can work with contacts, you need to create a card for each contact you want to manage. There are several ways to capture contact information on cards in Address Book.

One way is to manually create a card and add contact information to it. This is easy to do and you can choose the specific information you add for a new contact.

① Click the **Add Card** button (➕).

A new, empty card appears in the Card pane.

② Type the contact's first name in the First field, which is highlighted.

③ Press Tab.

④ Type the contact's last name in the Last field.

⑤ Press Tab.

⑥ Type the contact's company in the Company field.

*Note: If the card is for a company, check the **Company** check box and type the company name; first and last name information is optional for companies.*

⑦ Press Tab.

⑧ Click the pop-up menu (⬍) next to the first field (work, by default).

⑨ Select the type of contact information you want to enter.

⑩ Type the selected information in the field, such as a phone number or e-mail address.

*Note: When you select a data type, Address Book automatically creates a field of the right format, such as for phone numbers when you select **mobile**.*

⑪ Repeat Steps **7** to **10** to enter information into each field to which you want to add information.

⑫ To remove a field from the card, click the **Delete** button (⊖).

⑬ To add another field of the same type to a card, click the **Add** button (⊕).

⑭ To add an image to the card, drag it from the desktop and drop it onto the Image Well.

A sheet that enables you to resize the image pops up automatically.

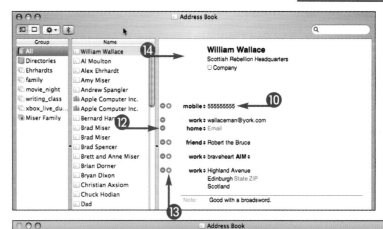

⑮ Drag the slider to the left to make the image smaller, or to the right to make it larger.

⑯ Drag the image so that the part you want to be displayed on the card is contained within the box.

⑰ Repeat Steps **15** and **16** until the image is sized and placed as you want it to be.

⑱ Click **Set**.

The image is saved and the sheet closes.

⑲ Click **Edit**.

The card is saved and only fields containing information are shown.

 TIPS

What if the information I want to enter is not available on a pop-up menu?

Open a pop-up menu and choose **Custom**. Type the label for the field you want to add, and click **OK**. You return to the card and the custom label appears on the card. Enter the information for that field. The custom field is added to the card.

How can I configure the default information that appears on new cards?

Open the **Address Book** menu and choose **Preferences**. Click **Template**. Remove fields you do not want to appear by default by clicking the **Delete** button (⊖). Add more fields of an existing type by clicking the **Add** button (⊕) next to that type. Add fields that do not appear at all by clicking **Add Field** and then choosing the field you want to add to the template. Close the Preferences dialog.

Work with vCards

Many applications, including Address Book, use vCards to store contact information such as contact managers and e-mail.

You can add contacts to Address Book using vCards other people send to you; once you have added these cards, you can use them just like those you create in Address Book manually. You can also create a vCard for yourself to send to others so they can easily add your data to their contact information.

Work with vCards

ADD CONTACTS WITH VCARDS

1 Drag the vCard file onto your desktop.

Note: *One of the most common ways to receive vCards is through e-mail as attachments. Simply drag the vCard from the e-mail onto your desktop. vCard files have .vcf as their filename extension.*

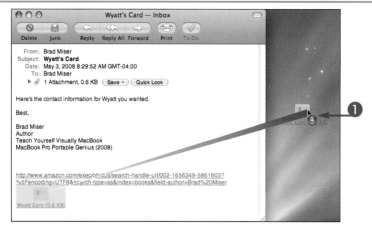

2 Drag the vCard file from the desktop onto the Name pane of the Address Book window.

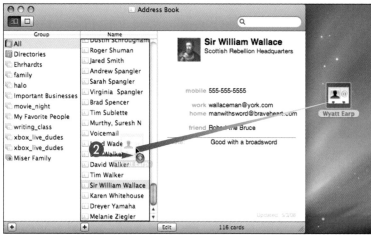

A sheet appears, confirming that you are adding a new card.

3 Click **Add**.

● The vCard is added to Address Book; you can work with it just like cards you create within Address Book.

CREATE VCARDS FROM ADDRESS BOOK CARDS

① Search or browse for the cards for which you want to create vCards.

Note: *To quickly find your card, open the **Card** menu and choose **Go to My Card**. Your card, which is marked with a silhouette icon, appears in the Card pane.*

② Drag the card from Address Book onto your desktop.

Note: *The filename of the vCard is the name of the contact.*

The vCard is created, and you can provide it to other people. They can then add its contact information to their contact manager.

TIPS

Can I use a vCard from Microsoft Outlook or some other contact manager?
vCards are a standard file format used by almost all applications that deal with contact information. You should be able to add a vCard to Address Book, regardless of the program used to create that vCard. One caveat is that not all information stored in all applications can be moved into Address Book using vCards, but you almost always get the most important information. You can always add information to the cards you create from a vCard at any time.

How can I add contact information to Address Book from e-mails when a vCard is not attached?
When you receive an e-mail in Mail, you can add the sender's name and e-mail address to Address Book. Position the pointer over the address shown next to "From," and when the address becomes highlighted, click the trackpad button to open the action menu. Choose **Add to Address Book**. A new card is created with as much information as Address Book can extract, usually the first and last name along with an e-mail address. Using Address Book, you can add other information to the card as needed.

Find Contact Information

The whole point of having contact information is being able to find and use the information you need. Address Book makes it simple to quickly find information you are interested in.

You can find information by browsing your contacts. Or, you can search for specific contact information.

BROWSE FOR A CONTACT

① Select the group that you want to browse; to browse all of your contacts, click **All**.

● The cards in the selected group appear in the Name pane.

② Use the scroll bar to browse up and down the list of names.

③ Select the name for the contact information you want to view or to use, such as someone to whom you want to send an e-mail.

● The card containing contact information appears in the Card pane.

SEARCH FOR A CONTACT

① Select the group that you want to search; to search all of your contacts, click **All**.

● All the cards in the selected group appear in the Name pane.

② Type search text in the Search field.

Note: *Address Book searches all the fields at the same time, and so you do not need to define what you are searching for, such as a name instead of an address.*

As you type, Address Book starts searching all the fields in the cards and reduces those shown in the Name pane so that it contains only those that match your search.

③ Continue typing in the Search field until the card you want appears in the Name pane.

④ Select the card.

● The card's information appears in the Card pane.

● The part of the card that matches your search is highlighted in gray.

⑤ Clear the Search field by clicking the **Stop Search** button ().

All the cards in the selected group appear again.

TIPS

Can I search for contact information by phone number or e-mail address?

When you search in Address Book, it searches all the fields on all your cards simultaneously. If it finds a match in any of these fields, a card is included in the search results shown in the Name pane. For example, if you enter text, it looks for matches by searching name fields, e-mail addresses, and other fields that include text. Likewise, if you type numbers, Address Book searches phone numbers, addresses, and so on.

Can I browse or search in multiple groups at the same time?

You cannot browse the cards in multiple groups at the same time; you can only browse one group at a time by selecting the group you want to browse. You can search more than one group at a time, but you will get better results if you only search with the All group selected.

Create an
Address Group

A group is useful because it enables you to store many cards within it. Then you can take an action on the group and it affects all the cards included in the group.

For example, when you want to send an e-mail to everyone in a group, you can do so easily and quickly by sending one message to the group instead of adding each person's e-mail address individually.

Create an Address Group

① Click the **Add Group** button ( ).

● A new group appears in the Group pane with its name ready to be edited.

② Type a name for the group.

③ Press `Return`.

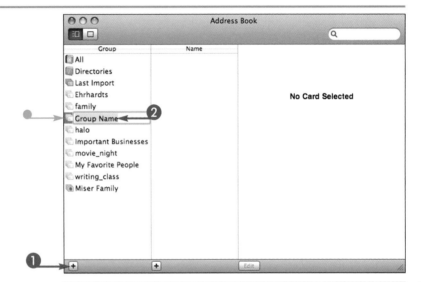

● The group is created and is ready for you to add cards to it.

④ Click **All**.

All the cards in Address Book are shown in the Name pane.

⑤ Browse or search for the first card you want to add to the group.

Note: *See the previous task, "Find Contact Information," for the steps to browse and search.*

⑥ Select a card that you want to add to the group.

● The card appears in the Card pane.

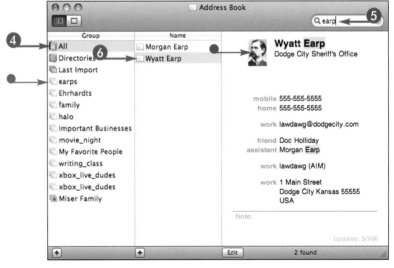

7 Drag the card from the Name pane and drop it onto the group to which you want to add it.

Note: *When you drag a card over a group, a green circle containing a plus sign appears below the card's icon (⊕). When the group into which you want to place the card is highlighted, release the trackpad button.*

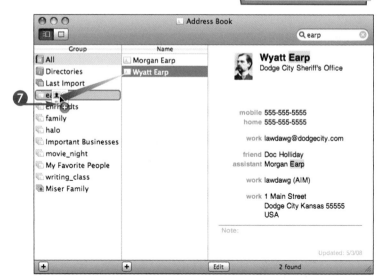

8 Select the group to which you added cards.

● The cards included in the group are shown in the Name pane.

TIPS

Can I add more than one card to a group at the same time?
Yes. To add multiple cards to a group at the same time, press and hold the ⌘ key while you click each card that you want to add to the group. Then you can drag all of the cards you have selected onto the group at the same time.

How do I create a smart group?
Open the **File** menu and choose **New Smart Group**. Type the name of the group. Use the pop-up menus and other controls to configure the first criterion, such as "Name includes Smith." Click the **Add** button (⊞) to create more criteria until you have defined all the criteria you want to use. Choose **all** if you require that all the criteria be met, or **any** if you want only one criterion to be required. Click **OK**. The smart group is created and all the cards that meet the criteria you defined are added to it automatically.

Use Address
Cards and Groups

After you have added all that great contact information, Address Book will help you use your contacts in many ways. Check out the following tricks that Address Book can do for you.

ADDRESS E-MAIL

① Find the card for the person you want to e-mail.

② `Control`+click the e-mail address to which you want to send a message.

The contextual menu appears.

③ Choose **Send Email**.

Your default e-mail application opens, and a new message to the address you selected in Step **2** is created.

VISIT WEB SITES

① Find a card with a home page or other Web page URL on it.

② Click the URL you want to visit.

Your default Web application takes you to the URL you clicked.

MAP A PHYSICAL ADDRESS

① Find the card containing the address you want to map.

② **Control**+click the address you want to see on a map.

The contextual menu appears.

③ Choose **Map Of**.

Your default Web application takes you to a Google map showing the address you clicked.

PRINT AN ENVELOPE OR MAILING LABEL

① Find the card containing the address for which you want a mailing label.

② **Control**+click the address you want to place on an envelope or label.

The contextual menu appears.

③ Choose **Copy mailing label**.

④ Open the application you use to print envelopes or labels.

This example uses a widget called EasyEnvelopes from Ambrosia Software.

⑤ If the address is not inserted automatically, open the **Edit** menu and then select **Paste**, or press ⌘+**V** to insert the address.

Once the address is in the application, use the application's printing feature to print the envelope or label.

TIPS

How do I know what actions are available for a card or a group?

Each type of information on an address card has a different set of actions available for it. To see what actions are available for specific information on a card, simply **Control**+click that information. To see what actions are available for a card or group, **Control**+click the card or group. On the resulting pop-up menus, you see all of the actions that are available.

Can I share my Address Book with other people?

You can easily share your Address Book with people who also have a MobileMe account. Open the **Address Book** menu and choose **Preferences**. Click the **Sharing** tab. Check the **Share your Address Book** check box. Click ➕ and select the other MobileMe users with whom you want to share your Address Book. Click **OK**. If you want those people to be able to change your Address Book, check the **Allow Editing** check box.

Change or Delete
Address Cards or Groups

Over time, you want to be able to update your Address Book by adding new information, changing existing information, or removing information you no longer need. Fortunately, with Address Book, all these tasks are simple.

You can change information for cards or groups that you want to continue to use. When you decide you do not want a card or group anymore, you can delete them.

Change or Delete Address Cards or Groups

CHANGE ADDRESS CARDS

① Search or browse for the card you want to change.

② Click the **Edit** button.

Existing fields become editable and the Delete (⊖) and Add (⊕) buttons appear.

③ Click the information you want to change.

④ Make changes to that information.

Note: *You move between fields on a card by pressing the* Return *or the* Tab *key.*

⑤ To delete information from the card, click ⊖.

The field clears; after you exit the Edit mode, that field no longer appears on the card.

⑥ To add information to the card, click ⊕ next to the type of information you want to add.

⑦ Choose a label for the new field on the pop-up menu.

8 Type information into the new field.

9 After you have made all the changes to the card, click **Edit**.

The changes you made to the card are saved.

Note: When the Edit button is blue, you are in Edit mode. When it is black, you are in View mode.

DELETE CARDS FROM ADDRESS GROUPS

1 Select the group you want to change.

2 Select a card you want to remove from the group.

3 Press Delete.

A warning sheet appears.

4 Click **Remove from Group**.

If you started with a manually created group, the card is removed from the group, but remains in Address Book. If you started with a smart group, the card is deleted from Address Book, so be careful not to delete a card from a smart group that you want to keep.

How do I delete a card I do not need anymore?
Select the card you want to remove and press Delete. Click **Delete** in the confirmation sheet. The card is removed from Address Book.

How do I delete a group I do not need?
Select the group you want to delete and press Delete. Click **Delete** in the confirmation sheet. The group is removed from Address Book; however, the cards in that group remain in Address Book.

Explore iCal

iCal is a full-featured calendar application of Mac OS X. As you can guess, you can use it to record To Do items and events; however, iCal goes beyond these basics.

One of the best things about iCal is that you can publish your calendars on the Web so that other people can view them. By subscribing to other people's calendars, you can see what they are up to, which makes coordinating events among a group of people much easier.

● **Back and Forward buttons**

Click these buttons to move back or forward in the calendar

● **View selection buttons**

Use these buttons to determine how you view the calendar, such as by day, week, or month

● **Search tool**

Enables you to search events and To Do items

● **To Do items**

Tasks that you need to do

● **Personal calendars**

The calendars you create and manage

● **Subscribed calendars**

Calendars other people or organizations have created to which you have subscribed; when a calendar's check box is checked, you see it in the iCal window.

● **Mini-Month pane**

A miniature view of the month; the current date is shown in dark blue and the date in focus is shown in a lighter blue.

● **Events**

Colored bars represent events; the color matches the calendar's color on which those events are stored.

● **Show/Hide Mini-Month**

Opens or closes the Mini-Month pane

● **Show/Hide Notifications**

Opens or closes the Notifications pane

Add a Calendar

In iCal, you store events and To Do items on a calendar. You can have as many calendars as you want. For example, you might want one calendar for work information and another for family events.

Events on a calendar whose check box is checked appear in the iCal window. When you uncheck a calendar's check box, its events are hidden. Each calendar has its own color so that you can easily see which events and To Do items are associated with it.

Add a Calendar

1. Launch iCal by clicking its icon on the Dock.

   The iCal window opens and you see two default calendars, labeled Home and Work, on the Calendars list.

2. Click the **Add** button (➕).

   A new calendar appears on the list, and its name is highlighted so that you know it is ready to edit.

3. Type the name of the calendar and press Return to save it.

4. Select the new calendar.

5. On the iCal toolbar menu, click **File** and then click **Get Info**.

The calendar's Info sheet appears.

6. Type a description of the calendar in the Description field.

7. If you want alarms on the calendar to be ignored, check the **Ignore alarms** check box.

8. Choose the color you want to associate with the calendar on the **Color** pop-up menu.

9. Click **OK**.

   The sheet closes and the new calendar is ready to use.

Add an Event to a Calendar

An event in iCal is some period of time for which you want to plan, such as a meeting, recurring activity, vacation, or other period of time that is important to you. Events are associated with a specific period of time and a specific calendar within iCal.

You can create events on a calendar and then configure them in many ways, such as the time, date, and alarms. If you want other people to attend an event, you can easily invite them to it.

Add an Event to a Calendar

① Select the calendar to which you want to add an event.

② Move the calendar view so the date on which the event starts is shown.

③ When viewing by week or day, drag over the time period for the event; drag across multiple days if the event extends beyond one day.

④ Release the trackpad button.

● The new event is created and its name is highlighted.

⑤ Type the name of the event.

⑥ Press **Return** to save it.

⑦ Double-click the event.

The event's Info window appears. Here you see the name of the event and the time period it includes.

8 Click **Edit**.

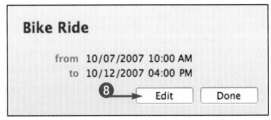

Bike Ride

from 10/07/2007 10:00 AM
to 10/12/2007 04:00 PM

8 ▶ Edit | Done

The window moves into Edit mode.

9 Edit the name, if needed.

10 Enter a location for the event.

11 If needed, change the event's dates and times using the date and time tools.

12 If the event repeats, choose the frequency of the event on the **repeat** pop-up menu, and set the last date on which the event should be scheduled on the **end** pop-up menu.

13 To change the calendar with which the event is associated, choose a different calendar on the **calendar** pop-up menu.

14 To set alarms for the event, choose the kind of alarm on the **alarm** pop-up menu, and then configure it using the controls that appear (these are based on the kind of alarm you select).

15 To send an invitation to other people, click **Add Attendees** and enter the e-mail addresses for each invitee separated by commas.

16 To store a file on the event, click **Add File** and select the file you want to attach.

17 To include a URL with the event, type it in the url field.

18 Type notes for the event in the note field.

19 Click **Send** if you included attendees, or **Done** if you have not.

The event is saved on the calendar, and, if they were added, invitations are sent to other invitees.

Note: To delete an event, select it and press Delete .

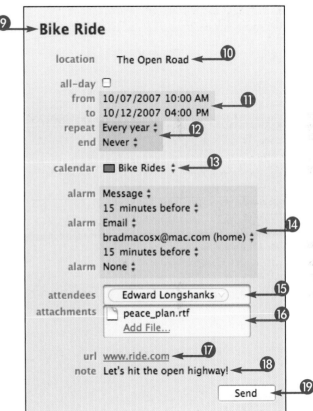

9 ▶ **Bike Ride**

location   The Open Road ◀ **10**

all–day ☐

from 10/07/2007 10:00 AM ◀ **11**
to 10/12/2007 04:00 PM

repeat Every year ⬍ ◀ **12**
end Never ⬍

calendar ▪ Bike Rides ⬍ ◀ **13**

alarm Message ⬍
15 minutes before ⬍

alarm Email ⬍
bradmacosx@mac.com (home) ⬍ ◀ **14**
15 minutes before ⬍

alarm None ⬍

attendees (Edward Longshanks ∨) ◀ **15**
attachments ▯ peace_plan.rtf ◀ **16**
Add File...

url www.ride.com ◀ **17**
note Let's hit the open highway! ◀ **18**

Send ◀ **19**

TIPS

I often forget what the date is. Is there an easy to way to see the current date?
Yes. iCal displays the current month and date in its icon on the Dock.

When I invite someone to an event, what does that person receive?
Each invitee receives an e-mail containing information about the event with a calendar item as an attachment. If the invitees also use iCal or another compatible calendar application, they can double-click the attachment to add the event to their own calendar in iCal.

Add a To Do Item to a Calendar

While events are periods of time for which you want to plan and that you want to manage, To Do items are specific actions that you want to perform. To Do items can contain basic information about a task, such as a description, along with information to associate the action with a date, including the date the action is due.

Like events, you can add To Do items to iCal, and you can associate them with specific calendars. You can also configure To Do items with alarms, a priority, and related information.

Add a To Do Item to a Calendar

CREATE A TO DO ITEM

1. Select the calendar with which you want the To Do item to be associated.

2. On the iCal toolbar menu, click **File** and then click **New To Do**.

● A new untitled To Do item appears on the To Do list.

Note: If you do not see the To Do list, open the **View** menu, and then select **Show To Do List**.

3. Type the name of the To Do item; in most cases, this is a description of what you need to do.

4. Press Return.
   The new name is saved.

5. Double-click the To Do item.

The Info window appears.

6 Edit the name if needed.

7 Use the **priority** pop-up menu to assign a priority to the item.

The priority you assign impacts how the item is displayed on the To Do list.

8 To assign a due date to the item, check the **due date** check box and set the due date.

9 To set alarms for the item, choose the kind of alarm on the **alarm** pop-up menu and then configure it.

Alarms are reminders to help you remember the task.

10 To change the calendar with which the item is associated, choose a different calendar on the **calendar** pop-up menu.

11 To include a URL with the item, type it in the url field.

12 Type notes for the event in the note field.

13 Click **Done**.

The item is saved on the To Do list.

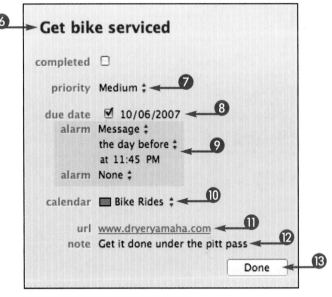

MANAGE TO DO ITEMS

● As events become due, their completion check box changes to an exclamation point.

1 After you have completed a task, check its check box.

2 To sort the list of tasks, choose how you want them sorted on the **To Do Items by** pop-up menu at the top of the list.

When I open Mail, I also see To Do items. Are these related to the items in iCal?

Mail and iCal share To Do items. Any To Do items you create in one application show up in the other one as well. Likewise, if you mark an item as complete in iCal, it also gets marked as complete in Mail. To work with To Do items in Mail, open the **Mailbox** menu, select **Go To**, and then select **To Do**. If you add To Do items in Mail, they appear under a section labeled with your e-mail address.

How can I set iCal to remove older completed items so that the list is not cluttered with them?

Open the iCal Preferences dialog and click the **Advanced** pane. Check the **Hide To Do items days after they have been completed** check box and enter the number of days that should pass before a completed item is removed from the list. When that number of days passes since an item was marked as completed, it is removed from the list.

Publish Calendars

iCal's publishing tools make sharing your calendars with other people fast and easy.

If you have a MobileMe account, you can publish your calendars to the Web. Other people can then view your calendars in a Web browser or subscribe to them so that they can see them in their iCal application. You can also view your published calendars on the Web without iCal, such as from a Windows computer. For more information about subscribing to calendars, see the next section, "Subscribe to Calendars."

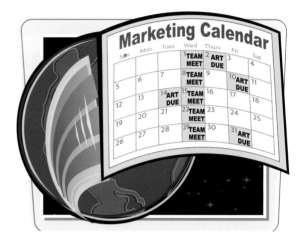

Publish Calendars

① Select the calendar you want to publish.

② Choose **Calendar** on the iCal toolbar menu, and then click **Publish**.

The Publish calendar sheet appears.

③ Type the name of the published version of the calendar in the Publish calendar as field.

④ On the Publish on pop-up menu, choose **MobileMe**.

⑤ If you want changes you make to be published automatically, check the **Publish changes automatically** check box.

⑥ If you want both titles and notes to be included, check the **Publish titles and notes** check box.

⑦ If you want to publish the To Do items associated with the calendar, check the **Publish To Do items** check box.

⑧ If you want alarms to be included, check the **Publish alarms** check box.

⑨ If you want attachments to be available on the published version, check the **Publish attachments** check box.

⑩ Click **Publish**.

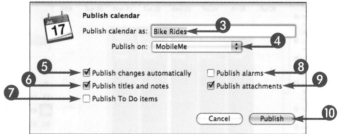

iCal publishes the calendar. When the process is complete, you see the Calendar Published dialog.

(11) To send the URL and subscription invitation to someone, click **Send Mail**.

An e-mail message with the information about the published calendar is sent so that the recipient can subscribe to the calendar.

(12) To see how the calendar appears on the Web, click **Visit Page**.

● Your Web browser opens and you see the Web version of the calendar.

TIPS

Do I really need a MobileMe account to publish my calendar?

No. If you do not have a MobileMe account, you can publish your calendars to a WebDAV server. There are several free iCal publishing services available on the Internet; a quick Google search for "publish iCal calendar" will lead you to information about these services. To be able to publish calendars to one of these servers, you need to know the URL for the server and have a username and password.

I like to have a hard copy of my calendar at times. Can iCal help?

Yes. Choose **File** on the iCal toolbar menu, and then click **Print**. In the resulting Print dialog, you can choose from many output options. For example, you can print a weekly or monthly view, choose a time range to include, and set the paper size.

Subscribe to Calendars

Other people who use iCal can publish their calendars as easily as you can publish yours. When someone sends his calendar information to you, you can subscribe to the calendar or visit it on the Web.

When you subscribe to a calendar, it is added as a calendar to iCal, and you can use iCal's tools to view it (you cannot make changes to someone else's calendar). When you visit a calendar on the Web, you view it through a Web browser, such as Safari.

Subscribe to Calendars

SUBSCRIBE TO A PUBLISHED CALENDAR IN ICAL

① Open an e-mail containing calendar subscription information.

② Click the link starting with **webcal://ical.me.com**.

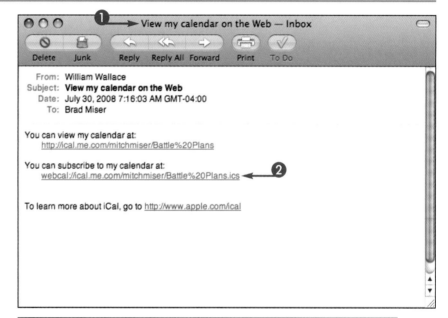

The subscribe sheet appears.

③ Review the URL for the calendar to make sure it is one to which you want to subscribe.

④ If so, click **Subscribe**.

iCal downloads the calendar information, and you see the calendar's Info sheet.

5 If you want to change the name of the calendar as it appears in your iCal application, edit the name in the **Name** field.

6 Use the **Color** pop-up menu to associate a color with the calendar.

7 Enter a description of the calendar in the **Description** field.

8 If you do not want alarms, attachments, or To Do items removed, uncheck the respective **Remove** check boxes.

9 On the **Auto-refresh** pop-up menu, choose how often you want the calendar's information updated.

10 Click **OK**.

● The calendar is added to iCal in the Subscriptions sections, and you see its events and other information.

VISIT A PUBLISHED CALENDAR ON THE WEB

1 Open an e-mail containing calendar information.

2 Click the link starting with **http://ical.me.com**.

Your default Web browser opens the calendar on the Web.

TIPS

Can I add events to a calendar to which I am subscribed?
No. Calendars published to iCal are read-only, meaning that you can view them, but you cannot change them.

Do organizations share their calendars?
Yes. Many organizations, such as professional sports teams, publish calendars to which you can subscribe in iCal. To find them, open the **Calendar** menu and then select **Find Shared Calendars**. You go to the iCal Library Web site, on which you can find and subscribe to many different kinds of calendars.

Configure iCal Preferences

You can further tailor how iCal works by changing its preferences. For example, on the General tab, you can determine whether weeks are five or seven days long and when days start. You can also configure the start and end time for the "working" part of the day.

On the Advanced tab, you can determine how To Do items are managed and control alarms for all iCal events and To Do items.

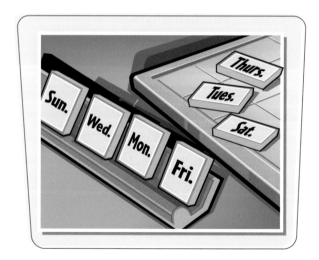

CONFIGURE GENERAL ICAL PREFERENCES

1 Press ⌘+,.

The iCal Preferences dialog opens.

2 Click the **General** tab.

3 On the **Days per week** pop-up menu, choose 5 if you want weeks to be shown as the five workdays, or 7 if you want to see all seven days.

4 On the **Start week on** pop-up menu, choose the first day of the week.

5 Use the **Day starts at** and **Day ends at** pop-up menus to define the times at which "work" days start and end.

6 On the **Show** pop-up menu, determine how many hours iCal shows at once.

7 If you want the timeline to be shown in the Month view, check the **Show time in month view** check box.

8 If you want the Birthdays calendar in iCal to be shown, check the **Show Birthdays calendar** check box.

9 If you want a default alarm for all events, check the **Add a default alarm to all new events and invitations** check box and enter the default number of minutes before the start time for the alarm to activate in the field.

CONFIGURE ADVANCED ICAL PREFERENCES

1 Press ⌘+,.

The iCal Preferences dialog opens.

2 Click the **Advanced** tab.

3 If you want to be able to manage events in different time zones, check the **Turn on time zone support** check box.

4 To manage how and when To Do items display on your calendars, select or deselect this section's check boxes and enter the appropriate number of days in the various fields.

5 To disable all iCal alarms, check the **Turn off all alarms** check box.

6 To disable alarms only when iCal is closed, check the **Turn off alarms only when iCal is not open** check box.

7 If you want Mail to automatically retrieve event invitations you receive, check the bottom check box.

TIPS

What is the Birthdays calendar?

One of the attributes you can collect for people in Address Book is **birthday**. If you enable the Birthdays calendar to be displayed, iCal creates events for each birthday captured in Address Book and presents them to you on the Birthdays calendar.

How does time zone support work?

When you enable time zone support, iCal can help you manage the often confusing situation when you are managing events across multiple time zones. When you create an event, you can associate it with a specific time zone. When viewing your calendars, you can set the current iCal time zone using the Time Zone pop-up menu located in the upper-right corner of the iCal window. When you set this, all events are shifted according to the relationship between their specific time zones and iCal's so that you see all events according to the current time zone. To see an event in a specific time zone (such as when you travel there), choose that time zone on the pop-up menu.

Understand Printers

Although we live in an electronic world, printing is an important part of using MacBook Air. There are a number of concepts you need to understand as you build a printing system for your MacBook Air and the network it is on.

Inkjet Printers

Inkjet printers create text and graphics by spraying droplets of ink on paper in various combinations. Inkjet printers produce high-quality output, especially when the output is matched to the right kind of paper. These printers are very inexpensive and many of them offer additional features such as scanning and faxing. Inkjet printers are less expensive than laser printers initially, but they consume large amounts of ink, which is relatively expensive. You can expect to pay a significant portion of the purchase price of the printer each time you replace one or more ink cartridges. Still, for many people, inkjet printers make a lot of sense.

Laser Printers

Laser printers use a laser, mirrors, and an imaging drum to transfer toner onto paper. Laser printers produce very high-quality output and are fast relative to inkjet printers. Although more expensive initially than an inkjet printer, the cost per page of a laser printer can actually be significantly less than that of an inkjet printer. Like inkjet printers, most laser printers print in color. Because they were previously very expensive and printed mostly in black and white, laser printers were primarily used in businesses and other organizations. However, with some careful shopping, you can often get a color laser printer for not much more than an inkjet printer.

Printer Connections

No matter what kind of printer you use, MacBook Air needs to be able to communicate with it to send documents to print. There are three basic ways to connect MacBook Air to a printer, and each model of printer can support one or all of these types of connections. First, some printers use USB to communicate. Second, networkable printers have an Ethernet port that you can use to connect MacBook Air directly to the printer, or more likely, to connect the printer to your network. The third, and most convenient, way to connect is wirelessly. Some printers support wireless connections directly; however, you can connect a printer to an AirPort Base Station (through an Ethernet port or its USB port) to print to it wirelessly.

Printer Sharing

If you have more than one computer, you can share the same printer with all the computers over a local network (wired, wireless, or both). The shared printer can be connected directly to a Mac through USB or Ethernet, or it can be connected to an AirPort Base Station (this is the best option because it does not depend on the Mac running for the printer to be available on the network). See Chapter 7 for information about setting up an AirPort network.

PDF

Adobe invented the Portable Document Format (PDF) as a means to share and print documents that does not depend on the specific applications or fonts installed on a computer. PDF is the standard format for electronic documents, no matter how they are distributed. This is good news for Mac users because support for PDF documents is built into Mac OS X. You can read any PDF document using the Preview application, but more importantly for this chapter, you can also print any document in the PDF format so that you can easily share it with others through e-mail or over the Web.

Install and Configure a USB Printer

Connecting a USB printer directly to MacBook Air is simple, and all inkjet printers, and some laser printers, support USB connections. After you have connected the printer to MacBook Air, you need to configure MacBook Air to use it.

Install and Configure a USB Printer

① Connect the printer to a power source and turn it on.

② Connect MacBook Air to the printer using a USB cable.

③ Open the System Preferences application.

④ Click the **Print & Fax** icon.

● The Print & Fax pane appears.

⑤ Click the **Add** button (➕).

The Printer Selection window appears with the Default tab selected.

⑥ Select the printer with USB shown in the Kind column.

⑦ If you want to give the printer a different name, edit the name shown in the Name field.

⑧ Describe the location of the printer in the Location field; in most cases, you should leave the default information.

● If the correct printer is shown on the Print Using pop-up menu, Mac OS X has found a driver for the printer.

⑨ Click **Add**.

The Printer Selection window closes.

● You return to the System Preferences application and see the printer you added.

⑩ If you want the printer to be MacBook Air's default, choose it on the **Default Printer** pop-up menu.

⑪ Choose the default paper size on the **Default Paper Size in Page Setup** pop-up menu.

⑫ Quit the System Preferences application.

⑬ Open any document and choose **Print** under the **File** menu.

The Print sheet appears.

⑭ Click the **Hide/Show Details** button (▲).

The sheet expands to present additional controls and a preview of the document you are printing.

⑮ Use the pop-up menus, radio buttons, and boxes on the print sheet to configure the print job (the menus vary, depending on the type of printer you are using).

⑯ Click **Print**.

The document prints.

TIPS

Can I use any printer with MacBook Air?

A compatible printer must support a connection technology that MacBook Air supports (which is true for almost all printers). More importantly, a printer must have Mac-compatible drivers; most printers do have Mac drivers available, and almost all of these are built into Mac OS X.

When I try to install a printer, I do not see a driver for it on the list of printer drivers installed with Mac OS X. What do I do now?

Go to the manufacturer's Web site, look for the Support page, and then look for the Downloads section; there you can search for a Mac driver for the printer. When you find it, you can download and install it. Then, add the printer again; this time, you will be able to select the appropriate driver.

Install and Configure a Networked Printer

Many printers, especially laser printers, are designed to be connected to a network so that any computer that can connect to that network can use the printer. This is especially useful when the hub provides a wireless network.

One way to connect a printer to a network is through Ethernet. This provides fast and trouble-free connections. The only downside is that the printer has to be within cable range of a hub, such as an AirPort Base Station.

Install and Configure a Networked Printer

① Connect the printer to a power source and turn it on.

② Connect the printer to a hub (such as an Airport Extreme Base Station) using an Ethernet cable.

③ Connect MacBook Air to the same network using AirPort or an Ethernet adapter and cable.

④ Open the System Preferences application.

⑤ Open the **Print & Fax** pane.

⑥ Click the **Add** button (+).

The Printer Selection window appears. The printers available on the network are scanned and presented on the list of printers.

⑦ Select the printer to which you want to connect; the Kind column should display Bonjour, indicating it is a network resource.

⑧ If you want to give the printer a name, edit the name shown in the Name field.

⑨ Describe the location of the printer in the Location field.

● If the correct printer is shown on the Print Using pop-up menu, Mac OS X has found a driver for the printer.

⑩ Click **Add**.

The Printer Selection window closes and you return to the System Preferences application.

● You see the printer you added in the Printers pane.

⑪ If you want the printer to be MacBook Air's default, choose it on the **Default Printer** pop-up menu.

⑫ Choose the default paper size on the **Default Paper Size in Page Setup** pop-up menu.

⑬ Quit the System Preferences application.

⑭ Open any document and choose **Print** under the **File** menu.

The Print sheet appears.

⑮ Click the **Hide/Show Details** button (▲).

The sheet expands to present additional controls and a preview of the document you are printing.

⑯ Use the pop-up menus on the print sheet to configure the print job (the menus vary, depending on the type of printer you are using).

⑰ Click **Print**.

The document prints.

TIPS

What is Bonjour?
Bonjour is the Mac OS X network discovery technology. When a device can use Bonjour, it broadcasts its identity on the network. When you connect to that network to search for a device, such as a printer, Bonjour devices are discovered automatically and you do not have to search for them or deal with their network addresses. You simply select the device you want to access and connect to it.

So, what is the best printer for me?
If you do not print very often or you mostly print pictures, an inkjet printer might be your best option, especially if you get one with additional capabilities, such as scanning. However, if you print a lot or print mostly text documents, a laser printer saves you money over the long run. For the ultimate in printing, get a color laser printer, which is not as expensive as it sounds (search on eBay and you can often find reconditioned printers for less than $100).

Connect to a Printer Wirelessly

If you have created a wireless network using an AirPort Extreme Base Station and have connected a printer to one of its Ethernet ports, you can print to that printer wirelessly without additional configuration (and you can skip the steps in this chapter). To print to a USB printer wirelessly, you can connect it to the Base Station's USB hub.

Every computer that prints to a Base Station–connected printer has to have the printer's software driver installed on it before it can use that printer. If the correct driver is not installed on MacBook Air, download and install it before configuring the Base Station to share a printer.

Connect to a Printer Wirelessly

CONFIGURE AN AIRPORT EXTREME BASE STATION TO SHARE A USB PRINTER

① Connect the printer to the USB port on the AirPort Extreme Base Station.

② Open the AirPort Utility application, located within the Utilities folder in the Applications folder.

③ Select the Base Station to which the printer is connected.

④ Click **Manual Setup**.

The Manual Configuration window appears.

⑤ Click the **Printers** tab.

⑥ Type a name for the printer in the USB Printers field.

⑦ Click **Update**.

The AirPort Utility updates the Base Station and restarts it.

⑧ Quit the AirPort Utility.

The printer is accessible wirelessly through AirPort and on a wired network connected to the Base Station.

CONNECT TO A PRINTER BEING SHARED BY AN AIRPORT BASE STATION

1 Open the **Print & Fax** pane of the System Preferences application.

2 Click ➕.

The Printer Selection window appears.

3 Select the printer to which you want to connect; the Kind column should display Bonjour, which indicates it is a network resource.

4 If you want to give the printer a name, edit the name shown in the Name field.

5 Describe the location of the printer in the Location field.

● If the correct printer is shown on the Print Using pop-up menu, Mac OS X has found a driver for the printer.

6 Click **Add**.

The printer is added to the Printers pane in the System Preferences. You can now print to it.

Can I share a printer connected to a computer over an AirPort network, or do I have to have an AirPort Base Station?
You can share a printer connected directly to a Mac using USB over an AirPort network as long as that Mac is connected to the AirPort network. This works just like sharing a printer connected to a Base Station except that the Mac always has to be running for the printer to be available.

Can I print wirelessly to an Ethernet printer by connecting it to a Base Station using an Ethernet cable?
Yes. If a printer is networkable through Ethernet, just connect it to one of the Base Station's Ethernet ports or to a hub on the network. It is added to the network as a network resource, and you can connect to it using the steps in the section "Install and Configure a Networked Printer," earlier in this chapter. You can print to the printer because an AirPort Station connects the wired and wireless networks together.

The Portable Document Format, or PDF, is a great way to distribute documents you create to other people. This is because PDF files appear correctly on any computer, regardless of the fonts or other formatting options installed on it, and people cannot easily change PDF documents you create.

Support for creating PDF documents is built into Mac OS X so that you can create a PDF file of any file you work with.

Print to PDF

① Open the document from which you want to create a PDF file.

② Choose **Print** from the document's **File** menu.

The Print dialog appears.

③ Open the **PDF** pop-up menu.

④ Choose **Save as PDF**.

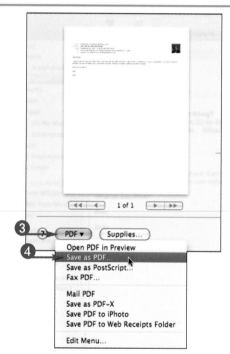

The Save dialog appears.

⑤ Type a name for the PDF file you are creating.

⑥ Choose the location in which you want to save the PDF file on the **Where** pop-up menu.

⑦ Type a title for the PDF file.

⑧ Type the author name.

⑨ If you want to enter an additional subject, do so in the Subject field.

⑩ Create keywords (used during Spotlight and other searches) in the Keywords field.

⑪ If you want to require passwords for the PDF file to be used, click **Security Options**.

The PDF Security Options dialog appears.

⑫ If you want people to have to enter a password to open the PDF file, check the **Require password to open document** check box and type the password in the Password and Verify fields.

⑬ If you want a password to be required for someone to copy content from the document, check the **Require password to copy text, images and other content** check box and type the password in the Password and Verify fields.

⑭ If you want a password to be required for the document to be printed, check the **Require password to print document** check box and type the password in the Password and Verify fields.

⑮ Click **OK**.

The dialog closes and you return to the Save dialog.

⑯ Click **Save**.

The PDF file is created.

⑰ Open the PDF file.

⑱ If the PDF file is password-protected, type the password at the prompt and press **Return**.

The document appears and is ready to send to other people through e-mail or to be posted on the Web.

PDF Security Options

☑ Require password to open document

⑫ → Password: ••••••••
Verify: ••••••••

⑬ → ☑ Require password to copy text, images and other content
⑭ ☑ Require password to print document

Password: ••••••••
Verify: ••••••••

(?)   (Cancel)   (OK) ← ⑮

Save

Save As: My_PDF.pdf

Where: 📁 Documents

Title: Can't We All Just Get Along?

Author: Brad Miser

Subject: A suggestion for getting along

Keywords: peace, getting along

(Security Options...)

(Cancel)   (Save) ← ⑯

TIPS

What applications can open a PDF document?

By default, PDF documents open in the Mac OS X Preview application, which provides the basic set of tools you need to view and print them. A number of other applications can open PDF files as well, most notably the free Adobe Acrobat Reader application, available at www.adobe.com. Acrobat Reader offers more features for viewing and working with PDF documents, so if you view a lot of PDFs, try it to see if it works better for you than Preview.

What if I want to configure or change a PDF document?

One of the benefits of PDF documents is that they are hard to change. If you want to change a PDF or to create more sophisticated PDFs with features such as tables of contents, hyperlinks, and combinations of PDF documents in different formats, you can use Adobe Acrobat. This is also available on the Adobe Web site at www.adobe.com.

Keep Apple Software Current

Apple regularly issues updates for its applications to correct problems (hopefully before you experience them). Along with correcting problems, Apple also issues updates to improve its software by adding new features and capabilities.

Mac OS X includes built-in tools to make it simple to keep your Apple software (Mac OS X plus any Apple applications installed on MacBook Air) current. Keeping your software up-to-date is one of the most important things you can do to maintain MacBook Air and to prevent problems.

Keep Apple Software Current

UPDATE APPLE SOFTWARE MANUALLY

① From the **Apple** menu (🍎), choose **Software Update**.

The Software Update application launches, connects to the Internet, and compares the versions of Apple software installed on MacBook Air to the current versions.

Note: *If the current versions of Apple software are already installed, you see a message stating that no new software was found.*

② Select one of the available updates.

③ Read information about that update to understand what it includes.

④ To install an update, check its check box; to prevent an update from being installed, uncheck its check box.

⑤ Click **Install *X Items***, where *X* is the number of updates you have selected to install.

⑥ Type your administrator username (if required).

⑦ Type your password.

⑧ Click **OK**.

MacBook Air downloads and installs the selected updates.

Note: *Some updates require you to restart MacBook Air; click **Restart** at the prompt and skip the rest of these steps.*

When the process is complete, the Software Update window reappears.

● You see a green check mark () next to each update that was installed successfully.

● Updates you did not install do not have next to their names; you can install them by checking the **Install** check box and clicking the **Install** button.

UPDATE APPLE SOFTWARE AUTOMATICALLY

① Open the System Preferences application.

② Click the **Software Update** icon.

③ Click the **Scheduled Check** tab.

④ Check the **Check for updates** check box.

⑤ On the **Check for updates** pop-up menu, choose how frequently you want MacBook Air to check for new software.

For example, choose Weekly to check for updates on a weekly basis.

⑥ If you want important updates to be downloaded automatically, check the **Download important updates automatically** check box.

Note: *If you do not check this check box, you are prompted to download the updates when they are available.*

When the specified amount of time passes, Software Update checks for new software. When it is found, you are prompted to install it.

Should I install all updates to my software?

In general, you should install all updates as they become available. In rare situations, an update actually causes more problems than it solves; however, that is unusual, and in such cases the problematic update is immediately followed by one that corrects these problems. You can simplify the update process by configuring MacBook Air for automatic updates.

How do I know what updates have been installed?

Open the Software Update pane of the System Preferences application. Click the **Installed Updates** tab. A list of all the updates you have installed successfully appears.

Maintain and Update Third-Party Applications

The odds are great that you also have third-party software, such as Microsoft Office or Quicken from Intuit. Like Apple, other software companies also issue updates to their software to fix bugs and add features.

Unfortunately, support for these updates is not built into Mac OS X. Instead, each application provides its own tools to download and install updates. Most of these also support manual and automatic updates. This section show how to update Microsoft Office applications manually and Snapz Pro X from Ambrosia Software automatically; other third-party applications are updated similarly.

Maintain and Update Third-Party Applications

MANUALLY UPDATE A THIRD-PARTY APPLICATION

① After launching the application, choose **Check for Updates** from the **Help** menu.

The application checks for updates either using built-in tools or through a separate update application.

② Download and install the updates using the update application.

MAINTAIN AND UPDATE THIRD-PARTY APPLICATIONS AUTOMATICALLY

① After launching the application, open the application's Preferences tools.

② Select the option to check for updates automatically.

Note: *This command may use different wording for different applications.*

Each time you launch the application, it checks for newer versions. When one is found, you are prompted to download and install it.

Profile
MacBook Air

MacBook Air includes a lot of hardware components and many different kinds of software. Each of these has a specific version and set of capabilities. Most of the time, you do not need to worry about these details. However, there are times when these details can be very important, especially when you are trying to troubleshoot and solve problems.

Keeping a current profile of MacBook Air is a good idea so that you have detailed information about it when you need to solve a problem or evaluate your MacBook Air capabilities (such as if it meets the system requirements for hardware or software you are thinking about adding).

Profile MacBook Air

① From the **Apple** menu ( ), choose **About This Mac**.

● The **About This Mac** window appears.

Here, you see information about the version of Mac OS X you are running, the processor in MacBook Air, and the amount of RAM installed.

Note: Click the version information to switch to other details, such as the build number.

② Click **More Info**.

The System Profiler application appears.

● In the left pane, you see various categories of information about MacBook Air, such as hardware components.

③ Select an area about which you want detailed information.

● The details appear in the right pane of the window.

④ Continue to select items to get details about them.

● Details for the selected item appear in the lower part of the right pane in the window.

You may want to print the profile and store a hard copy for reference.

Monitor MacBook Air Activity

You cannot always tell what is happening with MacBook Air just by looking at its screen or observing how applications are performing. It is useful to be able to identify what is happening with MacBook Air in detail, especially when you are troubleshooting a problem.

With the Activity Monitor application, you can see the status of MacBook Air in a very detailed way. For example, you can see how much processing power specific applications are using, which can often tell you when an application is having a problem.

Monitor MacBook Air Activity

① Open the Utilities folder within the Applications folder (press ⌘ + Shift + U to jump to that folder).

② Double-click the **Activity Monitor** icon.

The Activity Monitor application opens.

③ Click the **CPU** tab.

● In the upper part of the window, you see a list of all the processes running on MacBook Air.

● At the bottom of the window, you see a graphical representation of the activity of various MacBook Air processes.

④ Click the **Disk Activity** tab.

● At the bottom of the window, you see how data is being read from and written to the disk.

⑤ Click the **CPU** column heading to sort the list of processes by amount of processor activity being used for each process.

Note: You can limit the processes shown in the window to be just for applications, which can make the window's information easier to interpret.

⑥ On the pop-up menu at the top of the window, choose **Windowed Processes**.

● The list is reduced so that it includes only processes associated with applications.

⑦ Click the **Disk Usage** tab.

⑧ Select the disk about which you want information on the pop-up menu.

● The information at the bottom of the window shows how much of the disk is being used.

TIPS

What do I do if a process is using a lot of the CPU for a long period of time?

This often indicates that an application is *hung*, meaning that its processes are locked up because it is having a problem. Switch to the application and try to quit it. If it does not quit, then it is hung. Go back to Activity Monitor, select the process, and click the **Quit Process** button. Click **Force Quit**; the process is stopped. Forcing an application to quit loses any unsaved data in it, so make sure the application is really hung before doing this (wait several minutes to be sure that it is not busy working on a task). Save your work in other open applications, and then restart MacBook Air.

How can I get even more detail about a specific process?

Select a process and click the **Inspect** button. The Inspect window opens and you see several tabs providing information about various aspects of the process such as its memory use, statistics about how it is working, and the files and ports it has open. Sometimes this information is useful when doing detailed troubleshooting. For example, you see the number of recent hangs the process has experienced, which can tell you if the process is problematic.

Maintain the MacBook Air Hard or Solid State Drive

If the MacBook Air drive is not performing optimally, MacBook Air is not at its best either.

You can do a lot for the MacBook Air drive by practicing good housekeeping on it to keep as much free space available as possible (see the first tip at the end of this section). If you have an external hard drive, create a second startup disk to use in case something happens to your primary startup disk. You can also use the Mac OS X Disk Utility application to maintain the MacBook Air drive and to solve some problems if they occur.

Maintain the MacBook Air Hard or Solid State Drive

CREATE AN ALTERNATE STARTUP DISK

1 Connect an external hard drive.

2 Insert the Mac OS X installation disk.

The Mac OS X Install DVD window opens.

3 Double-click the **Install Mac OS X** icon.

The Mac OS X installer application starts.

4 Follow the on-screen instructions to install Mac OS X on the external hard disk.

The installer completes the installation and MacBook Air restarts using the new startup disk.

5 Complete the configuration of Mac OS X by following the on-screen instructions. For example, you create a user account on the startup disk just as you did on the MacBook Air startup disk.

CHOOSE A STARTUP DISK

1 Open the System Preferences application and click the **Startup Disk** icon.

The Startup Disk pane appears, showing the available startup disks.

2 Select the startup disk to use.

3 Click **Restart**.

MacBook Air starts up from the disk you selected.

Note: *You can also choose a startup disk by restarting MacBook Air and holding the* Option *key down. When the startup disk icons appear, select the disc you want to use and press the* Return *key.*

MAINTAIN OR REPAIR A MACBOOK AIR DRIVE USING DISK UTILITY

① Open the Disk Utility application located in the Utilities folder within the Applications folder.

② Select the disk you want to maintain or repair, such as the MacBook Air internal disk.

Note: *You cannot repair the current startup disk with Disk Utility; you can only verify it. To repair it, you must start up using a different startup disk and then run Disk Utility to repair the previous startup disk.*

③ Click the **Verify Disk** button.

Note: *If you selected a disk that is not the current startup disk, click* **Repair Disk** *instead of Verify Disk because the verify function is part of the repair process.*

● Disk Utility checks the hard drive, and the progress appears in the window.

If no problems are found, you can skip the rest of these steps.

④ If problems are found, start MacBook Air from an alternate startup disk.

Note: *You can also restart using the Mac OS X DVD as the startup disk. When the installation process starts, choose* **Disk Utility** *from the* **Utilities** *menu. You can the run Disk Utility to repair the startup disk. However, this uses the old version installed on the DVD, and so you are better off creating an alternate startup disk that you can keep current.*

⑤ Repeat Steps **1** and **2**.

⑥ Click **Repair Disk**.

Disk Utility attempts to repair problems it finds. If it is successful, you see a message telling you so. If the problems cannot be fixed, you have to do some more work (more details on this later in this chapter).

TIPS

What are good housekeeping practices for a disk?
When you are done with folders or files, move them off the internal drive. You can do this by deleting them if you are sure you will not need them again, or by archiving them by burning them onto a CD or DVD and then deleting them from the hard drive. You should try to keep your folders and files well organized so that you have a better idea of what you have stored on the disk. You should also make sure that you keep a good backup for all the important files on your internal drive.

Should I have and use a third-party disk maintenance application?
Disk Utility is a capable disk maintenance application, but it certainly cannot repair all problems that can occur on a disk. If Disk Utility is unable to repair a disk, you can purchase a more sophisticated disk maintenance application, such as Tech Tool Pro (mincromat.com). These applications usually include a DVD from which you can start up in order to repair your startup disk.

Back Up with Time Machine and a USB Hard Drive

If something really bad happens to MacBook Air, you can lose all the files it contains. This includes music from the iTunes Store (you have to pay for it again if you want it back) along with other content such as applications you have downloaded. However, what is worse is losing data you create, such as your photos, movies, and documents. Much of this data simply cannot be replaced at any cost.

The way to minimize the risk of losing important data is to back it up. The Mac OS X Time Machine application is designed to make it easy for you to do this so you can recover important files when you need to. All you need is an external hard drive on which to store your backups.

Back Up with Time Machine and a USB Hard Drive

① With an external hard drive connected, open the System Preferences application.

Note: See Chapter 9 for information about connecting MacBook Air to an external hard disk.

② Click the **Time Machine** icon.

The Time Machine pane opens.

③ Drag the slider to the **On** position.

Time Machine activates.

④ Click **Choose Backup Disk**.

The Select Drive sheet appears.

⑤ Select the drive on which you want to store the backed-up information.

⑥ Click **Use for Backup**.

Note: When you use a hard drive for Time Machine, the hard drive's icon becomes the Time Machine icon.

The sheet closes and you return to the Time Machine pane.

● The drive you selected is shown at the top of the pane along with status information about the backup process.

7 Click **Options**.

Time Machine

Name: Back Up Disk
Available: 232.5 GB of 232.6 GB
Oldest Backup: --
Latest Backup: --
Next Backup: 88 seconds...

Change Disk...
Options...

Time Machine

OFF [ ] ON

Time Machine keeps
• Hourly backups for the past 24 hours
• Daily backups for the past month
• Weekly backups until your backup disk is full

☑ Show Time Machine status in the menu bar

Click the lock to prevent further changes.

The Do not back up sheet appears, where you can exclude files from the backup process. This is useful because you can exclude files that do not need to be backed up to make your backups smaller.

8 Click the **Add** button (➕).

Do not back up:

Back Up Disk   107.7 MB

Total Included: 51.4 GB

+ −

☑ Warn when old backups are deleted

Cancel   Done

TIPS

Why would I exclude files from my backups?

Backing up files requires disk space, just as storing them does. The more and larger files you back up, the more room each backup consumes on your backup disk, resulting in fewer backups being stored. This lessens the amount of time you can move "back in time" to restore files from the backup. By excluding files, you make your backups smaller, which means you can go further back in time to restore files. You have to trade off the total amount of data you back up versus the number of backups you want to maintain.

What kind of files should I exclude from backups?

Files that you have stored on a disc are ideal candidates for exclusion, as are files you did not create or will not need in the future. For example, you should have Mac OS X on a DVD, and so you can exclude the Mac OS X files from the backups. Should something happen to the Mac OS, you can re-install it from the DVD (you have to reconfigure and update it, too). Likewise, if you have applications on a disc, you do not need to back up the Applications folder, which can save a lot of space on the backup disk.

continued

Many Mac users do not create a backup system, even though it is very easy to do with Time Machine, and after a few minutes of setup time, backing up is automatic. If you do not back up your files, you will eventually lose data. It is not a question of "If," but "When."

At some point, you will lose files that you either have to pay to get again (iTunes Store content) or cannot recreate at all (your iPhoto collection). With a backup system in place, recovering these files is a simple exercise. Without one, it might be impossible.

Back Up with Time Machine and a USB Hard Drive *(continued)*

The select sheet appears.

⑨ Navigate to and select the folders or files you want to exclude from the backup.

⑩ Click **Exclude**.

⑪ If you selected system files, click **Exclude System Folder Only** to exclude only files in the System folder, or click **Exclude All System Files** to exclude system files no matter where they are stored.

Note: *Exclude All System Files is usually the better option.*

● You return to the Exclude sheet and see the files you have excluded from the backup.

⑫ Click **Done**.

Do not back up:

💾 Back Up Disk	107.7 MB
📁 Applications	2.9 GB
📁 Developer	0 KB
📁 Library	6.6 GB
📁 System Files and Applications	Calculating Size

＋ －　　　　　　　Total Included: Calculating Size

☑ Warn when old backups are deleted

(?)　　　　　　　　　(Cancel)　(Done)　⑫

You return to the Time Machine pane, and Time Machine starts a countdown to the backup process. When the timer reaches zero, the backup process starts.

● You see status information about your backups in the pane, such as the time and date of the most current backup.

Time Machine automatically backs up your data every hour.

Note: *After you disconnect the external hard drive so you can move MacBook Air around, the next time you reconnect the external hard drive, the next backup is made. You should connect the backup drive frequently to ensure your backups are current.*

Time Machine

◄ ► Show All

Time Machine

OFF ▭ ON

→ Name: Valiant

Available: 52.6 GB of 465.8 GB

Oldest Backup: April 16, 2008

(Change Disk...)　Latest Backup: Today, 10:42 AM

(Options...)　Next Backup: Today, 11:42 AM

Time Machine keeps
• Hourly backups for the past 24 hours
• Daily backups for the past month
• Weekly backups until your backup disk is full

☑ Show Time Machine status in the menu bar

🔒 Click the lock to prevent further changes.　(?)

TIPS

How long is my data protected?
Time Machine backs up your data for as long as it can until the backup hard drive is full. It stores hourly backups for the past 24 hours. It stores daily backups for the past month. It stores monthly backups until the backup disk is full. To protect yourself as long as possible, use the largest hard drive you can afford, and exclude files that you do not need to back up (such as System files if you have the Mac OS X installation disc) to save space on the backup drive.

How else should I protect my data?
Hard disks can fail, and no matter how large your backup drive is, it fills up at some point and you will not be able to back up all the files you might need. You should also back up important files in a second way, such as to DVD. You can do this by burning files to a disc from the Finder (see Chapter 9) and from within some applications (such as iTunes, from which you can back up your iTunes Library onto disc).

Back Up Wirelessly with a Time Capsule

The Apple Time Capsule device combines an AirPort Extreme Base Station with a hard drive. This makes wireless backups simple because the Time Capsule provides the wireless network you use so that any computer on the network can also access the Time Capsule's hard drive to back up data.

To start backing up wirelessly, install a Time Capsule on your network. Then, configure Time Machine on MacBook Air to back up to it.

INSTALL AND CONFIGURE A TIME CAPSULE

1 Install a Time Capsule on your network.

Note: See Chapter 7 for details on Time Capsule.

Note: If you already use an AirPort Extreme Base Station as the primary hub for your network, replace it with the Time Capsule and use the WDS capability to connect the two base stations.

2 Open a Finder window.

3 If necessary, expand the Shared section.

   Time Capsule appears as a shared hard drive.

4 Select the Time Capsule.

5 Click **Connect As**.

   The Connect dialog appears.

6 Type the Time Capsule's password.

7 Check the **Remember this password in my keychain** check box.

8 Click **Connect**.

● The status changes to Connected and you see a folder on the Time Capsule.

   You are ready to back up to the Time Capsule.

BACK UP TO A TIME CAPSULE

Note: *Because backups typically involve a lot of data and even fast wireless networks are relatively slow, the first time you back up will require a long time during which the performance of your network will slow. When you configure Time Machine, choose a time during which other network activity is low.*

1 Open the System Preferences application.

2 Click the **Time Machine** icon.

3 Drag the slider to the **On** position.

The Select Drive sheet appears.

4 Select the Time Capsule.

5 Click **Use for Backup**.

6 Type the Time Capsule's password.

7 Click **Connect**.

You return to the Time Machine pane and the Time Capsule is shown as the backup disk.

8 Click **Options**.

The Do not back up sheet appears.

9 Use the Do not back up sheet to exclude files from backups.

Note: *For more details, see Steps 8 to 12 in the section "Back Up with Time Machine and a USB Hard Drive."*

10 Click **Done**.

You return to the Time Machine and a countdown to the backup process starts. When the timer reaches zero, the backup process starts.

Time Machine automatically backs up your data every hour.

TIPS

Can I back up wirelessly to my iDisk?

If you can access the Internet wirelessly, you can always copy files to your iDisk to back them up. This is ideal because the backups are stored on the Apple Web site, which makes them very secure, keeping them isolated from the locations in which you use MacBook Air. To back up files to your iDisk, simply copy them there. For better results, use a backup application to automate the process. If you are going to back up a lot of data, you probably need to increase the size of your iDisk.

What other backup applications should I use?

If you have a MobileMe account, you can download and use the Apple Backup application. This application enables you to create more complex backup strategies and also enables you to schedule your backups. You can also use a variety of backup storage locations, including a hard drive, DVD/CD, and your iDisk. To try using Backup, move to the Member Central area when you log in to your MobileMe account.

Restore Files with Time Machine

If you have used Time Machine to keep MacBook Air backed up, losing data from MacBook Air is not a big deal. (If you do not have your data backed up, it can be a very, very big deal.) You can use Time Machine to restore files that are included in your backups. You can restore files and folders from the Finder and you can recover individual items from within some applications (such as photos from within iPhoto).

Even if you have not actually lost files, you should try restoring files regularly to make sure your backup system is working correctly.

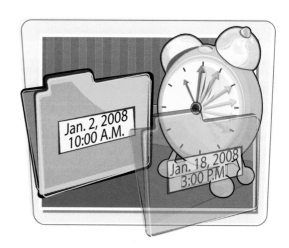

Restore Files with Time Machine

RESTORE FILES IN THE FINDER

1. Open a Finder window showing the location where the files you want to recover were stored.

2. Launch the Time Machine application by clicking its icon (◉) on the Dock, or by double-clicking its icon in the Applications folder.

   The desktop disappears and the Time Machine window fills the entire space.

● The Finder window that you opened in Step 1 appears in the center of the screen. Behind it, you see all the versions of that window that are stored in your backup from the current version as far back in time as the backups go.

● Along the right side of the window, you see the timeline for your backups.

● The Time Machine controls appear at the bottom.

● The time of the front-most window appears in the center at the bottom.

3. Click the date and time on the timeline when the version of the files you need were available.

   The date and time of the backup you select are shown in the center of the Time Machine toolbar.

4. When you reach the files or folders you want to restore, select them.

5. Click **Restore**.

   The files and folders you selected are returned to their prior locations.

RESTORE FILES IN APPLICATIONS

① Open the application containing the files you want to recover.

② Launch the Time Machine application by clicking its icon (⊙) on the Dock, or by double-clicking its icon in the Applications folder.

The desktop disappears and the Time Machine window fills the entire space.

● Versions of the application window appear in the Time Machine, with the most current version being front-most. Previous versions extend back in time.

③ Click the date and time on the timeline when the version of the files you need were available.

The date and time of the backup you select are shown in the center of the Time Machine toolbar.

As you go back in time, you see the versions of the application window that are saved in the backup.

④ When you get to the files you want to restore, select them.

⑤ Click **Restore**.

Note: To restore all of the files in the front-most window, click Restore All.

The files are returned to the application and you can use them as if they had never been lost.

What other ways can I use to move back in time in Time Machine?

In addition to using the timeline to move back in time, you can also click the windows behind the front-most window; each time you click a window, it moves to the front and becomes the active window. You can also click the large backward and forward arrows in the lower-right corner of the Time Machine window to move back or ahead in time, respectively.

What if an application I use does not support Time Machine? Can I still restore files for it?

Not all applications support Time Machine; currently only some Apple applications support the ability to back up and restore individual files within an application. Hopefully, more applications will support this technology over time. However, you can always use Time Machine to restore files being managed in an application by including them in the backups you create and then restoring the individual files from the Finder. This is not as easy as using a supported application such as iPhoto or iTunes, but it works well.

Troubleshoot and Solve MacBook Air Problems

Once in a while, MacBook Air is not going to cooperate with you. You might experience applications that hang (they stop doing anything while displaying the spinning color wheel icon) or quit unexpectedly; or, something odd might happen and you cannot quite identify it. In the most extreme case, you might not be able to get MacBook Air to start up at all.

The first step in solving any problem is understanding when and how it happens. Part of this is determining if the problem is general or related to a specific user account. Once you have some idea of how and when the problem occurs, you can try to solve it.

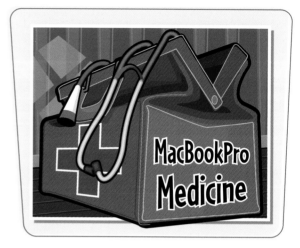

Troubleshoot and Solve MacBook Air Problems

FIND THE CAUSE

Note: *Restarting MacBook Air solves many problems you might experience. Because restarting is easy to do, it should always be one of the first things you try. Except for a minute or two of your time, there is no downside to restarting.*

1️⃣ Restart MacBook Air by choosing **Restart** from the **Apple** menu (🍎).

Note: *If MacBook Air does not respond to any commands or keys, press and hold the **Power** button until MacBook Air shuts off. Press the **Power** button again to restart it. This causes all unsaved data to be lost, so let MacBook Air sit in the "hung" state for a while to make sure you need to restart before you actually do it.*

2️⃣ Try to replicate the problem by doing the same things you did when it first occurred.

3️⃣ If you cannot cause the problem to happen again, assume it was solved by the restart, and you can continue working.

4️⃣ If you can cause the problem to happen again, use Activity Monitor to see if any applications or processes appear to be consuming large amounts of resources (such as more than 90 percent of CPU activity). (To learn about Activity Monitor, see "Monitor MacBook Air Activity," earlier in this chapter.) If they are, you have found a likely source of the problem.

5️⃣ Use Activity Monitor to check if the hard drive is too full.

If the drive is close to being full, it can be a cause of problems. You need to remove files to make more space available on the drive.

⑥ To see if your problem might have to do with newly installed software, generate a MacBook Air profile. (To learn how, see "Profile MacBook Air," earlier in this chapter.)

Note: *A MacBook Air profile includes such information as all the applications you have installed.*

⑦ Look for any applications you installed just before you started having problems.

The detailed information you collected should give you an idea of the cause of the problem.

DETERMINE IF A PROBLEM IS SYSTEMWIDE OR USER-SPECIFIC

① Log in to your troubleshooting user account.

Note: *You should create a troubleshooting user account that you only use when you are trying to isolate and solve problems. See Chapter 6 for more details.*

② Try to replicate the problem under the new account.

If you can repeat the problem, it is systemic rather than being specific to a user account.

If you cannot repeat the problem, it is likely related to an issue with your user account. In most cases, the issue is related to a preference file that has been corrupted.

What are the most important things I can do to protect myself from MacBook Air problems?
Back up your data. You should always have current backups of your data because losing data is the most severe consequence of any MacBook Air problem you might encounter. Losing data is not just something that might happen to you; it will happen to you at some point. Second to keeping good backups of data, is maintaining an alternate startup drive. If something happens to the system software on MacBook Air, you can restart from the alternate hard drive and get back to work, not to mention having a much better chance of fixing the problem. Third, keep your Mac OS X software installation disc available. If you need to restore your MacBook Air system software, you need this disc.

When it comes to effective troubleshooting and problem solving, a cool, calm state is your best friend. Unfortunately, problems tend to be very frustrating, especially when you are working under a deadline. Stress and frustration can lead to being unable to take the time and logical approach to problem solving that will get solutions more quickly. And, an emotional state can lead to rash actions that can make problems worse.

Sometimes, the most important step in troubleshooting is taking a break. Getting away from a problem for a while can clear your head and make a solution come much more quickly than just continuing to work through it.

Troubleshoot and Solve MacBook Air Problems *(continued)*

③ Navigate to your Home folder.

④ Open the **Library** folder.

⑤ Open the **Preferences** folder.

⑥ Delete the preferences files for the application you are having trouble with.

Note: The application's name is part of the preference's filename.

⑦ Try to replicate the problem. If you cannot repeat it, you have likely solved the problem.

If you can replicate the problem, continue to the next steps.

SOLVE THE "HUNG APPLICATION" PROBLEM

① Identify the application that is hung.

Note: You can recognize a hung application by the spinning color wheel icon appearing on the screen for a long period of time.

② Press ⌘ + Option + Esc.

③ In the Force Quit Applications window, select the hung application.

Note: A hung application's name appears in red in the Force Quit window and the text "(Not Responding)" appears next to it.

④ Click **Force Quit**.

Note: If the Finder is hung, when you select it, the button becomes Relaunch, which attempts to restart the Finder.

⑤ At the prompt, click **Force Quit**.

The application is forced to shut down.

6 Restart MacBook Air.

If the application works normally, the problem is solved. If the application continues to hang, you should update it.

Note: See the sections "Keep Apple Software Current" and "Maintain and Update Third-Party Applications."

If the update solves the problem, you are done. If not, get help for the problem.

SOLVE THE "MACBOOK AIR WILL NOT START UP" PROBLEM

1 Make sure MacBook Air is either connected to power or has a full battery.

2 Connect the alternate startup disk.

Note: See the section "Create an Alternate Startup Disk."

*Note: If MacBook Air has begun the startup process, but does not complete it, press and hold the **Power** button until it shuts down.*

3 Press the **Power** button.

4 Press and hold the Option key.

After a few moments, the valid startup disks are shown.

5 Select the alternate startup disk.

● MacBook Air starts up from the selected disk.

If MacBook Air starts up, you know the problem is probably with the system software installed on the primary startup disk. Reinstall the system software on the primary startup disk.

6 Insert the Mac OS X installation disc.

7 Launch the Install Mac OS X application.

8 Follow the on-screen steps to reinstall or repair the system software on the primary startup disk.

Note: If you do not have an alternate startup disk, you can start up from the Mac OS X installation disc by inserting it, restarting MacBook Air, and holding down the C key. MacBook Air restarts in the Mac OS X Installation application.

There are a lot more problems possible than just these two specific ones. Why have you listed only these two?
Many different problems are possible, but you are likely to experience only a few. There is really no way to provide a comprehensive list of problems in a short section like this one. If you can understand how to describe a problem and know where to go for help (see the last section in this chapter), then you will be able to solve most problems you encounter.

I thought Mac OS X was supposed to be reliable and stable. Why should I have to worry about this?
Most experts agree that Mac OS X is the most reliable and stable operating system there is, and you are not likely to have very many problems (especially when compared to that "other" operating system). However, a MacBook Air is a complex system of hardware and software with many permutations depending on the specific applications you install and how you use them. It is inevitable that problems occur once in a while. Fortunately, most are readily solved with the steps in this section.

Capture a Screenshot

When you experience a problem, capturing a screenshot is a great way to describe and document the problem for yourself. It is even more useful when you ask for help because you can give the screenshots to the person from whom you are asking help.

There are two built-in ways to capture a screenshot under Mac OS X. You can use keyboard shortcuts, or for more sophisticated shots, you can use the Grab application.

Capture a Screenshot

CAPTURE A SCREENSHOT WITH A KEYBOARD SHORTCUT

1 Open the window that you want to capture.

2 To capture the entire desktop, press
⌘+Shift+3.

An image file is created on the desktop.

3 To capture a portion of the screen, press
⌘+Shift+4.

4 Drag over the area of the screen you want to capture; release the trackpad button when the area you want to capture is highlighted.

An image file is created on the desktop.

5 Open the image file you created; it is named Picture *Z*, where *Z* is a sequential number.

The file opens in Preview.

CAPTURE A TIMED SCREENSHOT WITH GRAB

1 Open the Grab application (within the Utilities folder in the Applications folder).

When you launch Grab, its menu appears, but it does not have any windows until you take a screenshot.

2 Open the window that you want to capture.

3 Switch back into Grab.

4 On the **Capture** menu, choose **Timed Screen**.

5 In the Timed Screen Grab dialog, click **Start Timer**.

You have 10 seconds until the screen is captured; the timer in the dialog counts down.

6 While the countdown is ongoing, get the screen as you want it to be captured.

When the timer ends, the screenshot is taken and opens in Grab.

Get Help with MacBook Air Problems

One of the most important troubleshooting skills is to be able to ask for help in the right places and in the right way. Many problems you encounter have been experienced and solved by someone else already.

Get Help with MacBook Air Problems

① If the problem is related to Apple hardware or software, visit www.apple.com/support.

② Search for the issue you are having.

③ Browse the information on the Search Results page to locate the problem and its solution.

Note: *If you purchased AppleCare, you can use that technical support service. See your documentation for contact information.*

④ If you do not find what you need, go to www.google.com.

⑤ Search for the problem you are experiencing.

⑥ Browse the results of the search to find the information you need.

Note: *If you live near an Apple retail store, call or visit Apple's Web site for an appointment at the Genius bar. You can often get excellent technical support for no cost if the problem can be solved in the store.*

PART

V

Having Fun

One of the great things about MacBook Air is that it comes with some amazing applications, especially those in the iLife Suite. Two of the best of these applications are iTunes and iPhoto. iTunes is a very powerful application for digital audio and video, and, of course, it is the companion software for iPods and iPhones. iPhoto is an excellent application for storing, organizing, and being creative with your digital photos. These applications make having a MacBook Air a lot of fun.

iTunes enables you to organize and enjoy a lot of content right on MacBook Air, an iPod, or an iPhone. With iTunes' integration to the iTunes Store, it is easy to add great audio and video to your iTunes Library whenever you want.

Although it is incredibly powerful, iTunes is also very well designed so that it is easy to use. In fact, the application is so well designed that a number of its interface elements have been adopted in other applications, including the Mac OS X Finder.

● **Source pane**

Shows all the sources of content available to you

● **Library**

Stores and organizes all the content you manage in iTunes

● **Categories**

The types of content included in your library

● **Cover Flow view**

Shows content in the selected source as album covers that you can flip through

● **View buttons**

Use these to change views

● **Search tool**

Enables you to search the selected source

● **Source information**

Shows information about the source you have selected, including how long the content will play and how much disk space it consumes

● **Content pane**

Shows detailed information about the content of the selected source

● **Artwork/Video viewer**

Shows album art when you listen to audio, or video when you play video content

● **List view**

Presents content in the selected source in a list

● **Browser**

Enables you to browse the selected source quickly and easily

● **Playback controls**

Use these to control audio and video content

● **Information window**

Displays information about what you are doing

● **Album view**

Shows content in the selected source, organized by group

● **Column headings**

Identifies information about content; you can organize the columns.

● **Eject**

Click to eject something, such as an iPod or audio CD

● **Show/Hide Browser**

Shows or hides the Browser

● **Output source**

Enables you to choose where you want iTunes output to play, such as on MacBook Air or on speakers attached to an AirPort Express Base Station

● **Show/Hide Artwork/ Video Viewer**

Opens or closes the Artwork/ Video Viewer window

● **Repeat**

Causes content in the selected source to repeat

● **Shuffle**

When active, iTunes randomly chooses content in the selected source to play

● **Create playlist**

Enables you to create playlists and smart playlists

Understand the iTunes Library

Before you can enjoy content in iTunes, it has to be available there. The iTunes Library is where you store all of your audio and video content, including music, podcasts, movies, and TV shows. Once content is stored in your iTunes Library, you can use iTunes tools to keep that content organized so that it is easily accessible to you.

Categories

The content in your Library is organized automatically by categories, including Music, Movies, TV Shows, and Podcasts. Within the Library source, you see an icon for each category. When you select a category, the content it includes is shown in the right part of the iTunes window where you browse and search it. When you find the content you want, you can listen to it, view it, create playlists, or burn it to disc.

Devices

iTunes considers sources of content stored outside of its database to be devices. If you use an iPod or iPhone with iTunes, they appear in the Devices section when connected to MacBook Air. Devices also include audio CDs. Like other sources, you select a device to work with it. For example, to configure an iPod's content, you select its icon and its settings tools appear in the right part of the window.

Tracks

Although it is easy to think of tracks as the songs on a CD, iTunes considers everything that you listen to or watch to be a track. So, each episode in a season of a TV series you download from the iTunes Store is a track, as is each section of an audiobook. Tracks are what you see in each row in the Content pane.

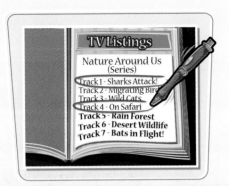

Tags

A lot of information is associated with the content in the iTunes Library. This includes artist, track name, track number, album, genre, and rating. Each of these data elements is called a tag. Each tag can be shown in a column in the Content pane, and you can view all of the tags for a track in the Info window. Tags are important because they are how you identify and organize content. Fortunately, iTunes automatically tags most of the content you will work with, but you can add or change tags yourself when you need to.

Playlists

One of the best things about iTunes is that you can create custom collections of content you want to listen to or watch. These collections are called playlists. Playlists can include any combination of content organized in any way. There are two kinds of playlists. You manually place content into a playlist, or when you create a smart playlist, you define criteria for content and iTunes automatically places the appropriate content into it. After you have created a playlist, you can listen to it, burn it to disc, or move it to an iPod or iPhone.

The iTunes Way

Although iTunes enables you to work with a lot of different kinds of content (such as music, audiobooks, movies, and music videos), it uses a consistent process to work with any kind of content. First, select the source of the content you want to work with; this can be a Library category, device, or playlist. Second, browse or search for content you want within the selected source if it is not ready for you immediately. Third, select the specific track you want to use. Fourth, use iTunes controls to play the content. This process is consistent, no matter what kind of content you want to use, and so once you get used to it, you can quickly enjoy any content you want.

Browse or Search for iTunes Content

Before you can enjoy audio or video content, you need to find that content so that you can select it. There are two ways to find content: by browsing or by searching.

Browsing is a good way to find something when you are not quite sure what you want to listen to or watch. Searching is useful when you know exactly what you want, but are not quite sure where it is.

Browse or Search for iTunes Content

BROWSE FOR ITUNES CONTENT

Note: The iTunes window has several views; this section assumes that you are using the List view.

① In the Source pane, select the source of content you want to browse, such as **Music**.

*Note: If the Browser does not appear, click **View** and then click **Show Browser**.*

② Browse the list of genres in the Genre column.

③ In the Genre column, select the genre you want to browse.

④ Browse the artist list, which shows only those artists with music in the selected genre.

⑤ Select the artist whose music you want to browse.

● All the albums by that artist in the Library are shown in the Album column.

⑥ Select the album you want to browse.

The tracks on that album appear in the Content pane.

⑦ Select the track you want to hear.

⑧ Use the playback controls to play the track.

Note: You can double-click a track to play it.

SEARCH FOR ITUNES CONTENT

1 In the Source pane, select the source of content you want to search, such as **TV Shows**.

2 Type the text or numbers for which you want to search in the Search tool.

● As you type, only content that meets your search criterion appears in the Content pane.

3 Continue typing until the content for which you are searching appears in the Content pane.

4 Select the content you want to listen to or watch.

5 Use the playback controls to play the content.

 TIPS

I do not see the Genre column in the Browser. Where did it go?

You can use the Browser with or without the Genre column. If it is not shown, click **iTunes**, and then choose **Preferences**. Click the **General** tab. Check the **Show genre when browsing** check box. Click **OK**.

Why does the Browser disappear when I select some sources?

The Browser is not all that useful for some sources, such as an Audio CD, because you can usually see all of the content on the source in the Content pane. When you select such a source, the Browser is hidden. You can show it again by clicking the **Show Browser** button at the bottom of the iTunes window.

Browse the Library with Cover Flow View

The List view is very functional and efficient, but it is not all that pretty, nor is it that exciting to browse.

The Cover Flow view makes browsing for music like flipping through a stack of CDs (only easier). You view content by its cover art, and you can flip through the content available to you until you see something that you like.

Browse the Library with the Cover Flow View

① Select the source you want to browse, such as **Music**.

② Click the **Cover Flow View** button (▥▥).

③ To change the size of the Cover Flow pane, drag the resize handle up or down.

④ To move through the content quickly, drag the scroll bar to the left or right.

Note: You can also click album covers to jump to specific collections.

As you drag, the covers flip quickly.

● The content in the collection that is directly facing you appears on the content list, where you can listen to or watch it.

⑤ To browse in full-screen mode, click the **Full Screen** button.

The Cover Flow pane fills the desktop.

⑥ Browse the content by using the scroll bar or clicking to the left or right of the artwork facing you.

⑦ Control the content with the playback controls.

⑧ To return to the iTunes window, click the **Full Screen** button.

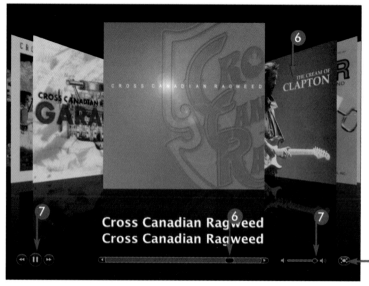

Browse the Library with Group View

The Group view is sort of a combination of the List and Cover Flow views.

You can see the Browser and lists as in the List view, but the content is organized by collection and you see associated artwork as in the Cover Flow view.

Browse the Library with Group View

① Select the source you want to browse, such as **Music**.

② Click the **Group View** button (▤).

③ Open the Browser if it is not open already.

● The Browser appears at the top of the window.

● In the Content pane, you see the content in the source selected in the Browser grouped by collection, which can be a CD, a season of episodes for a TV show, or other grouping. The collection's artwork is shown on the left side of the pane.

● Within each collection, you see the content organized in a list.

④ Click the tag by which you want the collections to be sorted.

For example, to sort the groups by album, click the **Album** column, or to sort the groups by artist, click the **Artist** column.

● The content is rearranged so that the groups are sorted by the tag you selected.

⑤ Use the Browser to find the specific content in which you are interested.

Listen to Audio Content

If you have used any device to listen to audio content, you should be able to quickly listen to audio content in iTunes.

Of course, whereas most audio players give you just basic controls, iTunes really lets you fine-tune your audio experience by choosing exactly how you want to listen.

Listen to Audio Content

1 Browse or search for the audio content you want to hear.

2 Select the first track you want to hear.

3 Click the **Play** button (▶), double-click the track, or press the Spacebar.

The audio content begins to play.

● In the Information window, you see information about what is playing, such as the track name, artist, and a timeline.

● The track currently playing is highlighted and marked with a blue speaker icon (🔊).

The audio continues to play through each track in the selected source in the order they are shown in the pane (from top to bottom) until the last track plays or you stop playing (unless you have the repeat function turned on, in which case, the content repeats).

4 Click the **Pause** button (⏸ changes to ▶) or press the Spacebar to pause the audio.

5 Click the **Previous** button (⏮) to jump back to the previous track.

6 Click the **Next** button (⏭) to jump to the next track.

Note: You can also jump to the previous or next track by pressing the ← or → keys.

Watch Video Content

iTunes works as well for video content as it does for audio content. You can watch movies, TV shows, music videos, and video podcasts within the iTunes window or in full-screen mode.

Watching video content works according to the iTunes pattern: Find the content you want to view, select it, and use the iTunes controls to play the content.

Watch Video Content

① Browse or search for the video content you want to watch.

② Select the first video track you want to see.

③ Click the **Play** button (▶) or press the `Spacebar`.

Note: By default, iTunes remembers where you were in video content the last time you played it. So, if you stop video playback, when you return to the same content, you pick up right where you left off.

● The content fills the iTunes window and begins to play.

④ Position the mouse pointer over the video image.

● The video controls appear. You can watch the video in the iTunes window or you can expand it to full screen.

Note: To return to the iTunes window, click the **Close** button (⊗).

⑤ To expand the video to full screen, click the full screen button.

The video fills the desktop.

⑥ To expose video controls, move the pointer.

Video controls appear on the screen that you can use to control playback or return to the iTunes window.

Copy iTunes Content from Other Computers onto MacBook Air

If you have another computer with iTunes content on it, you can copy that content onto MacBook Air to build up your iTunes Library. This is a fast and simple way to fill your iTunes Library with a lot of audio and video that you can enjoy while you are on the move.

There are two steps to this process. The first is to use file sharing to copy the iTunes content from the source computer onto MacBook Air. The second is to add the content to the iTunes Library.

Copy iTunes Content from Other Computers onto MacBook Air

COPY ITUNES CONTENT FROM ANOTHER COMPUTER

Note: *For information about configuring and using the File Sharing feature, see Chapter 7.*

1. Configure file sharing on the source computer.

2. Log on to the source computer from MacBook Air using an account that has access permissions to the iTunes folder containing the music you want to move onto MacBook Air.

3. On the source computer, navigate to the user account's Home folder in which the music you want to move is stored (**Home**, **Music**, **iTunes**, and **iTunes Music**.

4. Open a second Finder window showing the iTunes Music folder within the iTunes folder that is within the Music folder in your Home folder on MacBook Air.

5. Drag the content you want to copy from the folder on the iTunes Music folder on the source computer to the iTunes Music folder on MacBook Air.

ADD NEW CONTENT TO THE ITUNES LIBRARY

6. In iTunes, open the **File** menu and choose **Add to Library**.

   The Add To Library dialog appears.

7. Move to the iTunes Music folder located in the iTunes folder within the Music folder in your Home folder.

8. Select the content you copied from the source computer.

9. Click **Open**.

   The content you selected is added to your iTunes Library.

If you have an iPod that has content you have purchased from the iTunes Store, you can move that content from the iPod to MacBook Air. This makes it simple to build up your iTunes Library with content that already exists on your iPod.

In order to transfer purchased content from an iPod, MacBook Air must be authorized to play that content under the same account as it was purchased under.

Copy Purchased iTunes Content from an iPod onto MacBook Air

AUTHORIZE MACBOOK AIR

① On the **Store** menu, choose **Authorize Computer**.

The Authorize Computer dialog appears.

② Type the iTunes Store account under which the content that you want to move onto MacBook Air was purchased.

③ Type the account's password.

④ Click **Authorize**.

iTunes connects with the iTunes Store. As long as there are not already five or more other computers authorized for the account, MacBook Air is authorized for the content purchased under the account.

TRANSFER CONTENT FROM AN IPOD TO MACBOOK AIR

① Connect the iPod to MacBook Air.

After a moment, the iPod appears in the Source pane. If the iPod has been synchronized with another computer, you see a dialog enabling you to choose to transfer purchases from the iPod.

② Click **Transfer Purchases**.

iTunes searches the iPod for content purchased under the account for which you authorized MacBook Air. Any content it finds is copied to the iTunes Library on MacBook Air.

Add Audio CD Content to the iTunes Library

If you have a MacBook Air SuperDrive, one of the most useful ways to add content to iTunes is to import music from audio CDs. Once imported, this music becomes part of your iTunes Library and you can listen to it, add it to playlists, and put it on custom CDs you burn.

First, you need to do a one-time configuration of iTunes to import audio. Then you can import CDs to build up your iTunes Library.

Add Audio CD Content to the iTunes Library

PREPARE ITUNES TO IMPORT AUDIO CDS

Note: To import CDs, you need to first connect the MacBook Air SuperDrive. See Chapter 9 for details.

① Click **iTunes** and then click **Preferences**.

The Preferences dialog appears.

② Click the **Advanced** tab.

③ Click the **Importing** subtab.

④ From the **On CD Insert** pop-up menu, choose **Import CD and Eject**.

⑤ On the Import Using pop-up menu, choose **AAC Encoder**.

⑥ On the Setting pop-up menu, choose **Higher Quality**.

⑦ Check the **Automatically retrieve CD track names from Internet** check box.

⑧ Check the **Create file names with track number** check box.

⑨ Click **OK**.

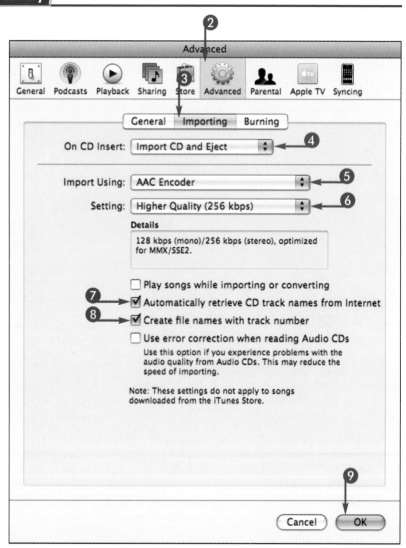

IMPORT AUDIO CDS TO THE ITUNES LIBRARY

① Insert a CD into the SuperDrive.

● iTunes connects to the Internet and identifies the CD you inserted.

The import process starts.

● The song currently being imported is marked with an orange circle ().

● You see information about the import process in the Information window.

● As songs are imported, they are marked with a green circle and check mark ().

When all the tracks on the disc have been imported, iTunes ejects the disc.

The tracks on the CD are now part of the iTunes Library.

 TIPS

How does iTunes recognize an audio CD?

When you insert an audio CD, iTunes connects to the Internet and looks up the CD in online CD databases. When it finds the CD, iTunes adds tags for the album including name, artist, and track titles. iTunes remembers CDs so that the next time you insert them; the information iTunes looked up is there automatically. For this to work, MacBook Air has to be able to connect to the Internet. If it cannot, new CDs show up as unknown with track titles such as Track 1 and Track 2.

iTunes supports many different types of formats when importing music. Should I use something other than AAC?

Although iTunes does support a number of audio formats, AAC (Advanced Audio Coding) is the best option for most people because AAC files provide good sound quality in relatively small file sizes. That is a good thing because you can store more content in your iTunes Library. If you demand the absolute highest audio quality, you can use the Apple Lossless format, which produces significantly larger files with slightly better sound quality. If you have a portable player other than an iPod, you might want to use the MP3 (Motion Picture Expert Group, Audio Layer 3) format, which is supported by all devices.

Explore the iTunes Store

Adding content you already have to the iTunes Library is easy. You can build your iTunes Library using content stored on another computer, an iPod, or audio CDs that you own. However, there is a better way. The Apple iTunes Store provides thousands of audio CDs, movies, TV shows, audiobooks, podcasts, and other content that you browse, preview, and purchase. As soon as you buy content from the iTunes Store, it is downloaded to your iTunes Library and is immediately ready for you to use. Because access to the iTunes Store is built into iTunes, shopping for audio and video could not be easier.

iTunes Store homepage

Links take you directly to specific content as well as to categories

Albums

Album covers and titles are links to those albums

Categories

Click these links to see the homepages for categories of content

Top lists

There are many kinds of lists in the iTunes Store, such as Top Movies and Top Albums

New Releases

This area shows content that is new to the iTunes Store

Page buttons and arrows

Use the page buttons and arrows to move among pages of content in a specific section

Content page

Displays information about a specific item

Buy button

You can buy an item by clicking its Buy button

Related links

Various links take you to related information

Tracks

The contents of the current item are shown in the bottom of the window

Buy buttons

You can use a track's Buy button to buy only that track

Artist links

Click these links to visit the artist's homepage

Path

Shows your current location in the store

Obtain and Log in to an iTunes Store Account

To be able to purchase content from the iTunes Store, you need to have an iTunes account and be logged in to it (you can browse, search, and preview content without being logged in to an account).

Like other aspects of the iTunes Store, you can get an account from within iTunes.

Obtain and Log in to an iTunes Store Account

① Click **iTunes Store** on the Source list.

iTunes connects to the iTunes Store and you see the Home page.

② Click **Sign In**.

The Sign In dialog appears.

③ Click **Create New Account**.

The Welcome to iTunes Store screen appears.

④ Follow the on-screen instructions to create your account.

When you have created your account, you will have an Apple ID and password. This enables you to log into your account on the iTunes Store and purchase content from it.

Sign In to download music from the iTunes Store
To create an Apple Account, click Create New Account.

③ → (Create New Account)

If you have an Apple Account (from the iTunes Store or .Mac, for example), enter your Apple ID and password. Otherwise, if you are an AOL member, enter your AOL screen name and password.

Apple ID:

Example: steve@mac.com

Password:

(Forgot Password?)

○ **AOL**

(Cancel) (Sign In)

Buy Music, TV, Movies, and More from the iTunes Store

The iTunes Store has a lot of great content that you can easily preview, purchase, and download to MacBook Air, where it is added to your iTunes Library automatically. When you are interested in content, you can preview 30 seconds of it to decide if you want it or not.

There are two ways to shop in the iTunes Store. Using the 1-Click method, you can purchase content with a single click. Using the Shopping Cart method, you place content in a shopping cart; when you are ready to buy, you go to your shopping cart and purchase the content you want to obtain.

Buy Music, TV, Movies, and More from the iTunes Store

CONFIGURE YOUR SHOPPING PREFERENCE

① Press ⌘+⎵.

The iTunes Preferences dialog appears.

② Click the **Store** tab.

③ Click the **Buy using a Shopping Cart** radio button.

④ Check the **Automatically download prepurchased content** check box if you intend to buy content before it is released and want that content to be downloaded automatically when it is available in the store.

⑤ Check the **Automatically create playlists when buying song collections** check box.

When you buy collections, playlists for those collections are created automatically.

⑥ If you have a slow Internet connection, check the **Load complete preview before playing** check box.

⑦ Click **OK**.

You are ready to shop.

BROWSE THE ITUNES STORE

① Click the **iTunes Store** link on the Source list.

The iTunes Store home page fills the right part of the window.

② Click the **Browse** link.

③ In the Store Browser, click a category.

④ Select a genre.

⑤ Select a subgenre.

⑥ Select an artist.

⑦ Select an album.

● The contents of the selected album appear in the bottom pane of the window. You are ready to preview and purchase content.

SEARCH THE ITUNES STORE

① Click the **iTunes Store** link on the Source list.

The iTunes Store home page fills the right part of the window.

② Type information for which you want to search.

As you type, iTunes attempts to match what you are typing and presents the matches on a pop-up menu.

③ If a match is found, select it on the pop-up menu to perform the search.

● The results of your search appear.

④ To see the results in a specific category, click the **See All** link for that category.

You are ready to preview and purchase content.

*Note: Much of the content purchased from the iTunes Store is protected; a computer must be authorized to play it. If you attempt to play content for which a computer is not authorized, the Authorization dialog opens. The Apple ID shown is the one under which the content was purchased. Enter the password for that account and click **Authorize**. You can see how many computers are currently authorized to play that content (the computer on which you purchased the content is authorized automatically). If five computers are already authorized, you must deauthorize one to authorize another (click **Store** and then choose **Deauthorize Computer**).*

continued ▶

There are two kinds of content in the iTunes Store: protected content and unprotected content (called *iTunes Plus* content). There are certain restrictions on the protected content that somewhat limit how you can use that content. iTunes Plus content, marked with a plus sign in a box, has no restrictions and you can use it however you want.

Over time, the restrictions on the content you purchase from the iTunes Store have been lessened (this is determined by the content owners, not Apple) as providers feel more comfortable with electronic distribution of their copyrighted material. Hopefully, before too long, all content in the iTunes Store will be unprotected.

Buy Music, TV, Movies, and More from the iTunes Store *(continued)*

PREVIEW ITUNES STORE CONTENT

① Select the item you want to preview.

② Click the **Play** button (▶) or press the `Spacebar`.

A 30-second preview plays. If the content is audio, you hear it. If it includes video, you see the video too.

You can control previews with the same controls you use to play content in your iTunes Library.

BUY AND DOWNLOAD CONTENT FROM THE ITUNES STORE

① Preview the content in which you are interested.

Note: If you see Buy buttons instead of Add buttons, you are using the 1-Click method; as soon as you click a Buy button, you immediately buy and download that content.

② Click **Add Album** to add the album to your shopping cart.

③ Click **Add Song** to add an individual song.

④ Click **Shopping Cart** on the Source list.

● Your Shopping Cart appears in the right part of the window and you see the content you have placed there.

⑤ To buy individual tracks, albums, movies, or seasons of TV shows, click their **Buy** buttons.

⑥ To expand an album or season of a TV show, click its expansion triangle (▶ changes to ▼).

The item expands and you can buy items it contains individually.

⑦ To buy all of the content in the shopping cart, click the **Buy Now** button.

Note: You can see the total cost of the items in your cart next to the Buy Now button.

The Sign In dialog appears.

⑧ Type your Apple ID or AOL password and click **Buy**.

The content you selected is purchased and downloaded to your iTunes Library.

⑨ Click **Purchased** on the iTunes Source list.

● Content you have downloaded from the iTunes Store is shown ready to use.

You can play the content and move it into playlists.

TIPS

What are the restrictions on content I purchase from the iTunes Store?

Currently, most iTunes Store content is digitally protected, which is actually not very restricting. For protected content, you can use it on up to five computers at the same time, and you can burn unique playlists to a disc up to seven times. To be able to access protected content, you must authorize a computer to play that content. Each authorized computer counts as one against the five-computer limit.

iTunes Plus
NO RESTRICTIONS
iTunes
NO MORE THAN 5
COMPUTERS AT ONCE.
BURN TO DISC NO MORE
THAN 7 TIMES.

What about iTunes Plus content?

iTunes Plus content is not restricted by any limitations, and so you can have and use it on as many computers as you want, and burn it to as many discs as you want. Content that is iTunes Plus in the iTunes Store is marked with a plus sign icon (⊞). iTunes Plus content is the same price as protected iTunes content.

Rent Movies from the iTunes Store

You can rent movies from the iTunes Store. This process is very similar to purchasing movies and other content from the iTunes Store, but there are a couple of differences.

You can rent movies for less than it costs to buy them. New releases are typically $2.99, while older movies are $1.99 or sometimes less. When you rent a movie, you have it for up to 30 days, but you can only watch it for a 24-hour period. Once you start watching a movie, the timer starts and when 24 hours have passed, the movie is deleted from your computer automatically.

Rent Movies from the iTunes Store

① Click the **iTunes Store** link on the Source list.

The iTunes Store Home page fills the right part of the window.

② Click the **Movies** link in the iTunes Store section.

● The Movies Home page appears.

③ Browse for a movie that you want to rent.

④ Click the movie's icon or link.

The movie's home page appears.

⑤ Preview the movie or view its trailer.

⑥ Click **Rent Movie**.

Note: If the Rent Movie button does not appear, the movie is not available for rental. You can buy it if you want.

7 Type your Apple ID or AOL password.

8 Click **Rent**.

9 In the resulting confirmation dialog, click **Rent**.

The movie downloads to MacBook Air.

The Rented Movies category is added to the Source list.

10 Click **Rented Movies** on the Source list.

The movies you have rented appear.

11 Select the movie you want to watch.

12 Click [▶] or press the Spacebar.

The movie plays.

When 24 hours pass from the time you started playing the movie, it is deleted from MacBook Air automatically.

Explain how the 30-day and 24-hour rental periods work?

Movies that you rent remain on your computer up to 30 days. However, you rent the movie only for a 24-hour viewing period. Once you start playing the movie, the 24-hour period starts. When 24 hours have passed since you first played the movie, the movie is deleted from your computer whether you have finished watching it or not. (You can watch the movie within the 24-hour period as much as you want.) The movie is also automatically deleted at the end of the 30-day rental period, again whether you have watched it or not.

Does what I paid for rent count against purchasing the same movie?

No. In the iTunes Store, renting and buying are totally separate activities. If you rent a movie and later want to buy it, you have to pay the full purchase price.

Subscribe to Podcasts

Podcasts are episodic audio or video programs that you can listen to or watch. Many podcasts are like radio shows, and in fact, many *are* radio shows. Most radio shows offer podcast versions that you can download to MacBook Air and copy to an iPod. Podcasts go way beyond just radio shows, however. You can find podcasts on many different topics.

You can subscribe to many different podcasts in the iTunes Store. Once you have subscribed, episodes are downloaded for you automatically so that they are available for you to listen to or watch, which you do in the same way as other content in the Library.

Subscribe to Podcasts

1. Click **iTunes Store**.

   The iTunes Store fills the Content pane.

2. Click **Podcasts**.

   The Podcasts home page appears.

3. Click the **Browse** link.

The Browser opens.

4. Click a category.

5. Click a subcategory.

6. Select a podcast.

7. Click the **Play** button, or just double-click the podcast (▶ changes to ■).

   The podcast plays.

Note: *Because most podcasts are free, the entire episode plays instead of just a preview.*

8. When you find a podcast that you want to listen to regularly, click its **Subscribe** button.

9. Click **Subscribe** in the confirmation prompt.

10. Continue to subscribe to other podcasts until you have subscribed to all those of interest to you.

LISTEN TO PODCASTS

1 Click the **Podcasts** source in the Source list.

● You see all the podcasts to which you have subscribed.

2 Select and play an episode of a podcast just like other content.

Note: Podcasts you have not played are marked with a blue dot (●).

3 If an episode you want to listen to has not been downloaded yet, click its **Get** button.

4 Click **Get All** to get all the episodes in a podcast.

CONFIGURE PODCAST SETTINGS

1 Click **Podcasts** in the Source list.

2 Click **Settings**.

The Podcasts tab of the iTunes Preferences dialog appears.

3 On the **Check for new episodes** pop-up menu, choose how often iTunes looks for new episodes.

4 On the **When new episodes are available** pop-up menu, choose what you want iTunes to do.

5 On the **Keep** pop-up menu, choose how you want iTunes to manage your podcasts.

6 Click **OK**.

TIPS

What if a podcast I want to subscribe to is not available in the iTunes Store?

For various reasons, mostly having to do with money, some podcasts are not available in the iTunes Store, which is too bad because that is definitely the easiest way to find and subscribe to podcasts. Some Web sites provide a URL to a podcast subscription; copy this, click **Advanced**, click **Subscribe to Podcast**, paste the URL in the dialog, and click **OK**. Others provide podcasts as MP3 files that you can download and add to the iTunes Library; you work with these files just like tracks from a CD.

A radio show I listen to has a podcast application; what does it do?

When shows offer podcasts as MP3 files for which you have to pay a fee to access, they often provide an application that downloads the files automatically. After you install and configure such an application, the show's MP3 files are downloaded to the location you specify. Add them to the iTunes Library by dragging them there or by clicking **File**, and then clicking **Add to Library**.

Create a Standard Playlist

Playlists enable you to create your own custom content collections (such as music, audiobooks, and video) that you can then play, burn to disc, or move to an iPod or iPhone. You can create as many playlists as you want, and they are completely customizable; you can include as many tracks as you want in the order you want them. You can even include the same track in a playlist multiple times for those tracks you just have to hear over and over again.

A standard playlist is one in which you manually place and organize songs.

Create a Standard Playlist

① Click the **Create Playlist** button (➕).

A new playlist is created, and its name is ready to be edited.

② Name the new playlist and press **Return**.

The playlist is renamed and moves to a location on the Source list based on its title (playlists are sorted alphabetically).

③ Select the playlist on the Source list.

● The content pane is empty because you have not added any songs to the playlist yet.

④ Select the category of content you want to add.

⑤ Browse or search for content you want to add to the playlist.

⑥ Drag tracks from the Content pane onto the playlist you created.

When you double-click a playlist, it opens in a separate window. This makes it easier to drag content from the Source pane into the playlist.

⑦ Select the playlist.

● Its contents appear in the Content pane.

⑧ Drag tracks up and down the playlist until they are in the order in which you want them to play.

As with other sources, when you play in order, tracks play from the top of the window to the bottom.

The playlist is complete.

TIPS

Can I sort the contents of a playlist?
You can sort a playlist that you create by clicking the column heading by which you want to sort the playlist just like any other source. However, when you sort a playlist you have organized manually so that the tracks play in a specific order, that order is lost. You have to manually place the tracks back in the order you want if sorting by one of the column headings does not create the order you want.

How can I create a playlist for an album I just downloaded from the iTunes Store?
Select all the tracks on the album. Click **File**, and then choose **New Playlist from Selection**. A new playlist is created, containing all the tracks you selected. If they are all from the same album, the name of the playlist is the name of the album.

Create a Smart Playlist

Standard playlists are great because you can easily create custom content collections, but you need to do some work to create and fill them. Why not let iTunes do the work for you? That is where a smart playlist comes in.

Instead of placing content into a playlist manually, you define the criteria for content and iTunes grabs the appropriate content from the Library and places it into the smart playlist for you automatically.

Create a Smart Playlist

1. Click **File** in the iTunes menu, and then click **New Smart Playlist**.

    The Smart Playlist dialog appears.

2. Select the first tag on which you want the smart playlist to be based in the Tag menu.

    For example, to include genre in the condition, select **Genre**.

3. Select the operand you want to use on the Operand menu, such as **is**, **is not**, or **contains**.

4. Type the condition you want to match in the Condition field.

    Your condition can include text or numbers.

    Note: As you type, iTunes attempts to match data in the Library to what you are typing. If a match is found, you can stop typing.

5. To add another condition to the smart playlist, click the **Add Condition** button (⊕).

    A new, empty condition appears.

6. Select a second tag.

7. Select an operand.

8. Type a condition you want to match in the Condition field.

9. Repeat Steps **5** to **8** until you have added all the conditions you want to include.

10. Select **all** on the pop-up menu at the top of the dialog if all the conditions must be met for a track to be included in the smart playlist, or select **any** if only one of them must be met.

⑪ If you want to limit the size of the playlist, check the **Limit to** check box; if not, skip to Step **15**.

⑫ Select the parameter by which you want to limit the playlist in the first menu, such as **hours**.

⑬ Type an appropriate amount for the limit you specified in the **Limit to** field, such as the number of hours.

⑭ Select how you want iTunes to choose the songs it includes based on the limit in the **selected by** menu.

⑮ To include only tracks whose check box in the Content pane is checked, check the **Match only checked items** check box.

⑯ If you want iTunes to update its contents over time, check the **Live updating** check box.

⑰ Click **OK**.

The smart playlist is added to the Source list, the tracks that meet the playlist's conditions are added to it, and its name is ready for you to edit.

⑱ Type the playlist's name and press Return.

The playlist is complete.

TIPS

How do I change the contents of a smart playlist?

If a smart playlist has live updating enabled, the contents of the playlist change over time as new content is added, content is removed, or content changes so it meets the playlist's criteria. If you want to change the contents of a smart playlist, you have to change the criteria for the list. To do so, select it, press and hold the Control key, and choose **Edit Smart Playlist**. Use the resulting Smart Playlist dialog to make changes to the conditions, which will change the playlist's content.

Can I drag the contents of a smart playlist onto another playlist to move it there?

The smart playlist does not actually contain the content you see or even pointers to that content, and so you cannot move tracks from a smart playlist to another playlist. Likewise, you cannot delete tracks from a smart playlist; you must change the list's criteria so the content no longer meets them, or delete the content from the Library (only do this if you are sure you do not want it).

Explore iPhoto

iPhoto is an amazing, powerful, and easy-to-use application that enables you to do a lot of cool things. From storing and organizing photos to publishing your photos to the Web to creating professional-quality photo books, iPhoto does it all for you.

You might think that iPhoto looks and works a lot like iTunes. If you think that, you are right. The two applications use similar interfaces and concepts, and so once you learn how to use one of them, using the other one comes quickly and easily.

STANDARD VIEW

Source list

The various sources in which your photos are stored and organized

Photos

When you select a source, the photos it contains appear in the right pane of the iPhoto window

Library

All the photos you add to iPhoto

Albums

Collections of photos you have created

Projects

Projects you created using your photos, such as photo books

Add

Enables you to add albums

Info

Opens the Information pane

Full Screen

Puts iPhoto in Full Screen mode

Search tool

Enables you to search for photos

Size slider

Changes the displayed size of photos (does not actually change the size of the photos themselves)

Play

Plays the photos in the selected source in a slide show

EDIT VIEW

● **Selected source**

Select a source of photos to work with them

● **Photos in selected source**

Thumbnails of the photos in the selected source

● **iPhoto in Edit mode**

Edit photos to fix problems or make improvements

● **Photo being edited**

Changes you make to photos are shown immediately

● **Editing tools**

Tools you can use to improve your photos

● **Size slider**

Increase the size at which the photo you are editing is displayed

PHOTO BOOK VIEW

● **Photo book**

A book you design containing a collection of photos that you select

● **Page thumbnails**

Represent each page in the book

● **Page view**

Where you work on individual pages

● **Layout tools**

Tools you use to design pages and the book

● **Buy Book**

Order professionally printed photo books from Apple

● **Next page/Previous page**

Move through the book's pages

Import Photos from a Digital Camera

To work with photos, you need to add them to the iPhoto Library. The most common way to do this is to import them from a digital camera. By default, when you connect a camera to MacBook Air, iPhoto opens and prepares to import the pictures stored in the camera's memory.

Once imported, photos are added to your iPhoto Library, at which point you can edit them, create photo books, and do all the other amazing things iPhoto empowers you to do.

Import Photos from a Digital Camera

1. Connect the digital camera to the MacBook Air USB port.

2. Turn the camera on and put it in playback or computer mode.

   iPhoto launches and mounts the camera.

● The camera is selected as the import source in the Devices section of the iPhoto Source list.

3. Type a name in the **Event Name** field for the collection of photos you are importing.

   When you import photos, they are automatically organized into events based on their time stamps.

4. Type a description of the photos in the **Description** field.

5. To have iPhoto automatically create events based on the dates of the photos, select the **Autosplit events after importing** check box.

   When you select this option, photos you import are placed into events based on when the photos were taken.

6. If you have already imported some of the photos on the camera, select the **Hide photos already imported** check box.

7. Click **Import All**.

   iPhoto begins to transfer photos from the camera to the computer.

● As each photo is imported, you see a preview in the iPhoto window.

● The progress of the import process and the number of photos remaining are shown at the bottom of the window.

⑧ When the import is complete, click **Delete Originals** to delete the photos from the camera, or click **Keep Originals** to leave the photos on the camera.

iPhoto completes the import process.

● The Last Import source is selected automatically and you see the photos you imported.

Note: *The Last Import source always contains the group of photos you imported most recently.*

⑨ Disconnect the camera.

If you selected the Autosplit events after the importing option in Step **5**, each group of photos is placed into a separate event. You can rename each event to make getting back to groups of photos easy.

⑩ Select the title of an event.

The event name becomes editable.

⑪ Type the event name.

⑫ Press Return.

The event name you typed is saved and you can always return to that group of photos by selecting the event. (Remember that events are groups of photos captured in the same timeframe.)

TIPS

How do I import photos taken on an iPhone?

When you connect an iPhone on which you captured photos to MacBook Air, it opens in iPhoto just like a digital camera does. The same steps you followed to import photos from a camera are used to import photos from an iPhone.

How can I import photos from other sources?

Click **File**, and then click **Import to Library**. Use the resulting dialog to move to and select the images you want to import. Then click **Import**. The image files are imported into the iPhoto Library where they can be used just like photos you import from a camera.

Browse and Search the iPhoto Library

One of the first steps for most of the projects you do in iPhoto is to find and select the photos with which you want to work. There are a couple of ways to do this: You can browse for photos, and you can search for photos by using information associated with those photos. After you find some photos, you can select them to work with them.

Finding photos through either method is easier when photos are properly labeled, which you learn about in the next section, "Label Photos."

Browse and Search the iPhoto Library

BROWSE FOR PHOTOS

① To browse photos grouped by the events with which they are associated, click **Events** in the Source list.

② To browse photos individually, click **Photos**.

③ To browse by one of the recent collections, such as **Last 12 Months**, click the collection you want to browse.

*Note: You can click **Last Import** to browse the photos you most recently imported.*

④ Drag the **Display Size** slider to make the thumbnails of the photos larger or smaller.

⑤ Drag the vertical scroll bar down to see more of the photos you are browsing.

● As you drag, the month and year of the photos currently shown in the window appear.

SEARCH FOR PHOTOS

① Click the source you want to search, such as **Last 12 Months**.

● The photos in the selected source appear.

② On the pop-up menu in the Search tool (🔍▾), choose the kind of information by which you want to search.

Note: *In this example,* **Keyword** *is selected. You can choose* **Date** *to search by date,* **Rating** *to search by your ratings, or* **All** *to search by all information.*

The search tool appropriate to the kind of information you select appears.

③ Select the values in the Search tool for which you want to search.

Note: *If you click* **All** *on the Search pop-up menu in Step 2, type the text or numbers for which you want to search in the Search field.*

● Only photos that meet your search criteria are shown in the window. For example, only photos associated with the keywords you clicked are shown.

<hr>

TIPS

What is an event?

iPhoto uses the concept of an event to group photos together. The application assumes that any photos captured within a specific amount of time (within 1 week, 1 day, the same 8-hour period, or the same 2-hour period, depending on the preference set on the Events tab of the iPhoto Preferences dialog) are part of the same event. By default, iPhoto automatically organizes photos into events based on the timeframe selected when you import them from a digital camera.

How do I browse an event?

When you browse events, you see a thumbnail for each event, which can include multiple photos. When you point to an event, the number of photos it contains and the associated date are shown. Drag within an event's thumbnail to browse the other photos it contains. Double-click an event to browse all of its photos in the iPhoto window.

Label Photos

As you accumulate large numbers of photos in iPhoto, it is important to label those photos so that you can more easily find and identify them.

There are two primary ways to label photos. First, you can associate combinations of keywords with images so that you can easily find images by searching for keywords. iPhoto includes a number of default keywords that you can use, and you can create your own keywords. A second way to label photos is by adding a title, description, and rating.

Label Photos

CONFIGURE KEYWORDS

① On the **Window** menu, select **Show Keywords**.

● The Keywords window appears, showing all the keywords that are currently available.

② Click **Edit Keywords**.

The Edit Keywords dialog appears.

③ Click the **Add** button (➕).

A new, blank keyword appears.

④ Type the keyword you want to create.

⑤ Press the Tab key to navigate to the Shortcut column.

⑥ Press the key that you want to use for the new keyword's shortcut.

Note: *By default, this is the first letter of the keyword.*

⑦ Press Return.

⑧ Repeat Steps **3** to **7** until you have configured the keywords you want to use.

⑨ Click **OK**.

ASSOCIATE KEYWORDS WITH PHOTOS

1 Browse or search for the photos with which you want to associate keywords.

2 Select the photos with which you want to associate keywords; photos you select are highlighted with a yellow box.

3 Press ⌘+K to open the Keywords window.

Keywords to which shortcuts are assigned appear at the top of the window; remaining keywords appear on the bottom.

4 Press the shortcut key for the keywords, or click the keywords that you want to associate with the selected photos; you can apply multiple keywords to each photo.

The keywords become highlighted to show they are associated with the photos.

● The check mark keyword (✓) is a generic marker that you can use to temporarily mark photos for a specific project.

You can search for photos by their keywords and you can create smart photo albums using the keywords you have applied to photos.

RATE AND DESCRIBE PHOTOS

1 Select a photo.

2 Click the **Info** button ([ⓘ]).

● The Information pane appears.

3 Type a title for the photo by clicking its default name and typing over it.

4 Rate the photo by clicking the dot corresponding to the number of stars you want to give the photo.

5 Type notes about the photo in the description area.

TIPS

What labels does iPhoto assign to photos automatically?

iPhoto enters a title for each photo you import, which is the filename for the photo file; you can change this to be any text you want. iPhoto also adds the date and time on which the photo was captured; you should usually leave this information alone unless there was a problem with the camera's date function when you took the photo. iPhoto also captures information about the kind of image, its resolution, and file size.

Typing all this information takes a long time; do I really need to do it?

Labeling photos is a bit laborious. However, when it comes time to do a project, the value of making photos easier to find becomes apparent when you need them. At the least, associate keywords with photos you import because even a single keyword helps you find photos easily. Applying several keywords enables you to locate specific photos even more quickly. It is a good idea to label photos as soon as you import them. If you do not, unlabeled photos accumulate, which makes creating projects harder than it needs to be.

Edit Photos

One of the great things about working with digital photos is that you can easily edit photos to make them better. Before you jump into a project, such as creating a photo book, take some time to edit the photos you are going to use to make them the best they can be. This makes the end project much better.

Using the Edit tools in iPhoto, you can rotate, crop, straighten, enhance, remove red-eye, and retouch. You can also apply effects and adjust specific aspects of photos. Each of these tools has specific functions that you can use to make improvements in your photos. The more common editing tasks of rotating, cropping, and removing red-eye are covered here.

Edit Photos

ROTATE AND CROP PHOTOS

1 Select the photos you want to edit.

Note: *This example shows photos grouped as Event collections.*

2 Click the **Edit** button (✏️).

iPhoto switches to Edit mode.

● Thumbnails of each photo you selected in Step 1 appear at the top of the window.

● The thumbnail of the currently selected photo is highlighted, and the photo appears in the Editing pane.

● The Edit tools appear at the bottom.

3 To rotate the photo in the counterclockwise direction, click the **Rotate** button (↺).

Note: *To rotate the photo clockwise, hold the* Option *key down and click* ↺.

4 To crop the photo, click the **Crop** button (▢).

The Crop tools appear.

5 Select the **Constrain** check box.

Note: If you do not want to limit how you crop the photo, leave the check box unchecked and skip to Step 7.

6 On the pop-up menu, choose the proportion you want to maintain.

For example, to keep the photo proportioned as for a 4-inch by 6-inch photo, choose **4 x 6**.

7 Drag the edges of the selection box until just the part of the photo you want to keep is in the box.

8 Click **Apply**.

The photo is cropped and the Crop tools close.

9 Click **Done** to save your changes.

REMOVE RED-EYE

1 Click the thumbnail of the image you want to edit.

2 Drag the **Display Size** slider to the right to zoom in on the photo.

3 Use the scroll bars to move the eyes that have red-eye to the center of the screen.

4 Click the **Red-Eye** button (⊗).

● The Red-Eye tool appears.

5 Click the eye from which you want to remove red.

● Red is replaced by black.

6 Repeat Step **5** until all the red-eyes have been corrected.

7 Click **Done** to save your changes.

TIPS

What do the other editing tools do?
The Straighten tool (◻) aligns the subject of a photo with a grid; this is typically used to improve a distorted photo. The Enhance tool (🔧) improves the color balance and other characteristics of a photo. The Retouch tool (✏) enables you to remove scratches and other imperfections. The Effects tool (▦) opens a palette of effects that you can apply to photos. The Adjust tool (🖼) opens a palette of tools that enable you to make very detailed changes, such as tint and sharpness.

Should I really edit photos before I collect them for a project?
In some cases, it makes sense to organize the photos you plan to use for a project before editing them, in which case you do the steps in the next section, "Organize the Photo Book's Photos in an Album," before you do those in this one. This way, you do not spend time editing photos you are not going to use anyway. And, sometimes the project in which you are going to use photos impacts how you edit them.

Organize the Photo Book's Photos in an Album

You use photo albums to gather and organize photos for various purposes, such as to make it easy to view the photos for a specific event, like a vacation. Creating a photo album is also a required step in most projects, such as creating a photo book. So, you first create the photo album from which you create the project.

There are two kinds of photo albums. For a standard photo album, you manually place photos into the album. For a smart album, you define criteria for the photos to be included, and iPhoto automatically finds the photos that match and places them in the album. The following steps show you how to create a standard photo album.

Organize the Photo Book's Photos in an Album

CREATE A STANDARD PHOTO ALBUM

① Open the **File** menu and select **New Album**.

The New Album sheet appears.

② Type a name for the album you are creating.

③ If you have already selected some photos to be included in the new album, select the **Use selected items in new album** check box.

④ Click **Create**.

The album is created and is selected on the Source list.

⑤ Drag photos from the Browse window onto the photo album you created.

⑥ Release the trackpad button when the album is highlighted.

The photos are placed into the album.

7 Select the album on the Source list.

All the photos in the album appear in the Browse window.

8 Drag the photos around the album until they are in the order you want them to be.

Photos are ordered from left to right and top to bottom.

9 To remove a photo from the album, select it and press Delete.

The deleted photo is removed from the album but remains in the Library so that you can use it again later.

CREATE A SMART PHOTO ALBUM

1 Open the **File** menu and select **New Smart Album**.

The New Smart Album sheet appears.

2 Enter a name for the smart album.

3 Configure the first condition for the smart album.

4 Click the **Add Condition** button ($\oplus$).

5 Configure the next condition.

6 Repeat Steps **4** and **5** until you have added all the conditions for the smart album.

7 On the **Match** pop-up menu, choose **all** if all the conditions must be met for a photo to be included, or **any** if only one of them must be met.

8 Click **OK**.

The album is created and all the photos in the iPhoto Library that meet the conditions are placed in it automatically.

What happens when I edit a photo in an album?

When you add a photo to an album, you are actually just adding a pointer to that photo instead of making a copy of it. Any changes you make to a photo in an album, such as cropping or rotating, are made on the photo everywhere it appears, including the Library and other albums. So, be careful if you use the same photos in multiple projects because changing a photo in one location changes it in every location.

What if I want to have multiple versions of the same photo?

To use different versions of the same photo in different projects, make a copy of it. Select the photo in the Library, open the **Photos** menu, and select **Duplicate**. The copies are independent, and so you can make different changes to each version and use them in multiple projects.

Create a Photo Book

A photo book is a great way to display a collection of photos. You can use the photo book on your computer, print it yourself, or for best results, send it to Apple where it is bound with a cover for a truly professional-looking result.

Once you have created a photo album in iPhoto, you can create a photo book of it. When you select the photo album, the photos it contains are placed in the new book. From there, you can choose from a variety of layouts, with each having a different printing price.

Create a Photo Book

1 Select an album.

2 Click the **Book** button ( ).

The Book sheet appears.

3 Click the **Book Type** pop-up menu.

4 Choose the type of book you want to create.

For example, to create an 11-inch x 8 1/2-inch book with a hard cover, select **Large – 11" x 8 1/2"**.

⑤ Click a layout from the list shown on the left pane of the sheet.

● A preview of the layout you select appears in the right pane.

Note: To see how much the type of book you want will cost to print, click the **Options + Prices** button to open a Web page that shows current pricing.

⑥ Click **Choose**.

● The photo book is created in the Projects section.

● The photo book window appears.

● At the top of the window, you see previews of the photos in the photo album you selected.

● In the center of the window, you see the page preview that you use to build each page; the first time you view a book, it shows the cover.

● At the bottom of the window, you see the book tools.

You are ready to lay out the book's pages (see the next task).

Do I have to have a book printed by Apple?
No, you can print photo books yourself. Except for resolution problems, Apple does not check a book when it is printed; what you send to be printed is what you get back. Print a draft copy or create a PDF to check the book before you print it. You can also take the PDF version to a local printing store to have it printed.

How much does printing a book cost?
At press time, 8 1/2 x 11-inch hardcover books were $29.99 for 20 pages (double-sided) or 10 pages (single-sided). Additional pages cost $.99 for a double-sided page (100 pages maximum) or $1.49 for a single-sided page (50 pages maximum). Check the Apple Web site for current prices for these options.

Lay Out a Photo Book

Laying out a photo book is definitely the most time-consuming part of the process. It is also the most important one. For each page in the book, you choose the photos that appear on the page, the page's theme, and other aspects of its design.

Fortunately, you can use the Autoflow tool to get started and then make manual adjustments from there as needed.

Lay Out a Photo Book

USE AUTOFLOW TO LAY OUT PAGES

1 Select the book on the Source list.

● You see the book's cover with a title.

2 Click the **Autoflow** button (🖼).

iPhoto places the photos in the book on various pages, starting with the first photo in the photo album being placed on the book's cover.

3 Click the **Show Pages** button (🖼) to show thumbnails of the pages in the book instead of the photos.

You can manually adjust the autoflow layout as needed.

Note: *When a photo is marked with an exclamation point, it means that the photo's resolution is too low to print properly at its current size. You need to fix resolution problems before you send the book to Apple for printing or you probably will not be pleased with the results.*

ADJUST EACH PAGE'S LAYOUT MANUALLY

1 Select the cover thumbnail.

The cover, along with its text, appears in the center pane of the window.

2 Click the cover page photo.

The size and placement tools appear.

3 Drag the slider to increase or decrease the size of the photo relative to the cover.

4 Click the **Hand** button (🖐).

5 Drag the photo to position the part that is visible in the frame.

⑥ Click the book's title to edit it.

Note: *The default title of the book is the name of the photo album you selected or the photo book's name.*

⑦ Click other text on the cover and edit it.

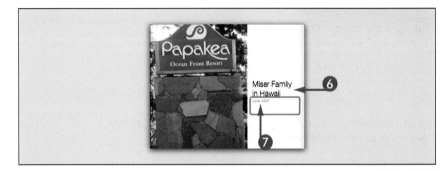

⑧ Click the thumbnail of the next page.

● The page appears in the editing area.

⑨ Drag the **Size** slider to zoom in or out so that you can work with the page effectively.

Note: *The Size slider only changes the size at which the page is being displayed.*

⑩ Use the scroll bars to change the part of the page you see.

⑪ Adjust the size and position of any photos on the page by clicking the photo you want to resize and dragging its edges until it is the size you want it to be.

⑫ Edit any text on the page.

⑬ Click the **Next** button (➡).

How do I fix photos that are marked with an exclamation point icon?

When a photo's resolution is too low to print with the best quality at its current size, it is flagged with an exclamation point icon. This means that the photo is sized too large for its resolution. If you have cropped the photo, uncrop it to restore more of the original photo so that its resolution is sufficient at its current size. You can also place the photo in a smaller frame on the same page or on a different page, or change the page's layout so that there are more photos on the page. If you have zoomed in on the photo, zoom out again to include more of the photo in the frame. If none of these solves the problem, remove the photo from the book or print it as is, realizing that its quality might not be very good.

Can I add more pages to a book after I have created it?

Yes. You can add more pages to a book by clicking the **Add Pages** button (🖥). When you do, two empty pages are added to the book (the number of pages in a book must be even). You can then add photos and design the layouts of the new pages. Realize that each page you add to the book also adds to the cost of the book, and so you want to make sure you do not add too many pages.

Lay Out a Photo Book *(continued)*

One of the reasons why laying out a book is time-consuming is that changes you make to pages in the book can impact the layout of other pages. For example, when you change the number of photos on a page, and the photos reflow, you might end up with blank spots on pages later in the book.

Laying a book out is an iterative process and usually requires several passes through the book, examining and working on each page as you go. You usually get to a better result quickly if you always work from the front of the book toward the back on each pass.

Lay Out a Photo Book *(continued)*

The next page of the book appears.

⑭ Select the first photo page in the book.

● The page you selected appears in the Layout pane.

⑮ To change the layout of the page, open the **Layout** (▣) pop-up menu.

⑯ Choose the page's layout.

Note: *The current layout of the page is marked with a check mark.*

Placeholders appear for each photo on the page.

⑰ To add a photo to the page, click the **Show Photos** button (▣).

● The photos in the book are shown.

⑱ Scroll through the photos to find one you want to add to the page.

⑲ Drag the photo onto the open position.

The photo is added to the page in the frame where you placed it.

⑳ To change the location of a photo on the same page, drag it on top of an existing photo.

The photos swap locations.

㉑ Move photos between pages by dragging them from one page to another.

Note: *If a photo exists in the new location, the photos swap places.*

㉒ Complete any text on the page.

㉓ Remove a photo from a page by dragging it from the page back onto the photo browser, or select it and press Delete.

Note: When you delete a photo from a book, it is only removed from the book and remains in the Library.

㉔ When you finish with pages being displayed, click the **Next** button (➡).

㉕ Continue moving through the pages in the book until you lay out all of them.

The book is now ready for an editing pass.

TIPS

Can I add photos to the book that are not in the photo album that I started with?

Yes. To add photos to the book that were not in the album you started with, find the photos you want to add in the Library or in a different album, and drag the photos onto the book icon on the Source list. The photos are added to the group, and appear at the far-right end of the Photo Browser pane. You can then place them in the book.

What if I need to edit a photo in a book?

Double-click a photo on a book page; it opens in the Edit window. After you edit the photo, click **Done**. You return to the photo in the book and the changes you made are reflected in the photo, whether you have already placed it on a page or not.

Edit a Photo Book

Once you have finished laying out a book, you should edit it to make sure that what you send to be printed is going to please you.

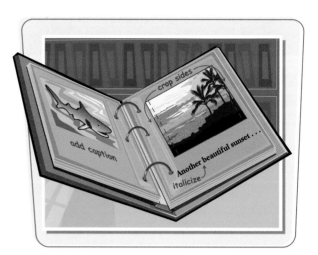

Editing passes are necessary to find those problems that you may have missed when you laid out the book, or you may decide that you want to improve some aspect of the layout that you might not have discovered while you were laying the book out. It is much better to discover problems when you can fix them easily and for free, rather than after you spend money on printing a book.

Edit a Photo Book

1. Select the photo book.
2. Set the preview size so that you can see all of the pages in the window.
3. Look for photo problems or layout issues.
4. Click the **Next** button (➡).

The next set of pages appears.

5. Use the Zoom slider and scroll bars to navigate the pages containing text so that you can read the text easily.
6. If you find a text problem, fix it.

Note: *iPhoto has a spell checker that underlines misspellings and suggests corrections.*

7 To apply a background to a page, click the **Background** button ( ).

8 Select a background from the pop-up menu.

The background is applied to the page.

9 When you get to the end of the book, note how many pages there are to determine how much the book costs.

10 If you want to remove pages, move to the page you want to remove, open the **Edit** menu, and select **Remove Page**.

The page is removed from the book.

11 Check whether deleting the page has affected the rest of the layout, and fix any problems you find.

Note: *If you are using a book with double-sided pages, you must add and delete pages two at a time.*

TIPS

Can I change a book's design after I lay it out?

Using the Themes menu, you can choose a different design for a book you have laid out. When you choose a new design, the pages are redone according to the new design. This can cause problems with some of the pages, especially if the pages have text on them. Do some additional editing passes with the new design to make sure the results are acceptable.

What does the Adjust button do?

When you select a photo and click the **Adjust** button ( ), the Adjust palette appears. The Adjust palette has tools that enable you to apply effects and adjust many aspects of the photo, such as brightness and color temperature. These are the same tools that are available in the Editing toolset.

ADJUST PALETTE

Configure a Photo Book's Settings

Each book has a set of configuration options that you can adjust. These include fonts and whether you want the Apple logo included on the book.

Before you are really done with a book, you need to configure these settings.

Configure a Photo Book's Settings

1. Select the photo book.

2. Click the **Settings** button ().

The Settings sheet appears.

3. Use the **Font** pop-up menus to set the fonts.

Note: *If you change the fonts significantly, review the book again to ensure that changes you make do not mess up the book's layout.*

4. If you do not want an Apple logo included on the book when it is printed, uncheck the **Include Apple logo** check box.

5. Check the **Automatically enter photo information** check box to have photo information such as titles added automatically.

6. Select the **Double-sided pages** check box to use double-sided pages.

Note: *Like font changes, if you add photo information or change to double-sided pages, review the impact of those changes on the book before you print it.*

7. Click **OK**.

Any changes you make are reflected in the book.

Print a Photo Book

You can print photo books yourself or have Apple print them for you.

Apple prints photo books using high-quality printers, binds the books for you, and even ships them to the locations of your choice. However, you should know how to print books yourself, so that you can proof a book before you send it to Apple for printing.

Print a Photo Book

PRINT PHOTO BOOKS YOURSELF

1. Select the photo book you want to print.
2. Open the **File** menu and select **Print**.

   The Print dialog appears.
3. Click the **Preview** button.

   A preview of your book appears in the Preview application.
4. Review the book in Preview.
5. If you want to make changes, go back into iPhoto and make the changes.
6. If you made changes, repeat Steps **2** to **4** to generate a new preview.
7. When you are ready to print the book, click **Print**.

   iPhoto prints the book using your selected printer.
8. Check the printed version and fix any problems you notice.

HAVE APPLE PRINT PHOTO BOOKS

1. Select the photo book you want to print.
2. Click **Buy Book**.

   The Order Book dialog appears.
3. Select the color of the cover on the **Cover Color** pop-up menu.
4. Select how many copies of the book you want in the **Quantity** field.
5. Select where and how to ship your book.
6. Click **Buy Now**.
7. Follow any on-screen instructions to complete the process.

   Your book is printed and shipped to the address you selected.

Note: *You need an Apple ID to order books. This is the same account you use to order from the online Apple Store and the iTunes Store.*

Index

Index

Index

Index

Index

Index